ASIAN WATERS

ASIAN WATERS

THE STRUGGLE OVER THE SOUTH CHINA SEA AND THE STRATEGY OF CHINESE EXPANSION

HUMPHREY HAWKSLEY

THE OVERLOOK PRESS
NEW YORK, NY

To Jonie

This edition first published in hardcover in the United States in 2018 by
The Overlook Press, Peter Mayer Publishers, Inc.
141 Wooster Street
New York, NY 10012
www.overlookpress.com
For bulk and special sales, please contact sales@overlookny.com
or write to us at the above address.

Cataloging-in-Publication Data is available from the Library of Congress

Book design and type formatting by Bernard Schleifer
Manufactured in the United States of America
FIRST EDITION
1 3 5 7 9 10 8 6 4 2
ISBN 978-1-4683-1478-6

Contents

Map 1. Asia-Pacific

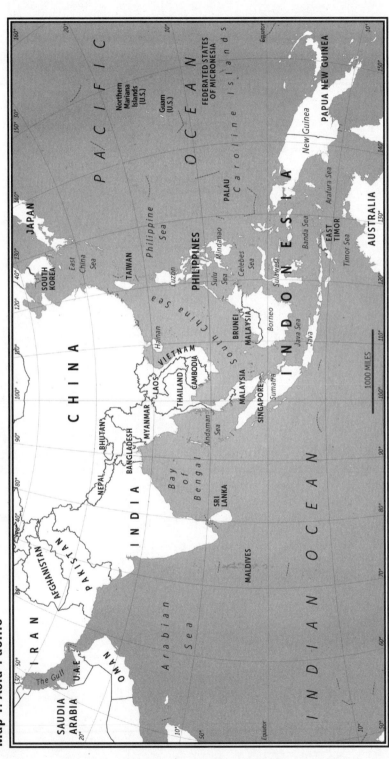

Map 2. China

Map 3. Southeast Asia

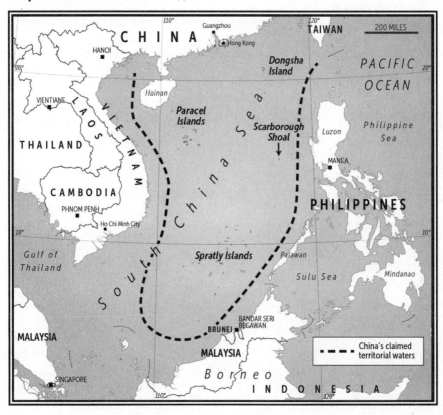

Map 4. South Asia

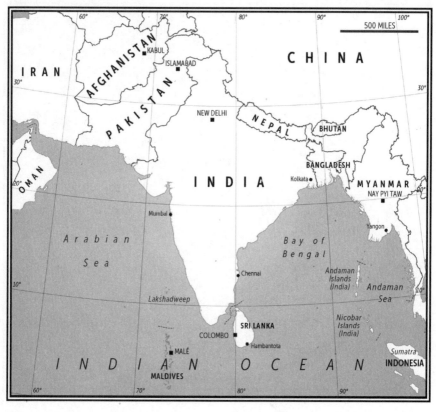

Map 5. East Asia

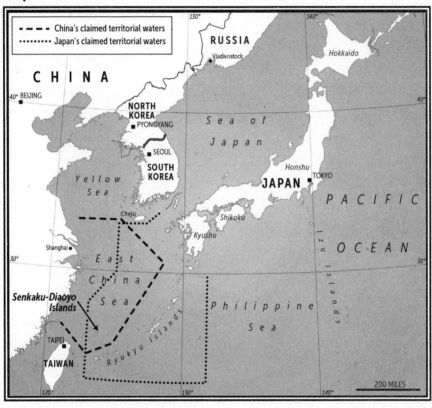

Preface

"Whosoever commands the sea commands the trade; whosoever com
mands the trade of the world commands the riches of the world, and
consequently the world itself."

— Sir Walter Raleigh, *The History of the World*,
Walter Burre, London, 1614

Imagine gazing down from the heavens on the continent of Asia as if
it were an elegant table laid out for a banquet, an array of dishes displayed for the feast about to take place. In taste, texture and position
on the table, each dish contributes to the overall well-being of the diners
who are to be satiated with good food and ambience. If one dish is too
highly spiced, too lightly cooked, or eaten out of sequence, the banquet
will not be the best. It might even fail.

Such is the way in which Europe gazed upon Asia in the nineteenth century, each tine of the fork polished and sharpened to pick at
what it wished. Japan followed in the early twentieth century, and after
that two rival powers fought over the banquet until the Soviet Union
got sick and only America was left at head of the table.

Now China examines the spread that Asia presents, because here
is the feast that it needs to own to keep its people secure. To take the
top seat, it plans to introduce a new style of table manners with Chinese
characteristics that reflect Asian culture. Whereas America—driven by
speed, certainty, and determination—cuts through with sharpened steak
knives, China approaches carefully, chopsticks raised, taking time to
think about which dishes it prefers and how the tastes and delicacies
should be blended together. For the moment, at least, it knows the table
must be shared between two hosts. But at some stage the other host
will have to leave because such is the cycle of life.

The Asian banquet in this current era will predominantly be a
seafood feast, so the waiters will replace American-style deep-fried

squid with delicacies of sharks'-fin soup and abalone. The new host will decide how many dishes it needs, of what quality and whether the table itself should to be expanded. Where the feast begins and ends can only be loosely defined because Asia is a continent without a cohesive identity.

Its vast shimmering waters stretch from the east coast of Africa to the west coast of America, from the Arctic and the Russian Far East down to the southern tip of New Zealand and to the Antarctic beyond. Its geographical frontiers of mountain ranges, rivers, and oceans are contradictory and clumsy. To the west, Turkey's narrow Bosphorus strait links the Sea of Marmara with the Black Sea and divides the country in two; Turkey is part Europe and part Asia. To the north, Asia rolls upward through the Himalayas, across the Muslim nations of the former Soviet Union, and into Russia, which itself straddles two continents. To the west it unfolds through India, China, and surrounding countries into Japan and the islands of the Pacific Ocean.

The name itself comes from no Asian language, but from the Greek, referring to "sunrise" or "east," thus placing Asia not within its own context but within Europe's. Yet, unlike in Europe and America, where Christianity predominates, Asia is not embedded by any one culture or religion. Buddhists, Hindus, and Muslims rub up against animists, Confucianists, and those of other sects. Asians communicate in more than two thousand languages, whereas Europeans have barely more than two hundred.

There is no basket of shared values, no single overarching system of government or common aspiration. Democracies jostle on equal ground with dictatorships and there are many shades in between. Asia's citizens are among the world's poorest and most repressed, but more billionaires live here than on any other continent. In one part of Asia, tribespeople hunt with bows and arrows. In another, a city gleams with high-rise office blocks. The world is now turning to this spread of dishes that Asia offers, for its ideas, its money, and its energy, and how Asia evolves in the coming years will impact all our lives.

Asian Waters covers only a small part of what is unfolding. But it is important to understand this backdrop to a region that is punching into the headlines with increasing frequency, whether about Asian money, North Korean bombs, or a tide-washed rock barely jutting from the surface of a faraway sea that can so quickly lead to talk of war.

Asia is a story about contested water as much as Europe is one about contested land. Asia's seas carry global trade in the trillions of dollars. Oil tankers from the Middle East deliver fuel needed for the continent's astounding growth, plying through the Indian Ocean and the South China Sea to huge ports in China, Japan, and elsewhere. Asia's factories send their products by sea to markets around the world, and any disruption to this free flow of maritime trade would shake us all.

Its array of bays, oceans and seas run across the equator and through the Tropics of Cancer and Capricorn, conjuring images of an exotic Orient, of typhoons and temples, of sun-drenched coral coastlines, of language, food, architecture, and culture. Some carry names that fire the imagination, like the Straits of Malacca and the Sea of Okhotsk. Others have more functional names like the East China Sea and the South China Sea, where crews of American and Chinese warships skirt suspiciously around each other, tasked with protecting their national interests.

Much mistrust stems of unresolved issues dating back to last century. Critical areas within these waters are contested between governments because there is no agreement on who owns what. China warns Japan; Vietnam challenges China; garrisons from China, Malaysia, the Philippines, Taiwan and Vietnam stake sovereign claims on remote atolls and rocks. Beijing has been upping the stakes by reclaiming land to build military bases far out in the South China Sea.

It is this issue, above all, that has acted as a new lightning rod of tension. In English, these rocks and reefs go by the names of colonial seafarers or their ships: Johnson, Mischief, Spratly, Woody, and so on. Over the centuries the British, Chinese, Filipinos, French, Japanese, Malays, Portuguese, and Vietnamese have raised national flags on them. There is no agreed-upon history. Old charts prove this and that; new ones are contentious. Legal rulings go one way or another. At first glance, disagreement is about alternative readings of history, ancient maps and tidal flows. But peel back that layer and these rocky islets represent a battle for the soul of Asia that is already rippling across thousands of miles to challenge governments on every continent. It is a contest that comprises opposing visions and values, shifting power, competition for control, and structures of government, and at stake is the familiar system that has dominated the global order for more than seventy years—since the end of the Second World War.

We are at the stage where the dishes of the banquet have been replenished and rearranged in a way that the rival host is being asked to move aside from its top table seat. China believes its turn has come—or, to be accurate, has come around again. The advance of China onto the world stage has been a step-by-step process: not one of invasion or colonization but instead of buying countries and winning control through trade. Its ambition is riddled with contradictions. China has become rich beyond its dreams precisely because of US predominance in Asia and its military security umbrella, which has mostly kept the peace since 1975. The US-led system of international law has also given China the freedom to sell to American and European markets.

Yet it is this system that China is now challenging. With its wealth it plans to reform the financial architecture by moving the renminbi to reduce the global dominance of the US dollar. In 2016 China won its first round when the International Monetary Fund awarded the renminbi the status of a reserve currency along with the US dollar, the euro, British sterling, and the yen, raising the question as to when we might switch from being an economy dominated by the greenback to one of the "redback."

With its military, China plans to ease American supremacy from the Pacific, match Russia's defense capabilities and replace the US security umbrella with a Chinese one. With its science, it intends to lead in everything from space exploration, nuclear energy, and environmental technology to combatting climate change.

For China, none of this ambition is seen as new; it is merely a return to its rightful position. This is not an American-style spearing of a rib-eye steak. This is the Middle Kingdom, with its millennia of experience, understanding the subtleties of spices and sauces, of seafood and vegetable, of culture, politics, and government. This is how it was before. Centuries earlier, China's technological and economic power had dwarfed that of Europe's. In the eleventh century, as the Normans conquered feudal Britain, China was the world's biggest producer of steel. Until the fifteenth century, it led the way in agriculture, health care, housing, transportation, and many other areas until overtaken—first by Italy and then by the rest of Europe.

China was the dominant global maritime power, sending large and sophisticated ships through Asia and across the Indian Ocean to Africa. Marco Polo, the thirteenth century Venetian explorer, reported seeing four-masted Chinese oceangoing junks with three hundred crew, far more robust than any European vessels. But by the end of the fifteenth century, in one of its political upheavals, China became inward looking and only now is seeking to rebuild its maritime presence.

China prides itself in having the world's oldest civilization, dating back five thousand years, earning it the title of Zhonghou, which translates as Middle (or Central) Kingdom. A China-ordered system dominated Asia until it was overtaken by the European one in the nineteenth century. The two systems stand at opposite poles. One believes the most efficient form of government emanates from a central command ruling a compliant population, while the other believes that power should be balanced through the rule of law, whether between nation-states or individuals. The West has rolled its system into the concept of democracy. China's has yet to be branded. It is not a dictatorship, and it governs through a series of mandates, reaching back into history and its ancient concept of the Mandate of Heaven, albeit using the term loosely, given the atheistic doctrine of the Communist Party.

Long ago, leaders from Korea, Vietnam, and elsewhere were expected to travel to China to pay tribute to its emperor. In return, the emperor would confer legitimacy on their rule, a protection and status that would be recognized by their subjects. As a resuscitated China grows, so we now see the modern Mandate of Heaven at work as power flows from Beijing to its provinces and then into smaller neighboring countries, expected to bend to the ruler's will. They become, in effect, vassal states and accepting Chinese control of the South China Sea is but one part of that process.

Embedded in China's thinking is securing itself against foreign intervention, thus correcting the weaknesses that allowed it to be invaded by European powers in the nineteenth century. The policy to militarize islands is drawn from a mind-set forged from historical experience that the country needs to be self-contained and able to protect itself.

As the world becomes more connected, China's arc of self-protection has to spread wider, far beyond its borders. To defend itself properly, it needs to establish from where it will gather its food, raw materials, and energy and how to keep its trade routes and supply chains safe. This expanding Chinese writ has sparked concern among neighbors and foreign governments, all of which have experienced the lethal consequences of the rise of Japan in the 1930s. For Beijing, it is self-protection. For Washington, DC, it is aggression.

Until the mid-nineteenth century, the predominant Han Chinese sheltered themselves from land intrusion in the north by controlling a series of buffer regions inhabited by different races, the Uighurs of Xinjiang in the far west, the Tibetans, the Mongolians, and so on. When the European threat came in the form of British gunboats in 1839, it had not yet constructed solid sea defenses and by then energy had drained from the Chinese empire. Political structures were shredded with corruption and lack of imagination. Science, technology, ambition, and military innovation no longer lay in China but in Europe.

The consequence of China's frailty led to the foreign occupation of its coastal cities, first by Britain and then by others, including Japan, the only Asian power that had developed a European-style industrial economy. The period from 1839 to 1949, when the Chinese Communist Party seized power, is referred to as the Century of Humiliation, a defeat that must never be allowed to happen again.

It was with this resolve that at the end of last century China turned its mind back to its coastal defenses. In 1995, fishermen raised the Chinese flag on the then little-known rocks of Mischief Reef off the coast of the Philippines. In 1999 Beijing declared an annual May–August fishing ban in areas of the South China Sea and still sends its coast guard to police it every year. In 2012 it deployed engineers to reclaim land in the Spratly Islands and build military bases, pitting itself not only against its immediate neighbors but also against the United States, which sees itself as the guarantor of security in the region. It was a brazen act of self-confidence, risky also because China needs American markets to sustain its wealth, and the US Navy can outgun China many times over.

One catalyst was an American announcement in 2011 that the United States would shift much of its military focus from the Middle East to the Pacific. China believed that the Pacific lay in its rightful arc of influence. The US policy became known as the Pivot to Asia, and the view from Beijing was that Washington aimed to contain China as it once had the Soviet Union.

There were other triggers, and if none had appeared, they would most likely have been found because as Rome, Athens, and Washington had before, Beijing felt strong and ambitious enough to disrupt the global status quo. The islands might have been an early military act of bald-faced audacity, but for decades soft power had been preparing the way.

More than a decade earlier, China had made its mark with multi-national companies such as the tech giant Huawei, which competes head-on with Apple in the smartphone industry while also providing critical software to Britain's telecom and Internet sectors. China's building of infrastructure is transforming landscapes of the developing world and has recently been consolidated into a single plan known as the Belt and Road Initiative. China now matches or has overtaken the United States as the biggest donor in international aid. President Xi Jinping is presenting himself as a global leader, talking up China's vision of joining hands to "march arm-in-arm toward a bright future." Industries and governments need to factor China into almost all their decisions. In Hollywood, should they change the villain from Chinese to Mexican so the movie can sell into China's billion-dollar market? In Vietnam, how much protest can be made over an illegal Chinese drilling rig off its coastline when it needs Beijing's support to sustain its economic growth?

China has marketed its philosophies of government by setting up some five hundred Confucius Institutes around the world explaining nondemocratic Chinese values across every continent, rivaling the British Council, the Goethe Institut, and the US Information Agency. Confucius, familiar for his long beard, flowing robes, and thoughtful eyes, was a Chinese statesman some two and half thousand years ago. Even today his pithy wisdom is widely quoted; for instance, "Real knowledge is to know the extent of one's ignorance." After being shelved for many years, he has been revived by the Communist Party to underpin its doctrine for good government, with an emphasis on hierarchy, community, and respect for age, tradition, and culture. Democracy is not a factor.

China has become—inescapably—a big country with vast power. All other countries are smaller. Indonesia's population of 260 million, even though three times that of Germany, is still five times smaller than China's 1.4 billion. Vietnam's population of less than 100 million is fifteen times smaller. Only India comes close in population size, but its billion-plus people have achieved little against China when it comes to economic or military might.

With this in mind, the present volume comprises five parts; the first four identify trends and triggers that, if activated, could change all our lives in a dramatic and possibly catastrophic way.

Part 1 examines the competing claims in the South China Sea and America's determination to uphold international law, defend its predominance, and protect the independence of smaller countries to prevent them becoming vassal states. It is here that the Chinese and US militaries routinely come face-to-face. From Beijing's side, I will illustrate the reasoning behind the military outposts and to what extent they do threaten international shipping routes.

Part 2 looks at Southeast Asia, which forms a horseshoe around the South China Sea and whose countries are once again having to choose between the will of opposing superpowers. Some have succumbed; others are putting up a fight. But unlike in the Cold War, when both Moscow and Washington were distant capitals, China is on the doorstep, indeed with its foot already inside the door. It is here where priorities and issues blur. Development, terrorism, and trade merge into defense and national security. China may be a partner in one and a threat in another. This is not Europe dealing with Russia. Each Southeast Asian country is having to make its own independent decision about China.

In part 3, I move to South Asia, where India views the South China Sea dispute as an early stage of China's military expansion into the Indian Ocean, the world's third largest body of water and crucial to shipping that serves the global economy. It is here that the massive democracies of America and India come together, with the United States describing India as "a key security and economic partner."[1] While China funds and builds Indian Ocean ports, America is selling India some of the latest defense systems. It is here, too, that Asian democracy will be tested. Can Australia, India, Indonesia, Japan, New Zealand, the Philippines, and South Korea create a cohesive enough front to prevent the South China Sea and Indian Ocean from falling under Chinese control? Or is Asia too diverse for democracy to be the force that bonds?

Part 4 covers East Asia, where China and Japan have revived their historic rivalry, using contested and uninhabited islands with no identifiable value as the fuse. The hostility underlines a truth that economic growth and rising living standards are not enough to bury bad and unresolved history. In East Asia lie two more triggers: North Korea and Taiwan. North Korea, with its bombs and concentration camps, has delivered us a real-life, dystopian scenario of nuclear war. The crisis draws in rival powers from opposing sides. But, North Korea is a strategic issue for Beijing, whereas Taiwan, that renegade leftover from the 1949 communist victory, is emotional and heartfelt, and invasion plans remain on the table. Taiwan is an energetic, lively, and rich democracy that sits across a narrow stretch of water as a robust reminder of China's failure to return it to the fold of the motherland. Taiwan is a symbol of Chinese weakness.

Part 5 ends the book with an attempt to show how these two parallel forces of western and eastern values might learn to live together or what the stakes would be if they choose to clash. As Western democracies become more inward-looking, so China is reaching out to sell its message around the world. There is wide agreement, that the current global architecture designed in the nineteen fifties is creaking to breaking point, but no understanding yet on how to fix it.

There has been much discussion on how the shifting power balance resembles that of the 1930s, or even Europe in the early years of the twentieth century. That is partly correct because of the cycle of some societies strengthening while others weaken. It is also very different because our thinking has changed about patriotism, race, loyalty, who we are, where and to whom we belong, and the way we communicate with each other.

---

1. President Donald Trump, televised address, August 21st 2017.

The dishes of the banquet are already being rearranged. The tines of the European fork are tarnished and weakened. The developed West is becoming fractured, inward-looking, with political populism, an uncertain Europe, and an unpredictable America. China is filling many voids.

But it has its own style and it is casting shadows of vulnerability over Asia because the continent itself does not speak with one voice, enjoy the same flavors or wish to be the obsequious guest of a new preeminent table host. The dishes are not yet in perfect sequence; spices and sauces jar to leave an uneasy taste. One day we hear of Chinese and Indian troops in a standoff high in the Himalayas; the next, the China Coast Guard has attacked a fishing boat. Then Chinese and Japanese warships lock guns on each other. China claims to lead the world in national strength and international influence. But how exactly will it lead, or will it even be allowed to?

In order to find a way forward there needs to be a clear-eyed understanding of the past, why governments do what they do, where they are heading, how we got it wrong before, and what we should do now. We know what China intends. Other governments have yet to work out how to deal with it. We also know from history that a single isolated event can signify that something far more dangerous is afoot, which is why *Asian Waters* begins with a fisherman being blasted by a Chinese water cannon.

PART 1

CHINA

If the US monopoly capitalist groups persist in pushing their policies of aggression and war, the day is bound to come when they will be hanged by the people of the whole world.

—MAO ZEDONG, founding father of the Peoples' Republic of China

CHAPTER 1

THE STORY OF
A SOUTH CHINA SEA
FISHERMAN

J URRICK OSON IS A BIG MAN, FORTY-SIX YEARS OLD, WITH MUSCLES bulging inside his bright purple sleeveless T-shirt. He was raised to work around nets, fish, tides, and weather, and his skin is leathery from a lifetime at sea. His boat had always been moored at the end of a dirt track, with shacks and small stalls on one side and the gently lapping sea on the other. It was a colorful, chaotic old vessel, painted in yellows, greens and blues, and she plied her trade as such boats had done for thousands of years.

There was no refrigeration on board. The catch was stored in iceboxes. Underwater lights to lure shoals of fish were made up of household lamps in glass coffee jars sealed by glue and tape and powered by old car batteries. Ropes and wires lashed different bits together around a narrow wooden hull, and bamboo stabilizers stretched out on each side like the wings of an albatross.

This was a pace and a way of life that could not last. The sea stretched westward, dappled with sunlight in a mix of bright tropical blues and murky grays toward Oson's fishing ground, Bajo de Masinloc. It was about a hundred miles away, and named after his rugged coastal community of Masinloc in the Philippines, whose fishermen had worked the same patch of sea for centuries.

There were echoes in Masinloc of the old steel towns of America, the long-closed textile mills of Britain: a community harboring a way of life whose time had passed. The village is a five-hour drive north of the capital Manila; part of the journey is along brand-new highways with service stations, sparkling restrooms, and coffee shops. Then, off the highway, Masinloc itself lies an hour or so down a narrow coast road with shanty shacks and old Spanish churches painted faded yellow and blue. It is place where change was bound to come and, in Oson's case, it arrived in the form of a water cannon from a Chinese gunboat.

"I am so angry," he said when I met him, his eyes flitting back and forth between the land and the sea. "If I'd had a gun, I'd have fought them." Shaking with fury, he told how in February 2014 he was on a routine fishing trip around Bajo de Masinloc when his boat was suddenly buzzed by Chinese helicopters. Men in speedboats cut across his boat's path, threatening his crew with weapons. Finally, a China Coast Guard vessel roared up to the wooden Philippine boat and opened up its powerful water cannon. "This powerful jet of water smashed into my boat," Oson said. "Then it hit me directly and I was thrown into the sea. I tried to scramble up, and they hit me again. It was as if they really wanted to kill me. If America supports us, we should go to war with them."

But America did not come to his rescue, and there was no war. And Oson has since been unable to work his traditional fishing grounds. I met him on the day he came back from his first fishing trip in more than three years. He told me how he had tried to make ends meet by taking passengers here and there in a little motorcycle taxi, a vehicle too small for his bulky frame, a job too humdrum for a man used to the challenges of the sea.

Eyes narrowed against the sun, face at ease with the elements, Oson explained that he had been unable to earn enough money to provide for his family. His wife, Melinda, became an overseas domestic worker and took a three-year contract in Saudi Arabia, sending money back every month. Oson was gutted, his esteem and confidence gone. Other families in the village had to do the same. The women, proud matriarchs, swallowed their pride to become servants in Middle Eastern households. Relatives and neighbors looked after the children while Oson, with little work and too much time on his hands, imagined going to war against China.

"The Chinese took our food and our income. Some days I wanted to kill myself. Wouldn't you feel bad?" he asked, his lip trembling. "I am a fisherman, like my father and my grandfather. It's who I am and what I do. How can a foreign country take that away from me?"

Oson's fishing ground of Bajo de Masinloc is better known in international political circles as Scarborough Shoal, a reef in the South China Sea named after a British East India Company ship that ran aground there in 1784. From the air it has a flatiron look, a narrow triangle of rocks and reefs forming the thirty-mile perimeter of a lagoon with just one way in. Scarborough Shoal lies well within the Philippines' UN-designated exclusive economic zone that stretches two hundred miles from the coastline. Under international law, the Chinese should have been nowhere near it.

But they were. China Coast Guard vessels arrived in 2012. There was standoff with the Philippines, which China won. Oson continued to fish there, but it was risky because a China Coast Guard vessel blocked the entrance to the calm lagoon where fishermen sought refuge in bad weather. Under Chinese protection, racketeers worked inside the lagoon, stripping the seabed of giant clams and other marine life to sell on black markets in Asia.

Oson's government was powerless to fight Beijing, so it compared China to Nazi Germany and filed a complaint in an international court. Meanwhile, Beijing carried out a rapid construction program to take over other reefs, rocks, and islands with colonial-era names like Johnson, Mischief, and Thomas. Within a few years Beijing had reclaimed enough land to build seven military bases in one of the world's most strategic waterways while no nation—not America, the Philippines, or any Asian country—nor the United Nations had taken any decisive step to stop it.

Had the ten governments of Southeast Asia been stronger and less corrupt; had they been given another fifty years to develop; had they been able to form a cohesive political and military bloc; had been less embroiled in the Middle East; had the much-heralded US Pivot to Asia of 2011 had time to take root; had a different style of US president been in office; had Europe not been so absorbed with its own problems; or had the many flows of history come together in a different way there might have been a stronger balance against China's extension of power.

But between 2013 and 2018 there was no such gathering of forces. Europe became weaker for Britain's leaving. America's Asian allies—Japan, the Philippines, South Korea, Taiwan, and Thailand—had little unity of purpose, and certainly nothing that began to resemble the US-led military umbrella that united Europe. All Asian defense threads led to Washington, DC, where President Barack Obama believed that American global interests were better served through cooperation with China, even if that risked diminishing US power in Asia. On his watch, China succeeded in militarizing the South China Sea with its newly built island bases. Yes, US military action could take them all out in less than an hour. But what would that achieve? Then again, if the Pentagon were to wait another ten years while the Chinese military developed further, it may not even be able to do that.

"We must recognize a new reality," Peter Dutton, director of the China Maritime Studies Institute at the US Naval Warfare College, told me. "Beijing controls this sea with its missiles and new airports. It now has the capacity to act against our interests of maintaining an open, international order."

The South China Sea, which Oson calls the West Philippine Sea, is the main shipping route between the Indian and Pacific Oceans. It carries $5 trillion worth of trade a year. Its fishing produces 12 percent of the global catch and it is the lifeblood for Southeast Asia's 620 million people and others far beyond. The South China Sea lies at the heart of Chinese global expansion. As China's tentacles spread around the world, the South China Sea and the building of islands there has become a test of how far China can push the boundaries of international law and get away with it.

Oson's plight over Scarborough Shoal, therefore, was one tiny stepping stone in Beijing's overall master plan. In 2013, a year after instigating the Scarborough Shoal dispute, President Xi Jinping announced a plan for massive infrastructure building across Asia into Europe in what has become known as the Belt and Road Initiative. Five years later, in 2017, he hosted a summit in Beijing with twenty-nine heads of government and star attractions from the global autocracies, including Russia's Vladimir Putin, Turkey's Recep Tayyip Erdoğan and Kazakhstan's Nursultan Nazarbayev. At a time when Western democracies were wrapped in their own problems, China took a global lead.

"Opening up brings progress while isolation results in backwardness," declared Xi. "Global growth requires new drivers, development needs to be more inclusive and balanced, and the gap between the rich and the poor needs to be narrowed."[2] Xi was speaking not as the strongman leader of a one-party state, but as a visionary statesman. Flanked by autocratic allies, he pitted their values directly against those of Western liberal democracy.

For more than a decade, the concept of liberty as seen through Western eyes has been diminishing. According to the US democracy watchdog, Freedom House, it is a far cry from the hopes of the early 1990s. The Arab Spring failed. Russia has turned back towards authoritarianism. Turkey has abandoned the European vision. Illiberal governments are becoming increasingly assertive and illiberal political movements are on the rise. While democracy is deeply embedded within American culture, it is a relatively new idea in most parts of the world, barely two hundred years old, one that emerged from the violent regimes which originally forged the now developed West. In China's eyes, through its millenia-long prism of history, the Western concept of democracy may well turn out to be just another cycle of history.

China's insistence on sovereignty over the South China Sea, and the building of islands, are merely the starting point for its global ambitions carried out with values that oppose those of the western democracies. The question is, if Beijing is not challenged now, when should it be? And what will happen if it is not?

"If Chinese claims are imposed by force or coercion, it will undermine over half a century of work to build international law," Gregory B. Poling, who runs the Asia Maritime Transparency Initiative at the Center for Strategic and International Studies, told me. "If China can claim a thousand miles from its shorelines because it has bigger boats and bigger guns, what will the Russians claim in the Arctic? What will the Iranians do in the Persian Gulf? Everyone will walk away from this system of global law, because if the Chinese are not bound by it, why should anyone else be?"

While Jurrick Oson—penniless, his dignity stripped—simmered with anger, China leveraged the Scarborough Shoal dispute in a way that it had done for centuries in order to keep its subjects in line. The strategy may first have been laid out by in the eleventh century BC by military analyst General T'ai Kung in his work *The Six Secret Teachings on the*

2. Chinese President Xi Jinping keynote speech May 14, 2017, opening ceremony of the Belt and Road Forum (BRF) for International Cooperation in Beijing, capital of China.

Way of Strategy. The method is to use the "certainty of reward" and "inevitability of punishment" to develop a bond of trust between the victor and the conquered. It is also advocated in the more famous *The Art of War* by the fifth century BC general Sun Tzu, who stated, "The supreme art of war is to subdue the enemy without fighting." T'ai Kung's teachings were passed down through the generations by word of mouth and only written down in the fourth century BC. What sets his work apart is that it is written from the perspective of a revolutionary aiming to overthrow a ruling regime, so it sits well with Chinese aspirations to overturn the American-led world order. One of T'ai Kung's points, as we will see later, is to instill a mission with strong sense of purpose. In China's case, this would be to protect the motherland against another Century of Humiliation, or, as the doctrine dictates, to follow the Chinese Dream.

Over Scarborough Shoal, China was about to deploy the teachings of both T'ai Kung and Sun Tzu, although to Western eyes, the strategy more resembled the Cold War technique of "salami slicing" whereby one side chips away little by little, but never enough to cause the other side to erupt.

When in July 2016 new Philippine president Rodrigo Duterte asked the American ambassador to Manila for help over Scarborough Shoal, he was told that the United States would not go to war over a fishing reef. So, after an initial bout of patriotic bluster, Duterte chose to cut a deal. He overturned his predecessor's antagonism and echoes of Chinese Nazism, flew to Beijing with a planeload of businessmen, signed deals for China to build infrastructure throughout the poorer part of his country, and declared that the future lay not with the United States but with China.

But he also attached a condition concerning Scarborough Shoal. As a senior Philippine diplomat told me, "The president made clear to the Chinese, 'If you want to mess with Scarborough Shoal, you need to see the fishermen right. If you don't do that, it's not going work because you'll be crossing me.'"

Within weeks a Chinese official from the Bureau of Fisheries arrived in Masinloc, reaching out a hand of friendship and offering to buy all of the fishermen's catch, thus guaranteeing the market price and a steady income to a community that could barely make ends meet. A delegation from the Masinloc Fishing Association was taken to China, all expenses paid, to see how the modern fishing industry worked.

Soon afterward, Oson was told he could head out to Scarborough Shoal again. When I met him in early 2017, there was a spring in his step. He had just returned from a week at sea. A China Coast Guard vessel guarded the entrance to the lagoon, barring Oson from going in. But he could fish. There were no water cannons or helicopters and, in those few days, he earned ten times what he could with his taxi tricycle. Life was good. The higher politics of sovereignty and superpower rivalry were not for him. Duterte and China had fixed things, and that was what Masinloc needed. No longer did Oson want to go to war.

"Now that I can fish again, I can make money," he said with a broad smile. "Melinda can come back and we can live as a family."

The Philippines had, in effect, surrendered the sovereignty of Scarborough Shoal to China, whose long-term plans for it were far from clear. The main cluster of new Chinese military bases lie four hundred miles to the south in the Spratly Islands, which are also claimed by Brunei, Malaysia, the Philippines, Taiwan, and Vietnam. There are other new bases on the Paracel Islands five hundred miles to the west, which China disputes with Vietnam, whose fishermen have, like Oson, suffered Chinese attacks. At the northern edges of the South China Sea is arguably the most strategic island of them all, Dongsha, which is garrisoned by coast guard forces from Taiwan.

Scarborough Shoal's geographical position could be crucial in China's military planning. Some months after Duterte struck his deal, new satellite images showed increased Chinese activity on the shoal amid reports that Beijing was planning to build a radar station. Here was another salami slice. Oson would keep fishing, and his catch would have a guaranteed buyer, so he asked himself, Why bite the hand that feeds you? As for the United States, having allowed China to build all those island bases and having so many common interests in banking, climate change, and combating terrorism, why should it risk a fight over one little radar station?

I FIRST TRAVELED through these seas more than forty years ago as a teenage deckhand on a freighter carrying iron ore from Angola in southern Africa to Japan in Northeast Asia. As part of a global supply chain in the 1970s we sailed in rough seas round the Cape of Good Hope and through the Indian Ocean, edged slowly into the busy, narrow Strait of Malacca between Indonesia and Malaysia, looped around Singapore, then headed out into the South China Sea, which sparkled with tropical sunlight, the air thick with humidity. This was the heart of Southeast Asia, once known as the Land Below the Winds because it lay beneath the typhoon belt of East Asia. I remember erratic winds whipping wave tops into a white swell as the huge propellers of our hundred-thousand-ton MV *Chelsea Bridge* bulk carrier took us north along these most vital of world shipping lanes.

We plied the same route as the Arab traders who centuries earlier had come to buy aromatic wood, bringing with them the teachings of Islam. Indians journeyed here too, with Buddhism, Hinduism, and such strength of personality that France aptly named its Southeast Asian colonies Indochina, the territory that lay between the vast countries of China and India. At the height of its colonial ambitions, Britain shipped Indian opium to China, forcing it ashore under a banner of free trade and international law underwritten by its gunboats. China regards its defeat by Britain in the First Opium War of 1839–42 as the start of its Century of Humiliation, and that is now central to just about every policy move it makes.

As we sailed north toward Yokohama on a vast expanse of sea with Vietnam to the west and the Philippines to the east, American and Soviet submariners played Cold War hide-and-seek with each other beneath the surface, just as Chinese submariners are doing now. We reached the East China Sea. Farther north lay the Yellow Sea and the Sea of Japan, all rich with the history of naval battles and war. Here is a region where the theater of war is mostly defined by the sea and its islands, a different style of contest and thinking than in the European land wars of the last century where territory was fought over trench by trench and village by village.

While a hostile army raising a flag across a land border in a neighbor's territory is likely to prompt a violent military response, China's building a string of artificial islands in the South China Sea, claiming it as its own, has been met mainly by diplomatic protests. On the other hand, the wrath of maritime warfare should not underestimated. In 1945 the United States did not invade Japan, but forced surrender with two nuclear strikes. The iconic Iwo Jima Memorial in Arlington Ridge Park close to the Pentagon shows victorious US Marines raising the Stars and Stripes on a barren uninhabited rock. Iwo Jima itself is remote, in the middle of the western Pacific Ocean, a thousand or more miles from anywhere, but strategically positioned with Japan to the north, the Philippines to the south, and China due east. That particular battle in February and March 1945 cost sixty-eight hundred American lives in a war caused by a new Asian power with ambitions to oust the United States from its region.

The officers of my bulk carrier in the 1970s were mostly British, but the deck crew were Hong Kong Chinese. They had decorated their mess room with posters of the revolutionary Mao Zedong, who at the time was waging his destructive Cultural Revolution and shutting the country behind its bamboo curtain. As we approached Yokohama, the Chinese bosun told me that he would not be going ashore. "I hate Japanese," he said. "I want to kill them."

That was not just the long-ago view of a single Chinese seaman; the enmity continues today. China has not forgiven Japan for its invasion, its occupation in the 1930s, and the massacre at Nanjing. Memories of Japanese aggression stalk every corridor of power in Beijing.

The weather had turned cold and, alongside the Yokohama jetty, I ignored driving snow while I unfurled thick docking ropes, spellbound by my first sighting of the neon lights of an Asian port, a glitter that in the following decades spread from skyline to skyline of city to megacity, a statement that trade and wealth creation could prevail over historical grievances. That may no longer be the case, however. The issues that led to such a bloodied history lie swept under a carpet and are still unresolved.

Just over twenty years after docking at Yokohama, as China was emerging from its isolation, I worked as BBC bureau chief in Beijing. A strange story emerged about bamboo scaffolding appearing inexplicably on an unknown islet in the South China Sea, hundreds of miles from the Chinese coastline. It was barely even an island, more a rock jutting a few inches above the surface. It turned out to be the colonially named Mischief Reef, part of the Spratly Islands, a cluster of rocks, reefs, and islands once so obscure that President Ronald Reagan mistakenly referred to them as the Broccoli Islands.

Beijing argues that it has sovereignty over 90 percent of the 1.5-million-square-mile South China Sea. Mischief Reef is now a full-size military base. Together with six other reefs, it comprises a series of airstrips and harbors built on reclaimed land, bristling with hi-tech military hardware. These might be remote, inhospitable places, but they have become a lightning rod testing the intricate relationship between America, China, and the countries of Asia. Barely a day goes by now without one point of friction or another reaching the headlines.

The seas of Asia spread much farther. China has built its first official overseas military base in Djibouti, on the Horn of Africa on the far western edges of the Indian Ocean. In 2017, in an unprecedented show of force in the Sea of Japan, the United States deployed three aircraft carrier groups against the North Korean missile threat. Beijing chose the Taiwan Strait, an unresolved trouble spot since 1949, to display its first aircraft carrier. Around a cluster of disputed and uninhabited islands in the East China Sea, Beijing and Tokyo now play a dangerous maritime cat-and-mouse game that world leaders have warned could escalate at any time.

All of these seas are attached to nations with their own cultures, history, and ambitions: India, with its chaotic democracy; China, with its authoritarian juggernaut; Japan, risen from the ashes of Hiroshima to become the democratic bedrock of America's regional domination; Indonesia, the world's biggest Muslim country, its untidy new democracy struggling to blunt Islamic extremism, like the Philippines, and now torn between the West and China. Singapore, the tautly controlled trading city-state, fighting to stay neutral; Malaysia, once hailed as an Asian tiger but now fractured by corruption, ethnic tension, and the pull of Islam; and the weaker countries of Cambodia and Laos, already under China's writ.

At the center of their stories lie the Chinese-occupied South China Sea islands, Johnson Reef, Mischief Reef, Subi Reef, and others. What China has achieved there has given it the confidence to press on to farther-flung parts of the world and what eventually unfolds around these islands will impact all our lives. In that respect, we may all someday be faced with the same decisions as Jurrick Oson and the fishing families of Masinloc.

CHAPTER 2

THE GREAT WALL
OF THE SEA

B EIJING'S CONSTRUCTION OF MILITARY BASES IN THE SOUTH CHINA SEA is the culmination of a plan that dates back to the seventh century BC and the first stages of the building of the Great Wall. Through Chinese eyes it is about protection, not aggression. "We are not trying to take over these islands and territory," Ruan Zongze of the China Institute of International Studies told me in Beijing. "What China is doing is to safeguard and defend its own legitimate rights, not like the Americans who start wars all over the world. China will never do that."

Over the centuries China created buffers against hostile neighbors by taking territory to its north, including Manchuria, now China's northeastern region that borders North Korea and Russia and is just across the water from Japan; Mongolia, which China split in two—Inner Mongolia, controlled by Beijing, and Outer Mongolia, now an independent nation, but governed under the wing of the Soviet Union during the Cold War; Xinjiang, the troubled Muslim region that leads through to Kazakhstan, Tajikistan, Kyrgyzstan, Afghanistan, and the insurgent-ridden Kashmir region, which is disputed between China and India.

What it failed to construct were southern and eastern maritime defenses to protect its coastline from foreign invasion by sea and, because of this, it received a brutal wake-up call in November 1839 when British troops stormed ashore near the southern port of Guangzhou, determined to increase Britain's opium exports into China from its colony in India.

In China's history, the First Opium War marks the start of its Century of Humiliation, which ended 110 years later in 1949 when Mao Zedong came to power. The defeat highlighted a weakness that China will never forget, and the story is told vividly in the amply funded Opium War and Sea Battle Museum in Humen, where the British invaded. Events are embedded in the mind of every student, from school to university and beyond. "It is not only at primary school that we are taught this," said Jinan University student Lu Chu Hau, who showed me around. "At middle school, at university, at home, at work, it is drummed into us so that we know that China must never be weak again."

A long elegant expressway bridge now spans the stretch of the Pearl River where British gunboats blasted their way in. Fortified ramparts still remain, with huge cannons in their original firing positions behind thick stone walls. They had a range of almost a mile, but not enough to prevent defeat. The ramparts were once part of a seawall designed to stop foreign warships. But they were only half built, and their original purpose has now been extended to the new South China Sea islands. The area where British redcoats and Chinese soldiers fought hand-to-hand has been turned into a parking lot filled with buses delivering schoolchildren to the museum to learn their nation's history.

Opium is a narcotic that gives short-term euphoria but slows the brain and damages health. In 1839 addiction levels were as high as 15 percent of the population, spanning all social classes. A modern-day photo montage of a lively, healthy young woman gradually being destroyed by opium is displayed at the museum entrance. You see her deteriorate from being vivacious and filled with energy to finally becoming listless, head hanging, skin blotched and eyes dulled.

The exhibits show how a legendary local viceroy, Lin Zexu, was uncompromising in his opposition to opium. His operations to arrest traffickers and burn drug hauls are reminiscent of drug wars today against Latin American cartels. Because of Lin's doggedness, Britain felt compelled to use force. Arguing that this was an issue of free trade, it deployed the military.

The invasion was not without controversy, and many parliamentarians viewed it as illegal. In 1840 the young Liberal Party member William Gladstone, who went on to become prime minister, told the House of Commons that the policy of trafficking narcotics covered his country in a "permanent disgrace." The British flag had become a pirate flag, he argued. But Parliament ignored him. The museum gives a prominent position to Gladstone's parliamentary address, with a cutout figure in full flow.

Although superior in firepower and military expertise, Britain took three years to force a surrender that was concluded with the 1842 Treaty of Nanking. The treaty made scant reference to opium and spoke euphemistically about "mercantile transactions," the emphasis being that Britain's action had given China an understanding of free trade and international law. The terms included China opening up Guangzhou and four other coastal cities to foreign trade, and China was made to pay compensation for the opium it had seized. Britain took the sovereignty of Hong Kong Island, to be controlled by two private opium exporters, William Jardine and James Matheson. Their company, Jardine Matheson, came to symbolize the power of the Taipan and British colonial rule in Asia and still operates today as a successful multinational company.

For China, it was as if a Mexican drug cartel had blasted its way into the southern United States, demanding that Arizona, California, New Mexico, and Texas open themselves up to cocaine sales while forcing a weakened America to sign agreements that defined an alternative, modern way in which trade and law operated.

Britain did not stop with the Treaty of Nanking. In 1856 it sought even deeper access within China. By now the West, uniting under the banners of Christianity and trade, claimed that its merchants and soldiers had the moral right to go anywhere they chose. Supported by France, Russia, and the United States, Britain launched the Second Opium War in which, among other acts of destruction, troops entered Beijing and sacked and looted the Summer Palace, a complex of imperial buildings, gardens, and lakes known as the Garden of Perfect Brightness.

China was powerless to stop them. This time fighting lasted fourteen years until China surrendered for the second time in 1860 with the Convention of Beijing. Swaths of coastal areas were handed over to colonizing Western powers, as if—to stay with the analogy—the drug cartels, having secured the southwestern part of the United States, pushed on to New York and Washington, DC.

Britain's National Maritime Museum at Greenwich, near London, also displays exhibits of the Opium Wars. They take up a small, uncrowded corner with the story told in the wider context of the colonization of India. The account is accurate, but as in the school curricula of Western democracies, the Opium Wars story is but a part, while for China this is the story that propels the policies it now implements. China has never hidden its own historical weaknesses. In a speech on July 1, 2017, to mark the twentieth anniversary of China regaining control of Hong Kong, President Xi Jinping raised the Opium Wars and put Britain's victory down to "a weak China under corrupt and incompetent feudal rule."[3]

After the consolidation (and then chaos) of Mao Zedong, and the economic reforms of Deng Xiaoping, Xi Jinping is regarded as a new strongman implementing policies to regain China's long-lost strength. He calls it "the great rejuvenation." Until seven hundred years ago China led the world in living standards, overtaken first by Italy,[4] and bit by bit the rot of corruption and bad governance set in. By the time British troops invaded, China had suffered centuries of misrule. "Sure, China was a victim of Western imperialism," notes China scholar Frank Ching. "But this was simply the last straw that broke the back of a dying camel."[5]

The Opium War Museum does not hide historical failures and displays face-to-face exhibits that show China's decline in parallel with the rise of Europe. On one side are images of a backward, feudal, agricultural society, and on the other telescopes, maps, clocks, and books, all of which gave the West the technology to win. While "science, democracy and the Industrial Revolution" were in full swing in the West, China's development was at a standstill, we are told, and I noted the deliberate use of the word "democracy" in a museum set up by a one-party state.

The emphasis of blame was not on an immoral use of strength, which echoes around much of the Middle East, but on China's weakness, a lesson learned in hindsight that instead of fighting Britain, it

---

3. Chinese President Xi Jinping July 1 2017 speech to mark the 20th anniversary of Hong Kong's handover.

4. China, Europe and the Great Divergence: Stephen Broadberry, Hanhui Guan, David Daokui Li, University of Oxford, April 2017.

5. *Ancestors:* The story of China told through the lives of an extraordinary family, Frank Ching.

would have been wiser to have embraced and learned from it. As we see later, this is what its Asian neighbor, Japan, did in 1854 when faced with a similar display of hostile Western firepower.

The museum fails to explain exactly how broken China was in the middle of the eighteenth century. For twenty years, from 1851 to 1871, the Taiping Rebellion, led by a man who claimed to be the younger brother of Jesus Christ, left millions dead in the southern part of the country. The casualties from Britain's military action were by comparison minuscule, but drove home the point that without a better internal system of government China would never be able to withstand foreign invasion.

It is this narrative of strong, forward-looking internal government coupled with effective military defense that mirrors much of China's argument today, which flows directly to Beijing's South China Sea activities and is causing antagonism.

"You cannot overestimate the impact of the Opium Wars," Milton Nong Ye, professor of history at Guangzhou's Jinan University, told me. "We learned then that the international world order is unfair." He drew a comparison between the Opium Wars and the compromises China had made to join the World Trade Organization in 2001. Only fifteen years later, thinking it had made all necessary concessions, China found that the Western power demanded more. It found itself excluded from the US-sponsored Trans-Pacific Partnership trade deal, from which Washington has now withdrawn.

"China is not safe and has been invaded many times," Ye said. "The way to protect ourselves is to build a great wall of the sea, and you do that with big ships and strong islands."

CHAPTER 3

WARS THAT NEVER END

EACH OF ASIA'S FAULT LINES CAN BE SOURCED BACK TO AN UNRESOLVED conflict (if not on paper, certainly in the minds of the participants), ranging from the Korean War, which ended in stalemate in 1953, to the Sino-Indian War of 1962, to Beijing's inability to reunite with what it sees as its breakaway province of Taiwan.

To understand why President Xi Jinping deployed military engineers to build island bases hundreds of miles from its coastline, we need to grasp each of these bits of Chinese modern history, of which Taiwan is the most emotive.

In 1949, Mao Zedong's communist forces defeated the US-backed nationalist government, which fled to Taiwan. Taiwan island itself is more than a hundred miles from the Chinese mainland, but the nationalists kept control of several islands much closer, some barely a mile from the mainland. Mao's victory, almost seventy years before the South China Sea became a global flashpoint, marked the resumption of China's attempt to secure its territory with an outer wall of defense. At the top of Beijing's list back then was Taiwan itself, whose loss was seen as unfinished business and remains so today. Taiwan has now become a wealthy, democratic, self-governing entity, but China continues to threaten military action should it ever declare full, sovereign independence.

In October 1949, from the entrance of the fifteenth-century Forbidden City overlooking Tiananmen Square, forty-six-year old Mao announced the creation of a new nation. He appeared on the terrace of the ornate Gate of Heavenly Peace with its decorative orange and red curving roofs, figurative lions outside to ward off evil spirits. The choice of venue was important. As a communist, he could have made an address from a farm or a factory. But by choosing the Gate of Heavenly Peace, he was stating that he was the new emperor of the Middle Kingdom who ruled with a mandate from heaven. In many ways, this image contradicted Mao's communist and atheistic ideology. But he understood China's history and how the need for a tough decisive leader was deeply entrenched in its culture.

Yet despite controlling a country more than three thousand miles wide, bigger than India or even the United States, Mao's forces had failed to capture these several outlying islands. Just three weeks after declaring victory on the mainland, he dispatched his exhausted troops to the island of Kinmen, barely a mile from the Chinese mainland, that was still held by nationalist forces. The hand-to-hand fighting around the northern village of Guningtou was brutal, with nationalist tank crews so low on ammunition that they ended up ramming straight into Chinese soldiers, crushing them under the tanks' treads. Finally, Mao's mainland troops were defeated. The Battle of Guningtou was fought over three days, October 25–27, 1949; it was essentially Asia's first hot battle of the Cold War, and China lost.

Mao continued to mop up with a few skirmishes, but there was no more hard fighting. In May 1950 he took Hainan in the south, followed by Zhoushan in the east. But Kinmen continued to elude him, together with the smaller Lieyu, or Lesser Kinmen; Dadan; Erdan; Matsu, farther to the north; the Yijiangshan Islands; and others that on clear days loomed tantalizingly within sight of the communist-controlled mainland. The biggest prize of all lay 160 miles to the east: the large mountainous island of Taiwan.

All this unfolded against a wider backdrop of disarray and the restructuring of the global order. The Allies had won the Second World War; Germany and Japan lay in rubble. The United States and the Soviet Union squared off as the new superpowers. Britain and Europe shed colonies while clinging to their fading influence. The big Asian beasts, China and India, grappled with new freedoms. This was a time for the underdog to rise up, left against right, poor against rich, communism against capitalism, colonized against colonizer. Many of the fault lines that appeared then are alive today.

Britain had left India in August 1947, partitioning it from Pak-

istan. After three wars and more than a million dead in communal violence, India and Pakistan are still fighting. In January 1948, Britain
gave independence to Burma, now Myanmar, which today is clawing
its way out of years of military dictatorship, or perhaps toward another
one. A month later, Ceylon, now Sri Lanka, won independence and
from the 1980s went on to suffer a quarter century of civil war. In May
1948, Britain's mandate in Palestine ended with the creation of the Jewish state of Israel in the Middle East; there is no calm there either. The
Netherlands pulled out of Indonesia in 1946, and the United States out
of the Philippines, while France battled independence movements in its
Indochina territories of Cambodia, Laos, and Vietnam. Over the following decades this would embroil America in the first war it would
ever lose.

Having failed to regain Taiwan, Mao targeted Tibet—which, like
Manchuria, Mongolia and Xinjiang, he planned to control as a buffer
state. In Tibet's case, the threat came from India. Mao invaded in October 1950, forcing a surrender that accepted Chinese sovereignty, but
allowed Tibetan autonomy with the Dalai Lama, then only fifteen years
old, as the Buddhist spiritual leader. There followed an uneasy quiet,
which would erupt nine years later when the Dalai Lama fled to India.
In the interim, Mao turned his attention toward the Korean Peninsula,
where he shared an interest with the Soviet Union.

Like Germany at the end of the Second World War, Korea had
been divided; Americans controlled the south and the Soviet Union the
north, which was run by an ambitious dictator, Kim Il-sung, who har-
bored ambitions to take back control of the whole country. If he succeeded, it would be a victory for the spread of communism. In June
1950 Moscow gave Kim the green light to move, and if Taiwan's Kinmen
was the arena for Cold War's first hot battle, then the Korean peninsula
became the theater for its first full-blown proxy conflict.

America used the United Nations, then less than five years old, to
authorize a US-led coalition force to repel the North Korean offensive,
which it did. The American military soon controlled most of the north,
unnerving Joseph Stalin, who asked for Mao's help. Mao was reluctant—he had enough on his plate with Taiwan and Tibet—but he also

needed to keep in with Stalin. American and Chinese troops fought brutally, face to face, often in close-quarter combat; so equally matched
were they that it took more than two years of further war before both
sides accepted a stalemate. Fighting ended on July 27, 1953, but with
a cease-fire, not a truce, and the hostile atmosphere continues today.

WITH THE KOREAN WAR over, China returned its attention to the far
more heartfelt problem of Taiwan, this time bringing the world to a
brink of a nuclear war. To forfeit North Korea would have been a
strategic setback, but to lose Taiwan would be unconscionable, and this
patriotic sentiment was carried by both Mao and the defeated nationalist dictator Chiang Kai-shek, now ensconced in the capital, Taipei.
Chiang nurtured a similar dream of taking back Beijing. He refused to
unpack cartons of priceless treasures hauled over from the mainland
on the grounds that they would soon be returned to their rightful home.
They are still stored in the air-conditioned and humidity-controlled
vaults of the Taiwan National Museum, so numerous that they are only
displayed in rotation.

Although the island of Taiwan itself is far from the Chinese coastline, Kinmen—where Mao's troops had been defeated four years earlier—
is within easy artillery range. Only twenty miles long and fifteen wide,
Kinmen is a low-lying island whose shape resembles a dragon's tongue.
During the 1950s the island suffered intensive artillery bombardment
to such an extent that in 1958 the United States drew up plans for nuclear strikes along China's eastern coastline. It had not used nuclear
weapons in the Korean War because it did not have enough. But, by
1958, its stockpiles were secure. As with South Korea, America viewed
any collapse of Taiwan as a trigger that would open the Asia-Pacific region to the control of Soviet communism.

Unbeknownst to the general public, in August and September 1958
China, Russia, and the United States became one presidential signature
away from nuclear conflict.[6] By mid-August 1958 the Pentagon had
moved five Strategic Air Command B-47 bombers to the region to carry
out nuclear attacks on the Chinese mainland with ten to fifteen kiloton

---

6. Walter Pincus, "Eisenhower Advisers Discussed Using Nuclear Weapons in
China," *Washington Post*, April 30, 2008.

bombs, each with a similar explosive force as was used on Hiroshima. The plan was to strike airfields around the main coastal city of Xiamen. As Chinese artillery pulverized Kinmen as if in preparation for an invasion, US Air Force headquarters sent a message to the Pacific Command in Hawaii signaling that it should prepare for the nuclear strike. "Assuming presidential approval, any Communist assault upon the offshore islands would trigger immediate nuclear retaliation," the message said.[7]

Then Premier Nikita Khrushchev of the Soviet Union intervened warning that if the United States attacked China there would be a nuclear retaliation: an attack on China would be considered an attack on the Soviet Union. The prospect of war with the Soviet Union unfolded a far more terrifying scenario than carrying out strikes against a non-nuclear China. Khrushchev followed up with a second letter underlining the risk of a third world war.[8]

The brinkmanship played out among these three global powers foreshadowed the much better-known Cuban Missile Crisis four years later, and only came to light when documents were declassified in 2008.[9] President Eisenhower overruled his military commanders and refused to approve a nuclear strike, citing the widespread casualties it would cause.

China did not invade, but the islanders of Kinmen lived in a state of siege. US warships in international waters loaded supplies onto high-speed Taiwanese craft that sped back and forth, often under Chinese fire. Artillery barrages continued on and off for another twenty years until January 1, 1979, when the current One China policy came into force whereby no government, nor the UN nor many international institutions, could recognize both Beijing and Taipei. For long spells China would send over artillery shells stuffed not with shrapnel and explosives but with propaganda flyers containing quotations from Mao's Little Red Book and proclaiming how Chinese families were so much better off, with shiny bicycles and color televisions.

---

7. National Security Archive, George Washington University, http://nsarchive.gwu.edu/nukevault/ebb249.

8. M. H. Halperin, *The 1958 Taiwan Straits Crisis: A Documented History (U)*, The Rand Corporation, December 1966 (declassified and abridged, March 18, 1975).

9. "Air Force Histories Released through Archive Lawsuit Show Cautious Presidents Overruling Air Force Plans for Early Use of Nuclear Weapons," National Security Archives, April 30, 2008.

But Taiwan remains a point of risk that routinely flares up. On December 2, 2016, while still president-elect and spurred on by hawkish advisers, Donald Trump took a congratulatory phone call from the new Taiwanese president, Tsai Ing-wen, smashing the protocol that had kept peace there for more than forty years. Moments later, in one of his famous tweets, Trump questioned the bedrock of the One China policy itself, although later, in April 2017, when meeting President Xi at his Mar-a-Lago resort in Florida, Trump switched back again. Both China and Taiwan constantly update their detailed plans for war, and Trump's actions indicated how swiftly something so crucial could fall apart. Later that year, he went further during his visit to Asia when he complimented Xi for being "a very special man" to whom Trump had an "incredibly warm" feeling. Less than a month earlier, at the Communist Party's 19th Congress, Xi had been anointed China's most powerful leader since Mao, presiding over an increasingly rigid authoritarian regime.

"Such scenes of an American president kowtowing in China to a Chinese president sent chills down the spines of Asia experts and United States allies who have relied on America to balance and sometimes counter an increasingly assertive China," wrote Susan Rice, Obama's National Security Adviser in a *New York Times* articles entitled 'Trump is Making China Great Again'. "The Chinese leadership played President Trump like a fiddle, catering to his insatiable ego and substituting pomp and circumstance for substance."

Trump's flip-flopping quickly proved disruptive as governments questioned US commitment to shoring up Asia's delicate balance. Trump also appeared to be discarding those American bedrocks of democracy and human rights and it cast new uncertainty over Taiwan. Trump's entrance into the foreign arena which began even before his presidency through his conversation with Taiwan's President Tsai indicated how swiftly a ballast of global balance like the One China policy could be pulled apart. Both China and Taiwan continue to update their plans for war.

In the 1950s the United States was squeezing China on two fronts. Just a few months after the nuclear standoff with Taiwan, Mao lost his patience with unrest in Tibet that was being fueled by a CIA operation based in India. In March 1959 he sent in troops and the Dalai Lama, still only twenty-one, fled to India, where he was given sanctuary. Mao was furious and in 1962 decided India needed to be taught a lesson. He took advantage of running tension on the disputed border to order a full-scale cross-border invasion.

What unfolded in those weeks defined America's future relationship with India. Beijing's offensive coincided with the far higher-profile crisis developing off the American coast with Cuba. China invaded India on October 20, 1962, the day President John F. Kennedy announced a naval blockade to stop Soviet warships delivering missiles to the communist Caribbean nation that lies only a hundred miles from the US mainland. The standoff between the two superpowers created a worldwide fear of nuclear war, and the remote border conflict between China and India received scant public attention. The motive for China's timing is not clear. One school of thought is that Mao was trying to win back Soviet favor by attaching the invasion to the wider cause of international communism. By 1962, the Sino-Soviet friendship had cooled and was no longer the force that had brought the Soviet Union to China's aid over Taiwan in 1958. But Premier Nikita Khrushchev's attention was on the Caribbean and not the Himalayas and the farthest Moscow went publicly was to publish support for China in the communist newspaper Pravda, blaming India for causing the war. Yet President Kennedy did view the Chinese invasion as part of the same fight against communism and immediately became involved.

Kennedy asked Indian prime minister, Jawaharlal Nehru, what help was needed and, just over a week after the Chinese invasion, US military advisers, weapons and other supplies began arriving at Indian military air bases. Washington let Beijing know that bomber and fighter squadrons based in the Philippines were being readied for strike. Although there is no evidence that the nuclear threat was raised, it remained fresh in the minds of the Chinese. "We were in an impossible position," retired general Xu Guangyu told me in Beijing, where he was then with the Chemical Defense Research Institute, tasked with protecting China against weapons of mass destruction. "China had no nuclear weapon. We had no idea how to protect our people from a nuclear attack. Over Taiwan and then India we were sure the Americans would strike. We had no choice but to pull back."

China announced a unilateral cease-fire on November 21, the day after the United States ended its Cuban blockade. It kept control of Aksai Chin in Ladakh, now governed as part of the Xinjiang Autonomous Region, but withdrew from Tawang in Arunchal Pradesh, which remains disputed territory but under Indian control.

By now the Cold War divide might have had the appearance of falling into a predictable pattern, the world's two biggest democracies lined up against the communist giants of China and the Soviet Union. But things did not unfold like that. India's primary enemy was Pakistan, whose growing relationship with China became pivotal to the global balance and remains so today.

A year after the border war, Pakistan ceded territory in Jammu and Kashmir to China as part of formal border agreement. The problem was that the four thousand square miles of Aksai Chin was also claimed by India. Pakistan then initiated a series of border skirmishes, until India responded with a full-scale invasion in 1965. The UN, the United States, and the Soviet Union were drawn into brokering a cease-fire. The fighting ended in less than three weeks, but it included the biggest tank battle since the Second World War.

Pakistan found itself in a unique position of being both an ally to China and to the United States, which paradoxically saw this Islamic country as a firewall against the spread of communism. When President Richard M. Nixon came to power in 1969, Pakistan's military leader, Mohammed Ayub Khan, acted as an unofficial emissary with Mao to test the waters on Sino-US rapprochement, an initiative that led to the current One China policy.

Nixon announced in 1971 that he would be visiting China, prompting India immediately to forge an alliance with the Soviet Union which in turn prompted Washington to view democratic India as a Cold War hostile power. India hit back at Pakistan by sponsoring an independence movement in West Pakistan (now Bangladesh). The resulting civil war once again skewed the global alliances. Pakistan's military operation to suppress the independence movement led to massacres of up to three million people.[10] Ten million refugees fled

---

10. Three million is a Bangladesh government figure that claims this was the biggest genocide since the Nazi Holocaust. Lower estimates go down to half a million.

to India, which intervened on the grounds that it needed to stop the killings.

The United States came down against India on the side of Pakistan, sending warships to the Bay of Bengal. India activated its new agreement with the Soviet Union, which deployed its own warships and submarines to deter the United States. Once again in 1971 the United States and Soviet Union were facing each other down, as they had in 1950 in North Korea, 1958 in Taiwan, and 1962 in Cuba.

Britain's Royal Navy reinforced the Americans, creating a situation whereby the world's two leading democracies were taking military action against the world's most populated democracy that was being protected by the most powerful communist dictatorship. In South Asia there was none of the Cold War clarity so talked up in recent years. Pakistan surrendered on December 17, 1971, and the new nation of Bangladesh was created.

The constant state of war and hostilities within Asia also prompted a nuclear arms race. China carried out its first test in 1964, two years after the border war with India. In 1974, three years after being threatened by American warships, India conducted its own test, driving it further from the United States.

After the 1962 war Mao embarked on his two destructive internal policies: the Great Leap Forward, aimed at reforming agriculture but leading to famine that killed tens of millions, which was followed by the murderous, ideologically-driven Cultural Revolution, which brought the country to paralysis. To the outside world China became the communist giant, sleeping behind the bamboo curtain until it emerged again in the late twentieth century.

The components that created the earlier balance of South Asia's power remain in place today. Moscow is India's main weapons supplier; Pakistan and India continue with their hostility; and there is deep suspicion between China and India. As America once again seeks black-and-white clarity, India veers toward the gray, one moment seeking strategic support, the next advocating its nonaligned independent status. Both the US and India governments have returned to the platform of being great democracies. Each is unsure if either can be relied upon when the chips are down.

Given China's aim to control the South China Sea, Delhi and Washington are concerned about its intentions in South Asia, where it is constructing a network of commercial and military havens across the Indian Ocean. Trade routes have always linked the Indian Ocean and the South China Sea, but the speeding up of reclamation work around the South China Sea's Spratly Islands in 2012 set off alarm bells.

CHAPTER 4

CHINESE ISLANDS

CONCERN ABOUT CHINA'S INTENTIONS TOWARD THE PARACEL AND Spratly Islands had been raised more than half a century earlier but it only echoed faintly through diplomatic corridors because of more pressing global crises, whether in Cuba, Korea, or Suez. Archival papers show how the Australian government was so worried about China's that it wanted either the United States or Britain to take control of the two islands groups. Neither London nor Washington wanted anything to do with them. A 1959 briefing note to Australia's Joint Intelligence Committee read, "If, in the longer term, the Communist Chinese were to develop the islands militarily, they could make a nuisance out of themselves on the international shipping and air routes on the pretext of infringements of territorial waters and air space and might even shoot down an aircraft occasionally. Again, there is little the West is likely to do, except protest." It went on to specify,

> Although it would be possible to build airfields on the larger islands, these would only be of limited value because of restrictions on the length of runways, maximum length would be about 5000' on Itu Aba (Taiwan's Taiping Island), and the direction of the prevailing winds. However, looking further ahead to vertical take-off fighters and surface-to-air and surface-to-surface missiles the islands could become more useful, provided, of course, the occupying power was able to guarantee adequate logistic support . . . If air warning radars or radio intercept stations were erected in the Paracels it would extend considerably the cover which the

Communist Chinese now enjoy from stations on Hainan and in North Vietnam. Bases in those islands would probably also have similar advantage to the West.[11]

Security analyst Elliott Brennan of the Stockholm-based Institute for Security and Development Policy, who studied the archives, found that Australia's appeal for US help fell on deaf ears. A cable from the Australian embassy in Washington, DC, said simply, "United States policy is one of 'let sleeping dogs lie,'" to which an Australian official scribbled a side note: "Politically, this is not a very satisfactory outcome."[12]

"The response from US officials left a lot to be desired," writes Brennan. "The previous 'let sleeping dogs lie' approach should be a prompt for today's decision makers to engage deeply with all parties on the issue, while continuing to conduct routine operations in and above the South China Sea. If this falters, the outcome will be very unsatisfactory indeed."[13]

The 1959 Australian intelligence note concluded, "Provided the United States maintains its present air and sea supremacy in the area, it could, if it wished, quickly neutralize any Communist Chinese military bases on the islands."[14]

Sixty years later, as the prophecy has materialized, the United States is drawing up military plans to create a security system known as the Quad with Australia, India, Japan and the US forming an alliance to balance China. Even so, the staunchest Western allies, Australia and New Zealand, find themselves, like many countries in the region, making delicate judgments on how to keep China onside for their economies while relying on the United States to maintain the international rule of law. Australia and New Zealand make up the traditional Five-Eyes intelligence-gathering network of English-speaking Western democracies together with the Canada, the United Kingdom, and the United States.

11. Elliot Brennan, *Out of the "Slipstream" of Power? Australian Grand Strategy and the South China Sea Disputes* (Stockholm: Institute for Security and Development Policy, 2017), 19–20.

12. Ibid., 20.

13. Elliott Brennan, "Australia's 60-Year-Old South China Sea Prophecy Comes True," *Diplomat*, June 12, 2017.

14. Brennan, *Out of the "Slipstream" of Power?*, 20.

Yet as of early 2018, Australia has been unclear as to whether it is following the United States policy in carrying out the freedom-of-navigation operations that within the twelve nautical miles of the China's reclaimed islands, although it has tested the Chinese cordon with aircraft. Australia is an Asia-reliant economy and China is its largest trading partner. New Zealand is in a similar position and in 2008 became the first developed country to sign a free trade agreement with China.

BEIJING'S CREATION OF military bases in the South China Sea concentrates on seven remote Spratly Islands reefs: Cuarteron, Fiery Cross, Gaven, Hughes, Johnson, Mischief, and Subi. It has also modernized its base on the Paracel Islands, which are claimed by Vietnam.

China measures its South China Sea claim through what is known as the Nine-Dash Line, a series of perforated lines that follow the contours of the Southeast Asian coastlines and brings about 90 percent of the maritime territory under its sovereign control. Regionally, the Nine-Dash Line is often referred to as the Cow's Tongue because of the fluid outline of the South China Sea. Beijing has never published the exact coordinates, preferring what it describes as "constructive ambiguity."

The Nine-Dash Line only came to international prominence in May 2009 when Malaysia and Vietnam submitted a joint application to the UN to extend their continental shelves—the underwater land that stretches out from their coastlines. If accepted, this would increase their sovereign maritime territories. Beijing immediately objected, saying that the claims violated its own sovereignty, and sent in a Nine-Dash Line map as evidence, prompting objections from most other Southeast Asian countries. "No one had heard of this until 2009 and we have never accepted this Nine-Dash Line," Nguyen Can Dong, director of Vietnam's National Boundary Commission, told me in Hanoi. "It has no legal basis."

In 2013, the Philippines, infuriated by China's intrusion at Scarborough Shoal, filed a case with an international maritime tribunal, the Permanent Court of Arbitration in The Hague. Three years later the tribunal found the Nine-Dash Line to be invalid under the UN Convention on the Law of the Sea and favored the Philippines on nearly every point. China had no entitlement in the disputed areas; it needed to "respect the rights and freedoms of the Philippines."

But, of course, it didn't. Beijing declared the ruling null and void. By then, with an incredible feat of engineering, China's island bases were up and running and there was no dismantling of jetties, hangars, and missile silos. Through commissioning regular satellite overflights, Gregory B. Poling at the Asia Maritime Transparency Initiative in Washington, DC, has chronicled how far and fast China transformed these seven reefs into thirty-two hundred acres of land to give it a significant military advantage in the region.

On July 27, 2012, Subi Reef looked like a barren tropical island, a circular reef in faded yellows and blues with a narrow entrance to a deep blue lagoon inside, very similar to Scarborough Shoal. It only peeked above the surface at low tide; at high tide the sea washed over and it disappeared. On the same day, the satellite captured an image of a Chinese military ship, big enough to have a helipad on the back, together with a small structure that looked like a fuel or water tank. Two and a half years later, on January 26, 2015, we see five dredgers and support vessels near Subi Reef. On March 17, less than two months later, there was a large area of reclaimed land with buildings, vehicles, a jetty, and a flotilla of ships around. Just over a year later, on July 24, 2016, a vast C shape of the reef covering 976 acres had been reclaimed. It now had a runway, roads, vehicles, accommodations, and fuel tanks, as well as structures for weapon silos, surface-to-air missile launchers, offensive radar, and much more.

Mischief Reef followed a similar trajectory. On January 24, 2012, it was circular, comprising a reef, a lagoon, an entrance, and a small man-made structure. By mid-2015, however, it was a hive of activity around what looked like a small city airport, a runway, taxiways, aircraft hangars, clusters of buildings, and—as best one can see with an unclassified satellite image—a large circular structure that could house missiles.

The reclamation was a fast, ambitious, and expensive project aimed at projecting Chinese power in a way never attempted before. And it worked. Spurred by the Philippines tribunal, reef after reef was built up: Johnson Reef, twenty-seven acres, a port and supply base;

Hughes Reef, nineteen acres, a long jetty and a wide docking bay; Gaven Reefs, thirty-four acres, two outstretched jetties, a tower, and dark shapes that make it look like a small container terminal; Fiery Cross Reef, 677 acres, resembling the front half of a warship, with a runway right along one side and rows of buildings just like on a military base; and Cuarteron Reef, fifty-six acres, ugly, square, and a work in progress.

The Spratly Islands reefs are isolated and jostle together cheek by jowl with rival occupants. Mischief Reef keeps watch on Second Thomas Shoal, occupied by the Philippines, which deliberately grounded a rusting old warship, garrisoned by Filipino marines to see off any Chinese approach. The Philippines and Vietnam keep troops on two tiny atolls, North East Cay and South West Cay, so close to each other that the Filipino marines can use the Vietnamese mobile phone signal and SIM cards.[15]

"The largest dozen or so of the Spratlys are legitimate islets," Poling told me. "But most are concrete pillboxes or huts built on stilts. The only way to get in and out is on boats, and the only place to walk around is on the little platform that surrounds your hut."

It is not, however, China but Vietnam that occupies most of the Spratly Islands, twenty-seven outposts in all. The Philippines controls eight, Malaysia five and Taiwan one (albeit the biggest and best equipped). China has only seven, but they are now designed with a very different aim in mind. "The clear purpose of the Chinese structures is to control the sea around them," notes Bill Hayton, a South China Sea specialist with the British think tank Chatham House. "They bristle with radar domes, satellite dishes and gun emplacements."[16]

By mid-2017 Poling's satellite images showed Chinese advanced surveillance and early warning radar facilities at Fiery Cross, Subi, and Cuarteron reefs, where photographs also revealed hardened shelters with retractable roofs for the launch of mobile surface-to-air and surface-to-ship missiles. On Fiery Cross there were hangars for twenty-four combat aircraft and three larger planes, including bombers.

---

15. *The South China Sea: The Struggle for Power in Asia*, Bill Hayton, 2014.
16. ibid.

Chinese militarization of the South China Sea has not been confined to the eastern Spratly Islands. On the other side, to the west, con-
struction has been far more advanced on the Paracels, an archipelago
of some 130 small islands and reefs that cover more than a hundred
miles of water. The Paracel Islands lie midway between the coasts of
China and Vietnam and are divided into two sections, the Crescent
Group to the southwest and closer to Vietnam, and the Amphitrite
Group to the northeast, toward China. The islands' names, such as
Duncan, Pattle, and Woody, were given by officers of Britain's East
India Company as they sailed back and forth between China and India
with their cargoes of opium, silver, and tea.

The biggest is Woody Island, which the Chinese call Yonxing or
Eternal Prosperity Land. It is one of the most populated in the South
China Sea, with a thousand people living there, mostly government or
military staffers on rotation and fishing families for whom Woody Island is their permanent home. It is probably China's best-equipped
base, with a twenty-seven-hundred-meter runway in operation since the
1990s, and in 2016 satellite images showed evidence of missiles deployed there. Defense analysts identified them as YJ-62 antiship cruise
missiles with a range of up to 250 miles and HQ-9 surface-to-air missiles with a range of about a hundred miles.

"We did not know that they had systems this big and this advanced
there," Poling said at the time. "This is militarization. The Chinese can
argue that it's only for defensive purposes, but if you are building giant
antiaircraft guns and systems to destroy incoming missiles and aircraft,
it means that you are prepping for a future conflict."

Over the decades China has built up a track record of using violence to get its way in the South China Sea, and not only with the water
cannon used against Jurrick Oson on Scarborough Shoal. Vietnam has
been the target, and islands were seized from Vietnam in three separate
military operations. The first came with the division of the country in
1956, just as elections in pro-American South Vietnam were due after
the expulsion of France as the colonizing power. Taking advantage of
Vietnam's instability, China moved into the Amphitrite Group in the
eastern section of the Paracels. There was no fighting, but South Vietnam responded by sending troops to the Crescent Group in the western

section. In January 1974, as South Vietnam was fractured and close to being defeated by North Vietnam, China took the Crescent Group, this time forcibly. It sank one Vietnamese ship and killed fifty-three sailors. In 1988 China moved again, this time across the South China Sea in the Spratly Islands, storming ashore at Johnson Reef, killing sixty-four Vietnamese troops. The reef is now a Chinese military supply base of twenty-seven acres of reclaimed land defended by antiaircraft and anti-missile systems.

The Philippines and Vietnam are the two Southeast Asian countries that have come into direct conflict with China in the South China Sea and the two most targeted by China's strategy of punishment and reward in dealing with the region. More recently, however, other Southeast Asian governments that have no claims have been drawn into China's quest for influence in Southeast Asia. In 2016 a freighter carrying Singaporean military vehicles from joint military exercises in Taiwan was intercepted and held in Chinese-controlled Hong Kong. Indonesia, increasingly irritated by incursions into its waters by Chinese, Malaysian, and Vietnamese fishing boats, has renamed that part of the South China Sea the North Natuna Sea, raising objections from Beijing. And the Association of Southeast Asian Nations grouping of ten governments has warned how China's policy risks undermining peace, stability, and security.

No region is more vulnerable to China's rise than Southeast Asia, which cannot challenge it militarily, needs its trade for its economies, and is uncertain how much it can rely on the United States or even if that would be a wise path to pursue. The echoing theme is that Southeast Asia does not want a throwback to the Cold War when each country was forced to choose between superpowers, although without clear thinking and straight talking, that is exactly what is unfolding now.

Part 2

SOUTHEAST ASIA

With few exceptions, democracy has not brought good government to new developing countries.

—Lee Kuan Yew, founding father of Singapore

CHAPTER 5

A TAPESTRY OF VALUES

T HE ASIAN CONTINENT HAS A MORE COMPLEX TAPESTRY THAN ANY other. Central Asia is made up mostly of the former Soviet republics, and was in Russia's arc of influence, but now is increasingly in China's. Geography divides India-dominated South Asia and the more prosperous East Asia, comprising a richer mix of cultures, including the economic and democratic successes of South Korea and Taiwan. In recent years, the frosty relationship between China and Japan has cast shadows over those achievements.

China chose initially to test its strength in the South China Sea and Southeast Asia which, unlike Europe, Latin America, or the Middle East, has no predominant culture, way of life, or standard of living. The gross domestic product (GDP) per capita of the city-state trading center of Singapore is close to $87,000, against Cambodia's $3,700. In the European Union the GDP of the poorest country—Bulgaria— stands at $20,100 against Luxembourg's $102,000, a difference of five to one against Southeast Asia's almost twenty-five to one.

In Europe, Christianity is by far the dominant religion, averaging more than 70 percent in most countries. Islam has the biggest following in Southeast Asia, but is followed by only about a third of its more than six hundred million people. The Philippines is mostly Christian. Indonesia and Malaysia are predominantly Islamic. Cambodia, Myanmar and Thailand are Buddhist. Nor are religions confined to national borders. The southern Philippines has a restless Muslim population, as does southern Thailand. Myanmar is weakened by numerous running ethnic insurgencies and stands accused internationally of repressing its sizable Muslim Rohingya population.

17. Central Intelligence Agency, *World Fact Book 2017*.

Amid all this live about some fifty million overseas Chinese whose communities drive the region's economy. Indonesia has more than 7 million out of a population of 250 million; Malaysia has 6.5 million among its 31 million people, and the Philippines has 1.3 million out of its nearly 100 million. The percentage varies greatly from country to country, as does the impact. Singapore was forced to separate from Malaysia in 1965 precisely because it was so predominantly Chinese. After race riots in 1969, Malaysia introduced laws that favored the native Malay population, and Indonesia has been wracked with anti-Chinese sentiment since the eighteenth century. In 1998, when anti-Chinese riots broke out in Jakarta, Beijing took the unprecedented step of ordering Jakarta to protect the Chinese community there. During the Cold War, Chinese throughout Southeast Asia were routinely accused of procommunist sentiment.

When Beijing's reforms began in the 1980s, China was bruised and poor from Mao's failed policies. These overseas Chinese families from Southeast Asia pioneered inward investment, laying the groundwork for its economic success today. "The idea of one China is deeply embedded in the minds of all Chinese people," writes former Singaporean cabinet minister George Yeo, arguing that this is down to the impact of Chinese Confucian culture which focuses on family and respect for hierarchy. "The Confucianist idea of society being one big happy family is programmed into young minds. The political idea of one China is also a cultural idea. This distinguishes Chinese cultures from other ancient cultures. For example, Jewish culture is as tenacious as Chinese culture but it does not put the same emphasis on political unity. While Hindu culture encompasses political ideals, it does not program into all Hindus the idea of one India, as Chinese culture does."[18]

Southeast Asia, therefore, is exposed to an expanding China that has a hold not only over its trade but also over its psychology. It believes it can call on the loyalty of the Chinese business communities, which have been so crucial in lifting the regional economy. China also has

---

18. George Yeo, "Special Lecture by George Yeo, Minister for Trade & Industry, Singapore, at the Golden Jubilee Anniversary of New Asia College, Hong Kong," October 29, 1999, Government of Singapore, http://www.nas.gov.sg/archivesonline /speeches/view-html?filename=1999102902.htm.

an added card when it comes to competing against Japan or Western powers. Like Southeast Asia, China suffered from the brutalities of colonialism.

After the Second World War, as Southeast Asian countries were gaining their independence, the United States attempted to forge a pro-Western defense alliance based on the new North Atlantic Treaty Organization, which was protecting Europe. The Southeast Asia Treaty Organization (SEATO) came about in 1955, but the region was too diverse, the governments too new, weak and corrupt to hold it together. In 1977 SEATO was officially dissolved, and further attempts to revive the idea of a regional defense alliance in Asia have failed to get off the ground.

Instead, there is the Association of Southeast Asian Nations (ASEAN), which was created in 1961 and carries an ambitious slogan, "One Vision, One Identity and One Community." This grouping has worked better. It has a policy of not interfering in the running of each country, has worked toward setting up a free trade area, declaring the region a nuclear-weapons-free zone, and has an emphasis on quiet, nonargumentative diplomacy and consensual decision making. ASEAN had been examining a gradual move to closer integration based on the European Union (EU), but that slowed after Britain's decision to leave the EU and uncertainty set in over Europe's long-term future.

Unlike the EU, ASEAN has a mix of government systems, and Western-style democracy has failed to take root in its member countries. The closest so far are Indonesia and the Philippines, both sprawling archipelagos with thousands of islands to control. Their per capita GDPs are twelve thousand dollars and eight thousand dollars, respectively, and they remain far from becoming developed societies. Both were controlled by American-backed Cold War dictators. The Philippines had President Ferdinand Marcos, who was overthrown in 1986, and Indonesia was ruled by President Suharto, who oversaw brutal anticommunist massacres in the 1960s and was ousted in 1998.

Thailand has veered back and forth from experimenting with democracy and retreating into military rule. Neighboring Myanmar is in the paradoxical position of being run by the military and the now tainted one-time democracy icon, Aung San Suu Kyi. Cambodia has been ruled by the same leader since 1979, and is one of the world's poorest and most corrupt countries. Next door, Laos remains a one-party communist state, as does the larger and more robust Vietnam, which, together with the Philippines, has openly challenged Beijing over the South China Sea. Tiny oil-rich Brunei, nestled within Malaysia on the northern Borneo coast, is run top-down by Sultan Hassannal Bolkiah. Malaysia's ruling party, the United Malays National Organisation, has been in power since independence in 1963, as has Singapore's People's Action Party. Both govern with authoritarian mechanisms set up under British colonialism and now criticized by Western democracies. Both have led the way in creating the concept of the Asian economic tiger.

In many respects, Singapore represents the geographical and intellectual heart of Southeast Asia.It lies at the mouth of the Strait of Malacca, the shipping artery that links the South China Sea and the Indian Ocean. More than 75 percent of its six million people are Chinese, and it is because of this demographic that Singapore was forced to separate from Malaysia in 1965. It had been simply one of the fourteen Malay states, but would have economically smothered the newly independent Malaysia. Here was evidence that Chinese communities and ethnic tensions were part and parcel of Southeast Asian life. Singapore went on to forge itself into an Asian trading hub. Its authoritarianism tempered racial tension and delivered an exceptionally high living standard. It is this Singaporean model that China drew upon when it embarked on its own reforms in the 1980s. Although far from being a compact city-state, China has achieved comparable levels of success, and now has the wealth and confidence to challenge a long-held Western argument that elections and democracy deliver the most stable form of government.

"With few exceptions, democracy has not brought good government to new developing countries," said the late Lee Kuan Yew, founding leader of Singapore, whose position over the decades had underpinned the intellectual argument for authoritarian government. "Asian values may not necessarily be what Americans or Europeans value. Westerners value the freedoms and liberties of the individual. As an Asian of Chinese cultural background, my values are for a government which is honest, effective and efficient."

In the maelstrom of Southeast Asia, Singapore is a tiny, lone star. Its government might be corruption-free, but others are not, leaving the region weak and unable to counter Beijing in the South China Sea and elsewhere. Cambodia and Laos are now regarded as little more than colonies and Chinese vassal states. Beijing's use of Cambodia is particularly telling. The Chinese government has been drawing Cambodia within its arc since the early 1990s, giving its former royal head of state, Prince Norodom Sihanouk, sanctuary and cancer treatment in Beijing until his death in 2012. It befriended the prime minister, Hun Sen, even though he had sided with Vietnam against China in the 1980s. Over the past decade, Chinese money has transformed Cambodia's landscape. Between 2011 and 2015, it accounted for 70 percent of all industrial investment. Long before that, in 2006, Hun Sen described China as Cambodia's "most trustworthy friend," a compliment returned by President Xi Jinping, who categorized Cambodia as "an iron clad friend." All three of the past Chinese presidents have visited.

Cambodia became a crucial diplomatic component in Beijing's South China Sea strategy, and its foresight paid off in February 2012 when ASEAN foreign ministers met in the capital Phnom Penh. At the top of the agenda was creating an agreed-upon negotiating position with China on the South China Sea. China had always insisted that negotiations should be bilateral. Hun Sen backed Beijing and, for the first time in its forty-five-year history, ASEAN failed to issue a joint statement at the end of the summit, giving Beijing a clear victory.

Since then China's grip on Cambodia has only tightened, and Beijing scored a clear win in 2017 when Cambodia canceled routine joint exercises with the United States and held them with China instead. Four months later, Cambodia expelled a small US Navy unit that had been involved in school and health projects for nine years. In return, it was given a billion dollars for a sports stadium, a new airport, and other projects.[19]

China has made inroads into Thailand since the military takeover in 2014. While the United States imposed sanctions and demanded a return to democracy, Beijing stepped in with money, plans for high-speed rail networks and other infrastructure building, and weapons (in-

---

19. "Cambodia Is Among the Latest of Several Asian Nations to Switch Partnerships from America to China," *Philadelphia Trumpet*, April 16, 2017.

cluding submarines). In return, Thailand has been earning its spurs by helping China round up dissidents who sought sanctuary there. They include a hundred Xinjiang Uighur activists who were forcibly repatriated to China on July 9, 2015. On August 17 a bomb at a Bangkok tourist attraction, the Erawan Shrine, killed twenty people and injured more than a hundred with suspicion falling on insurgents sympathetic to the Xinjiang independence movement. The Thai military government was also tacking an insurgency in the south of the country, highlighting a risk that its embrace of China may only have served to make the country more unstable.

Thailand's southern neighbor, Malaysia, has become vulnerable to China because of a corruption scandal in which hundreds of millions of dollars were stolen from a state-owned Malaysian investment fund. Malaysia was once hailed as a pioneering Asian tiger, but the scandal revealed a country rotten at the highest level. China stepped in with four billion dollars to buy out assets held by the broken fund.

Saudi Arabia, the biggest exporter of extremist Wahhabist Islamic doctrine, became involved with the discovery that it had made substantial deposits into the bank account of Malaysian prime minister Najib Tun Rajak. The Saudi involvement highlighted concerns about how Islam has slowly been taking a hold in Malaysia, and to retain power, the ruling party has been incorporating religion into mainstream legislation. In what used to be a relatively easygoing country for Muslims, there are now laws about fasting during Ramadan, premarital sex, and criticizing Islam. Malaysia's most successful prime minister was Mahatir Mohammed, in office during the boom years of 1981–2003, who concentrated on the economy. His successors' lack of leadership skills is blamed for Malaysia slipping back into high levels of corruption and religious politics.

Indonesia, the world's biggest Muslim country, is more unwieldy, has more people, and covers more territory, but in an attempt to embed its democracy, the government is having to make similar accommodations toward Islam. Early on in its transition from being a secular dictatorship, Indonesia decided to bring extremist Islamic groups into the political process. While this helped stabilize the nation, Islamic missionaries trained in Wahhabism are having an impact. Southeast Asia is unlikely to suffer the extreme divisions of the Middle East, but Islam is taking hold and challenging governments inclined toward developing democracy.

The influences of Confucian China and a hard-driving Middle East–inspired Islam are converging influences in Southeast Asia. Western hopes that the region could become a gathering of secular Asian democracies have long faded. It is now a question of keeping as many governments as possible either in a US-led camp or staying neutral, a challenge that could prove difficult.

IF SINGAPORE IS Southeast Asia's intellectual heart, Indonesia, with its eighteen thousand islands and 260 million people, is its litmus test. Forty percent of the population lives on less than two dollars a day. More than 85 percent are Muslim. Some seven million, just 3 per cent-percent, are Chinese, but various studies, often disputed, over the past quarter century have put the Chinese community as controlling up to 70 percent of the Indonesian economy. Indonesia swings between embracing and rejecting its Chinese community, and there has always been friction. During the Cold War, the Chinese were suspected of supporting communism. In the 1960s, they became targets of anticommunist killings in which at least half a million died. Muslim gangs were responsible for much of the slaughter. In 1998 riots originally aimed against the dictatorial rule of President Suharto also targeted Chinese businesses and in 2016 the governor of Jakarta, Basuki Tjahaja Purnama, sparked riots after arguing that the Koran did not ban Muslims from voting for non-Muslims. Basuki was elected to office in November 2014 after serving two years as deputy governor, but was then sentenced to two years in jail for blasphemy against Islam. His success at being elected showed that Chinese community leaders could break through into politics. His conviction exposed the tide of Islamization creeping into the country's once secular institutions.

As with the rest of Southeast Asia, Indonesia is faced with growing religious influence against a secular US-supported status quo and the pull of China as a new colonizing or hegemonic power. Only the brave and foolish would try to predict how this will develop.

Two views of Southeast Asia have emerged in recent years. One is of sun-drenched tourist beaches, cityscapes lined with glass-fronted skyscrapers, and busy factories feeding global supply chains while wealth spreads through communities. Southeast Asia prides itself on its development being far removed from the bloodshed of the Middle East and the poverty of Africa and South Asia. That is accurate just as another view is also accurate, of a region that has been trampled by outside powers for centuries, has failed to break through decisively on tackling the negative forces of poverty, corruption, and ethnic tension, and is now bracing itself for another Cold War–style conflict.

"Southeast Asia is cast as the nut between the giant arms of a geopolitical nutcracker," explains Michael Vatikiotis of the Singapore-based Centre for Humanitarian Dialogue. "Governments are not banking on a US defensive shield beyond a token military presence and the odd bout of sabre rattling from an Aegis destroyer or Nimitz-class carrier."[20]

Vatikiotis has long experience in attempting to mediate various Southeast Asian conflicts, such as the Muslim insurgency in southern Thailand. He envisages a Southeast Asia that a few decades from now will begin to resemble more the region it was before European powers arrived in the fifteenth century. "China's advantages of geographical and cultural proximity will be magnified by the weakening of strong centralized states and the emergence of smaller autonomous entities relying on trade orientated toward the Middle Kingdom," he argues.[21]

To some degree this is already happening. Beijing has a history of supporting insurgencies that weaken governments, whether it be through Pakistan into Kashmir or the Shan State, which operates under its own government within Myanmar. Already, the Islamic province of Aceh in northern Indonesia has a special autonomy arrangement, as does Mindanao in the Philippines. Other insurgencies will at some stage have to settle, including the Christian Karens and Muslim Rohingya in Myanmar, the Muslims in southern Thailand, possibly the Balinese Hindus, and the animists in Indonesian Papua. Each agreement would draw power away from the central government.

Indonesia has no claim to the South China Sea, but has found itself being drawn in because of fishing boat intrusions into its exclusive

---

20. Michael Vatikiotis, *Blood and Silk: Power and Conflict in Modern Southeast Asia* (London: Weidenfeld and Nicolson, 2017).
21. Ibid.

economic zone. As I will examine in chapter 16, many Chinese crews are tasked directly by the military to harass other boats and test borders. They are known to defense analysts as the maritime militia. Indonesia has captured and burned fishing boats from China and other countries and, in 2016, its navy fired warning shots at a Chinese vessel near the island of Natuna off the north Borneo coast. The message was that Indonesia would not allow breaches of its territory regardless of which country was responsible. Then in July 2017 it ratcheted things up by renaming the area of the South China Sea within its control as the North Natuna Sea, drawing objections from Beijing.

Malaysia has had lesser but similar problems and, surprisingly, in 2016 even Singapore found itself targeted. Beijing's operation also drew in the former British colony of Hong Kong, which under an international treaty should be able to operate independently of Beijing's interference until 2047.

In November 2016 Singapore shipped nine armored vehicles to Taiwan for joint military exercises. On their way back, the vehicles were seized when the ship carrying them docked in Hong Kong, with Beijing saying openly, "The Chinese government is firmly opposed to any forms of official interaction between Taiwan and countries that have diplomatic relations with us, military exchanges and cooperation included."[22] It took more than two months for Singapore to negotiate the vehicles' return.

Along with the Philippines and Vietnam, Singapore has been one of the loudest critics of Beijing's South China Sea policy. Shipping and trade are Singapore's lifeblood and should the Asian shipping lanes fall under Chinese control, the autonomy of this city-state could be under threat.

China had known about the annual Singapore-Taiwan exercises for years, but felt confident enough to intervene in a way that struck on three fronts: it targeted Taiwan in an attempt to isolate it further; it underlined to Hong Kong that, despite the treaty with Britain, China could step in at any time; and it sent a warning to Singapore and any other Southeast Asian country not to cross China. Beijing flatly refused to allow Singaporean prime minister Lee Hsien Loong to the May

22. Cal Wong, *The Diplomat*, November 29, 2016, https://thediplomat.co /2016 /11/china-protests-singapores-military-exercise-with-taiwan/.

2017 summit on the Belt and Road Initiative despite invitations issued to the leaders of Indonesia, Malaysia, Myanmar, and the Philippines.

All this raises a question as to why China would create more regional animosity by involving governments staying neutral in the South China Sea dispute. Unless, of course, it believed its economic and military weight were now enough to win around the region through the doctrine of punishment and reward.

The prompt that led to several Southeast Asian governments asking for US help came seven years earlier in 2009 when China submitted its Nine-Dash Line claim to the UN. There were already winds of unease about maritime sovereignty that led Malaysia and Vietnam to apply in May 2009 to extend the boundaries of their continental shelves. The United States answered the appeal when Secretary of State Hillary Clinton attended an ASEAN summit in Hanoi in July 2010, by which time she was already formulating a policy that became known as the American Pivot to Asia.

Clinton declared that the South China Sea was an area of American national interest, adding, "The US supports a collaborative diplomatic process by all claimants for resolving the various territorial disputes without coercion. We oppose the use or threat of force by any claimant."[23] The emphasis there was that the United States was very much involved and supported ASEAN working as one unit in negotiations with China. Her Chinese counterpart, the Chinese Yang Jiechi, was having none of it. "China is a big country and other countries are small countries, and that's just a fact,"[24] he said, throwing down the dividing gauntlet of a struggle for power in Southeast Asia.

In October 2011 Clinton elaborated on her theme with an article in the prestigious magazine *Foreign Policy*. "As the war in Iraq winds down and America begins to withdraw its forces from Afghanistan, the United States stands at a pivot point," she wrote. "In the next ten years, we need to be smart and systematic about where we invest time and energy. . . . One of the most important tasks of American statecraft over the next decade will therefore be to lock in a substantially increased in-

---

23. Secretary of State, Hillary Clinton, speaking at ASEAN Regional Forum in Hanoi, July 23, 2010.

24. Chinese Foreign Minister, Yang Jiechi, statement at ASEAN Regional Forum in Hanoi, July 26, 2010.

vestment—diplomatic, economic, strategic, and otherwise—in the Asia-Pacific region."[25]

A month later, President Barack Obama formally announced the Pivot to Asia in a speech to the Australian Parliament: "As we end today's wars, I have directed my national security team to make our presence and missions in the Asia-Pacific a top priority," he said, adding that marines would be based in the northern city of Darwin.[26]

The Pivot was immediately read as being a new US policy to contain or at least stop China's rise and expansion. It is not difficult to see how wires between China and the United States became so crossed over the Pivot.

"The declaration was a public-relations disaster," writes defense analyst Harlan Ullman. "Allies in Europe, the Middle East, and Asia were very concerned, if not frightened, by this seemingly dramatic shift, made without much prior consultation. China was angered, regarding the Pivot as a direct challenge to its sovereignty and standing."[27]

Kurt M. Campbell, who helped Hillary Clinton design it, has argued that the Pivot merely represented Asia's new reality in the world. "It is the leading destination for US exports, outpacing Europe by more than 50 percent," he writes. "The verdict on which economic principles will define the twenty-first century will be reached in Asia, home to three of the world's four largest economies and increasing levels of interdependence. On so many issues central to the world's future, Asia is at the center of the action."[28]

Obama, too, tried to stress that this was not an anti-China policy. "We'll seek more opportunities for co-operation with Beijing, including greater communication between our militaries, to promote understanding and avoid miscalculation," he told the Australian Parliament. "With most of the world's nuclear powers and some half of humanity, Asia will largely define whether the century ahead will be marked by conflict

25. Secretary of State, Hillary Clinton, Foreign Policy, *America's Pacific Century*, October 11, 2011.

26. President Barack Obama addressing Australian parliament, November 17, 2011.

27. Ullman, Harlan, *Anatomy of Failure: Why America Loses Every War It Starts*, Maryland, Naval Institute Press, 2017.

28. Kurt M. Campbell, *The Pivot: The Future of American Statecraft in Asia* (New York: Twelve, 2016).

or co-operation, needless suffering or human progress."[29]

Beijing was skeptical. Yes, there was cooperation with the United States at so many levels, including finance and climate change. But that didn't mean China wasn't still vulnerable to its defenses being breached, leading to another Century of Humiliation. "America's pivot to Asia sent a very wrong and confusing message," the International Studies Institute's Ruan Zongze told me. "It divides ASEAN countries, and damages the US-China relationship. We ask them, For what? What is this pivot? They tell us that the US only wants to reassure its allies in the region. We say, For what? So, they can think they have Uncle Sam behind them so they can kick China around?"

Whatever message the United States tried to get across, the Pivot announcement was a public relations disaster, not least because it would not end up deploying more American warships to Asia. US budget cuts in defense meant that even though the percentage of ships might rise (to 60 percent), there would be fewer naval vessels in the Asia-Pacific. Within a year, China Coast Guard crews were confronting the Philippines over Scarborough Shoal. Beijing intensified its island building in 2013 when the Philippines took the Scarborough Shoal case to an international tribunal while, fired up and confident, President Xi Jinping announced his Belt and Road Initiative to expand China's influence throughout Asia and across to Europe and Africa. There was no war, military or economic, but the gloves were off.

Southeast Asia's confrontation with China has been led by the Philippines and Vietnam, who were the region's bookends during the Cold War. Philippine troops fought with the Americans in Vietnam. American planes and warships were based in the Philippines, and Soviet ones in Vietnam. Both have put up a brave front against China, but both have already been forced into compromises. Yet neither is fainthearted when it comes to a fight, and China would have noted their histories. Vietnam was the first country to expel a colonial power through war, and went on to beat both America and China in further conflicts. The Philippines became the first country in this present cycle to overthrow a pro-American dictator through the "people power" of street protests.

---

29. President Barack Obama addressing Australian parliament, November 17, 2011.

CHAPTER 6

THE PHILIPPINES:
A PRECARIOUS TIGHTROPE

THE PHILIPPINES FIRST RAN INTO TROUBLE WITH CHINA OVER DISPUTED maritime territory in 1995, when Beijing raised the Chinese flag on Mischief Reef, which lies 134 miles off the Philippines Palawan Island and well inside its two hundred-mile exclusive economic zone. Four years later China began to move toward Second Thomas Shoal, shaped like a jagged knife blade just twenty miles away. It was then that the Philippines chose to act.

The Philippine Navy deliberately ran a rusting old warship, a former American 330-foot-long tank landing craft, the BRP *Sierra Madre*, aground on Second Thomas Shoal. Since then a small unit of Philippine marines has lived on the ship, tasked with stopping China's encroachment. The grounding of the *Sierra Madre* was a skillful move on two levels: first, it placed a public militarized cordon around Second Thomas Shoal; second, while dilapidated and unseaworthy, it was still a Philippine Navy ship, therefore protected by the Mutual Defense Treaty with the United States. If the marines on board came under attack, the Philippines could activate the treaty and America would be bound to come to its aid. China Coast Guard crews kept watch and on several occasions tried to harass supply lines to the *Sierra Madre*. But they did not directly confront.

At Scarborough Shoal there had been no Philippine Navy presence. Therefore, when the Masinloc fisherman Jurrick Oson, and his crew were pounded with water cannons and threatened with firearms, the US government did not get involved. At least, this was the explanation delivered by the US ambassador to both President Rodrigo Duterte and his predecessor, Benigno Aquino.

Each president reacted very differently, giving an insight into the character of the Philippines. If its democracy had become more embedded and its economy had grown in the thirty years since the ousting of Ferdinand Marcos, it might have been able to put up a stronger front. But the Philippines has gone through a roller coaster of economic slump, a paralyzed legislature, and not very good presidents, with the result that it has neither the military nor the economic wherewithal to challenge Beijing.

After losing Scarborough Shoal, President Aquino tore up the diplomatic rule book and compared China to Nazi Germany. "At what point do you say, 'Enough is enough'?" Aquino asked in a New York Times interview. "Well, the world has to say it—remember that the Sudetenland was given in an attempt to appease Hitler to prevent World War II."[30] He repeated the comparison during a visit to Japan: "Unfortunately, up to the annexation of the Sudetenland, Czechoslovakia . . . nobody said stop. If somebody said stop to Hitler at that point in time, or to Germany at that time, would we have avoided World War II?"[31]

Aquino's statement was an open challenge to the United States to do more to protect its long-standing ally and Southeast Asia from Chinese expansion. But there was little America could or was willing to do, and the Philippines discovered, as China had in the mid-nineteenth century, that it had no sea defenses against a hostile foreign power.

"We cannot promise people something on China that we can't deliver," Philippine senator Gregorio Honasan, chair of the National Security and Defense Committee, told me. "How can we promote sovereignty if we have no security policy, and how can we have a security policy if we do not have a strong economy?"

This stage of the Philippine embroilment in the South China Sea is a story involving three leaders, each cut from different cloth: Aquino, Duterte, and US president Barack Obama, each wrapped in America's long history with the Philippines, inadvertently inherited in 1898 from an anticolonial war against Spain in the faraway Caribbean.

---

30. "Philippine Leader Sounds Alarm on China," Keith Bradshaw, *New York Times*, February 2014.

31. "Philippines' Aquino revives comparison between China and Nazi Germany," Reuters, June 2015.

The urbane Benigno Aquino was part of a wealthy political dynasty that among its assets listed the Philippines' biggest sugar estate, Hacienda Luisita. Aquino's father, Ninoy, an icon of the democracy movement, was assassinated in 1983 on his return from exile to lead the opposition against Ferdinand Marcos. When Marcos was expelled in 1986, Ninoy's widow, Cory, who was Benigno's mother, became president and staved off repeated attempts to overthrow her. Her main success was overseeing the democratic transition to the next president, Fidel Ramos, a former chief of staff of the Philippine Armed Forces. From there the country darted to Joseph Estrada, an eccentric film star; Gloria Macapagal Arroyo, the daughter of another political dynasty; Benigno Aquino; and then seventy-one-year-old Duterte, cast from another mold altogether.

Duterte won power in May 2016 on a populist vote of the style that delivered Donald Trump to the White House and, two years earlier, Narendra Modi to India's top job. All three men appear to be rough-and-ready, sleeves-rolled-up leaders who can get things done. Duterte, an acknowledged killer, won by skirting conventional channels and speaking straight to the common people, often in the language of the grassroots villages with son-of-a-whore and son-of-a-bitch style swearing, whether about the American president or drug traffickers whom he had ordered to be shot dead without judicial process. Duterte had won by six million votes more than his closest rival, a huge electoral mandate that he used to justify his shoot-to-kill program with the aim of wiping out the drug trade.

"We will not stop until the last drug lord . . . and the last pusher have surrendered or are put either behind bars or below the ground, if they so wish," Duterte had declared in his June 30, 2016 inaugural address, unfolding a policy that rubbed badly against those who believed democratically elected governments did not do such things.[32]

He came across as a Clint Eastwood character from a spaghetti western, the guy who walked into town, guns blazing, to raise hell for the common good. Duterte had earned his spurs by grittily taming the

---

32. "The Killing Time: Inside Philippine President Rodrigo Duterte's War on Drugs," *Time*, August 2016 http://time.com/4462352/rodrigo-duterte-drug-war-drugs-philippines-killing/

vast unruly southern city of Davao, making it safe for families to take their kids to play in parks again. He had achieved that not by being nice but by gunning down the bad guys.

"I'd go around in Davao with a motorcycle, with a big bike, and I would just patrol the streets, looking for trouble," he told a group of businessmen, recounting his twenty-year tenure as mayor. "I was really looking for a confrontation so I could kill. I used to do it personally. Just to show to the guys (police) that if I can do it why can't you?"[33]

Duterte took office in June 2016, a month before the Permanent Court of Arbitration ruled in favor of the Philippines and against China over its South China Sea claims. His initial reaction was to warn of war with China. He spoke of it being bloody and of the bones of soldiers, including his own, being sacrificed for Philippine sovereignty. But within weeks of that bravado, Duterte switched his hostile sights from China to the United States, and it became personal. In September 2016, at a regional summit in the small, impoverished, communist-run country of Laos, the street-fighting mayor came head-to-head with the professorial President Obama. It should have been a meeting between the leaders of two democracies with shared values and a military alliance that helped protect Southeast Asia, but it wasn't.

By the time they both arrived in Laos, more than two thousand had been killed in Duterte's antidrug operation. The US government and human rights groups had already spoken out against the killings, and Obama said he would raise them with Duterte when they met. That was when the relationship began to fall apart. Despite his earthy, abrasive manner, Duterte's upbringing was far more privileged than Obama's. He came from a political family with a network of relatives and supporting clans. His father and cousin served as mayors in the central city of Cebu. He was sent to good private schools, although he was expelled from two, and he graduated with a political science degree from the prestigious Lyceum University of the Philippines in Manila. He went on to get his law degree from San Beda College of Law, which was run by Benedictine monks. From there he joined the prosecutor's office in Davao City.

---

33. BBC, "Philippines: Duterte Confirms He Personally Killed Three Men," December 16, 2016, http://www.bbc.com/news/world-asia-38337746.

Obama, on the other hand, came from a broken home with an American mother and an estranged Kenyan father who died in a car accident when Obama was twenty-one. Obama's primary school years were spent in Indonesia, giving him experience in Southeast Asia, and from there with help from scholarships he went on to law school, became a civil rights attorney, and was elected to the Illinois State Senate in 1996.

There is often friction of moral choices between a criminal prosecutor and a human rights attorney and, in the Laos showdown, it unfolded in the will of a democratic superpower against the needs of a poor, developing Asian country.

Duterte's first outburst came as he boarded his plane for Laos. Asked by reporters what he would do if Obama pressed him on the anti-drug killings, he said, "I am a president of a sovereign state and we have long ceased to be a colony." His voice was raised and he tapped his chest to make his point. "I do not have any master except the Filipino people, nobody, but nobody. You must be respectful. Don't just throw around questions." He switched to the local language, Tagalog, to say "Putang ina" (meaning "son of a bitch"), then continued in English: "I do not want to pick a quarrel with Obama but, certainly, I do not want to appear to be beholden to anybody."[34]

A story leapt around the world proclaiming that Duterte had called Obama a "son of a bitch," or "son of a whore," as some media outlets translated it. Obama canceled their scheduled meeting.

So, was this a real shift in Philippine foreign policy, or was it a lost-in-translation misunderstanding that got out of hand? It was a bit of both.

"So, the president says 'son of a whore,' like when something goes wrong you might say 'fuck' or 'goddamn it,'" a senior Philippine official told me in Manila. "He was cursing the situation, not Obama. Listen to it. He didn't say, '*you* son of a bitch,' and when he said '*you* must be respectful' he was talking about the reporters, not Obama. And if you hear Duterte speaking, he's one of those guys who swears all the time, son-of-a-bitch this, son-of-a-whore that."

---

34. President Rodrigo Duterte, live television press conference, Davao City, the Philippines September 5, 2016.

There was, though, an added layer that underpinned the shifting winds of Asia when it comes to American influence. Obama had gone to Laos from a G20 summit in Chengdu, China, arriving on a day when five world leaders, including Russian president Vladimir Putin, had been greeted flawlessly. In a calculated, public snub, Chinese airport staff failed to deliver steps and unroll a red carpet for Obama to disembark in presidential style from Air Force One. Hurried arrangements were made for him to leave by emergency steps lowered from the back of the aircraft, while Chinese and US officials exchanged sharp words on the tarmac. "This is our country. This is our airport," shouted one Chinese official in English, with all the anger that underpinned China's Century of Humiliation and the unwelcome wielding of American power in Asia.

There is common sentiment here with Duterte's declaration that the Philippines is "no longer a colony." A month later, in October 2016, this leader of America's oldest ally in the Asia-Pacific flew to Beijing with 250 business people. Duterte played up his own Chinese heritage (his grandfather came from Xiamen), declaring, "It's only China [that] can help us."[35] He started with handshakes and flags, signed agreements on fishing, trade, and Chinese investment, and concluded with a dramatic performance in the Great Hall of the People on Tiananmen Square. "In this venue, your honors," he told an array of the Chinese elite, "I announce my separation from the United States. . . . America has lost. I've realigned myself in your ideological flow, and maybe I will also go to Russia to talk to Putin and tell him that there are three of us against the world—China, Philippines, and Russia. It's the only way."[36]

Questions were raised as to whether, in its campaign to weaken the pro-Western alliance in Asia, Beijing had taken its first scalp.

THE PHILIPPINES HAD been down this anti-American road before. Like many developing countries, it loved baseball hats, green cards, Disney, and aid money but resented being told what to do and the sense of being beholden to a foreign country. Duterte's sudden switch of policy

---

35. Ed Adamczyk, "Philippines' Duterte: 'Only China Can Help us,'" UPI, October 18, 2016, https://www.upi.com/Top_News/World-News/2016/10/18/Philippines-Duterte-Only China-can-help-us/7641476798719/.

36. President Rodrigo Duterte speaking in Beijing October 20, 2016

was less the grinding of global tectonic plates and more a symptom of unpredictable democracy and the Philippines' own haphazard way of doing things. In March 2016, less than six months before dramatically shifting his allegiance from the United States to China, Manila and Washington, DC, had signed the Enhanced Defense Cooperation Agreement, a military support package that gave the United States the use of five air bases, specifically for South China Sea operations.[37]

The Philippines mattered to the United States because of its 1951 military treaty, and during its last significant anti-American spell in the early 1990s America ended up having to close two huge bases that had been pivotal to its Cold War regional defense.

First to go was Clark Air Base, fifty miles north of Manila, in what appeared to be an act of God. As the Philippines was debating the expulsion of the US military, the nearby Mount Pinatubo volcano erupted, covering Clark's sprawling fourteen-square-mile military metropolis with thick, impenetrable ash. The fifteen thousand people who lived there fled. At least a hundred buildings were destroyed; many more were damaged, weighed down by a coating of thick gray sludge. It would have taken up to $800 million to fix, and the Philippines was asking for another $800 million in annual rent.

America did not want to stay where it was not welcome. Communist insurgents were gunning down US servicemen. Activists protested outside the US embassy. The Cold War had just ended, the Soviet threat was gone, and China had not yet risen. The United States had military arrangements with Singapore and Thailand and maintained bases in Japan and South Korea. Farther east, it had huge facilities in Hawaii, home to the US Pacific Command, and Guam, a small island where munitions to fight a Pacific war are stockpiled and 27 percent of the population is the American military. Given the growing hostile mood, the expense, and the difficult negotiations, it made sense to downsize from the Philippines. The United States had been at Clark since 1903. It decided to leave.[38] Little did anyone imagine that only a

37. "These Are the Bases the US Will Use Near the South China Sea," *Washington Post*, March 21, 2016.

38. "These Are the Bases the US Will Use Near the South China Sea," *Washington Post*, March 21, 2016.

generation on Russia would be resurgent and China would have woken up as a menacing giant.

The naval base at Subic Bay, fifty miles from Clark, was next. Subic had also been hit by Mount Pinatubo, but not as badly, and the US preference was to stay. It negotiated the Treaty of Friendship, Peace and Cooperation to extend the lease. But, in a reflection of nationalistic sentiments running through the country, the Philippine Senate rejected it. The United States narrowed its aims to requesting a three-year extension. That failed too, because the Philippines insisted that the United States revealed if it kept nuclear weapons at Subic Bay. To have complied would have broken the policy of neither confirming nor denying whether its warships, submarines, or aircraft are carrying nuclear weapons.

By the end of 1991 all US military personnel were being ordered out of the Philippines. The naval base became the Subic Bay Freeport Zone, a magnet for tax-exempt auctions, imported vehicles, construction equipment, and the like. Today it is no bustling commercial port, but more an empty expanse of wide roads, huge jetties, and military barracks turned into fast food joints, hotels, and massage parlors. Its small airfield, with old planes, rusting hangars, and grass growing through the runway resembles the set of a 1980s mercenary movie. American warships visit, but none is based there and crews are not allowed into the town. During the Second World War, Vietnam, Korean, and Cold Wars, American servicemen raised hell and laughter along strips lined with bars, brothels, and beckoning girls. Those fresh-faced or war-damaged young sailors have long gone. A few bars have survived; many customers are veterans going down memory lane, some with wives in tow, or retired servicemen who are never able to leave.

The US bases were a lightning rod for nationalist Philippine discontent. But shutting them down didn't bring closure about the Philippines' history and its place in the world, the stigma exposed by Duterte of being treated like a colony. It was not too long before the government was asking the Americans back. For a moment, it was a win-win: America needed an extra foothold in Asia, and the Philippines needed help against Islamic extremism. The 9/11 attacks motivated a resurgence of centuries-old Islamic unrest in the south. American special forces became a fixture in training and intelligence gathering. Then came China's resurgence and the Scarborough Shoal incursion. That not only underlined the country's military weakness but also exposed how much the Philippines, indeed each Southeast Asian nation, relied so much on China for its economy.

Since 2012, Beijing had slapped sanctions on the Philippines' fruit exports, claiming they did not meet pest control standards. Thousands of tons were impounded and destroyed. The banana market alone was worth $60 million a year together with jobs and livelihoods. And that was just one industry. China deliberately kept Philippine exporters on edge. Some goods were let through; some were impounded. They never knew whether a shipment would make it, and it became clear that China's leverage could make or break the Philippines' development. The choice was either to sacrifice its economy or accept China's authority, its aid money, its building of infrastructure that could turn the Philippines into a modern Asian nation. On the one hand, the choice was clear cut because the United States could no longer fill the role. On the other, it was unacceptable to exchange one colonizer for another. The Philippines had been under the sway of foreign powers since the sixteenth century, and each time it tried to take control of its destiny something got in the way. As Senator Honasan argued and China itself discovered, first a country needs a strong government and economy. After that things can begin to fall into place.

America colonized the Philippines almost inadvertently when it won a swift war against the fading Spanish Empire in 1898. The fighting took place in the Caribbean, where the United States took Cuba and Puerto Rico. The Philippines, also ruled by Spain, came with the surrender treaty, establishing the United States as a Pacific force. America's decision to go into Cuba came after more than three years of guerilla insurgency that was disrupting trade, particularly in sugar. There was also political pressure because of atrocities being carried out by the Spanish colonial government. American victory was swift, a decisive blow against the old European order, and, by taking ownership of the Philippines, too, America unexpectedly became a Pacific power. The war against Spain, intervention in Cuba, and taking the Philippines marked the beginning of an ideological mission encompassing trade and human rights that continues to underpin so much of US foreign policy today.

Spain had run the Philippines for more than three hundred years, from 1521 to 1898, and US president William McKinley's thoughts at the time revealed his hesitancy and how unsure he was of how to handle the Philippines. He concluded that he could not argue the case for colonization; the American flag had not been planted on foreign soil to acquire more territory, he argued, but "for humanity's sake."

"When I realized that the Philippines had dropped into our laps, I confess I did not know what to do with them," McKinley said in a magazine interview.[39]

> And one night late, it came to me this way. One, that we could not give them (the Philippines) back to Spain. That would be cowardly and dishonorable. Two, that we could not turn them over to France and Germany, our commercial rivals in the Orient. That would be bad business and discreditable. Three, that we not leave them to themselves. They are unfit for self-government, and they would soon have anarchy and misrule over there worse than Spain's wars. And four, that there was nothing left for us to do but to take them all, and to educate the Filipinos, and uplift and civilize and Christianize them, and by God's grace do the very best we could by them, as our fellow-men for whom Christ also died.[40]

Significantly, more than a hundred years before George W. Bush ordered the invasion of Iraq, his predecessor had understood that regardless of the high moral purpose, freeing up a country too quickly was fraught with danger.

McKinley also inherited an ongoing Islamic insurgency. As soon as the United States took control in 1899, it found itself at war with Moro fighters who fought with such intensity that the United States appealed to the Ottoman Empire in Turkey to broker a peace deal. But the dogged Moros would not even listen to the mighty Ottomans. Fight-

---

39. General James Rusling, "Interview with President William McKinley," *The Christian Advocate*, January 1903.
40. Ibid.

ing lasted fourteen years, to 1913. American dead were fewer than a thousand. The Moro casualties were far higher because of their unwillingness to surrender. Another Moro war ran from 1972 to 1986, and at its peak in the mid-1970s, 80 percent of the Philippine military was deployed against more than thirty thousand Moro fighters. Casualties totaled more than fifty thousand.

There has never been real peace in the Moro areas of the southern Philippines. The insurgency comprises a mix of the old Moro groups who had fought the Spanish, Americans, and their own government for centuries, and newer groups inspired by the Islamic State and al-Qaeda from the Middle East. In 2017, fighters associating themselves with the Islamic State (commonly called ISIS) fought Philippine troops as they moved in and occupied large parts of the city of Marawi in the south, holding it from May to October 2017 and prompting Duterte to declare martial law in the area.

About 5 percent of the Philippine population, or four million, are Muslim. Most live in Mindanao, where a quarter of the twenty-five million people follow Islam. The heartland of the Moro Islamic insurgency lies on the Sulu Archipelago, which, strangely, has a long history of allegiance to China. One of its first rulers, Paduka Pahala, the East King of Sulu, is buried in the northern Chinese province of Shandong. In the early fifteenth century he led a three-hundred-strong delegation to China to pay tribute to the third emperor of the Ming dynasty, Zhu Di. Paduka Pahala became ill, died, and was buried in an intricately sculpted tomb that has become a key tourist attraction. Descendants of his delegation are now classed as part of the Hui Islamic minority.

The key islands of the Sulu Archipelago are Basilan, Jolo, and Tawi Tawi, where battles with high casualties have been fought between extremists and Philippine troops. This is as almost as much a no-go area for civilians as Raqqa was once in Syria or Mosul in Iraq, with visitors risking kidnap or murder. The archipelago stretches to the Malaysian state of Sabah and out toward Indonesia. Today much is controlled by the Abu Sayyaf affiliate of the Islamic State, which has gained notoriety by carrying out executions and kidnapping of foreign hostages.

Duterte is hoping that China can succeed where Spain and the United States failed and that the Philippines' new infrastructure of high-speed railways, roads, and airports can lift Mindanao's economy enough to show the next generation that fighting for Islam is not worth it.

The United States gave the Philippines full independence in July 1946 in the wake of the Second World War. But it retained its military bases, and very quickly the Cold War set in. The United States retained its grip, finally supporting the authoritarian rule of Ferdinand Marcos. It was not until Marcos was overthrown that the Philippines had a real chance to strike out on its own and become a strong democracy.

In early 1986, businessmen, nuns, grassroots activists and others joined together to force an end to Marcos's twenty-one-year rule. After he fled to Hawaii and protesters breached the walls of Malacañang Palace, the colorful symbol of Marcos's misrule came in the discovery of his wife's three thousand pairs of shoes alongside coffers of corrupt money, while outside malnutrition and disease were rife.

The Philippines became an early modern experiment in the tricky transition to democracy that we have seen so much of in recent years. Unfamiliar with the horse trading and compromises of the democratic process, a restless military staged coup attempt after coup attempt while communist and Islamic insurgents exploited the power vacuum with new campaigns. The West poured in money that vanished into corrupt pockets. In the ensuing years the authoritarian regimes of Southeast Asia forged ahead, while the Philippines foundered. The per capita annual income in 2016 was less than eight thousand dollars, only just ahead of India and way behind China, where it was almost double.[41] The Philippines had fallen behind in many other areas, too. Its infant mortality rate was twenty-two deaths per thousand births, twice that of China, and Filipinos lived on average five years less than the citizens of that autocratic superpower.

The pitfalls of the dictatorship-democracy transition are weak institutions, entrenched interests, ethnic divisions, and an ignorance of how legislative checks and balances are meant to work. The Philippines experience is comparable to that of Egypt, Iraq, Ukraine, and others. As President McKinley had feared, after the fall of Marcos, anarchy and misrule prevailed.

---

41. Central Intelligence Agency, *World Fact Book* *https://www.cia.gov/library/publications/the-world-factbook/*

CHAPTER 7

ASIAN DEMOCRACY:
WHY I DIDN'T SHOOT
THE PRESIDENT

SENATOR GREGORIO HONASAN, NOW A RESPECTED POLITICIAN, WAS a key figure in the Philippines' democratic transition, pivotal in the overthrow of President Ferdinand Marcos and after that in numerous attempts to overturn the civilian government and bring in military rule. Honasan offers an insight as to why the Philippines is so badly placed with China in its campaign for sovereignty in the South China Sea, and why so many attempts to install Western democracy in the developing world have failed.

In the 1980s, only in his thirties and the youngest colonel in the Philippine military, Honasan had been a pinup figure, slim, athletic, sexy, and driven, wearing his military fatigues like a fashion model and at ease with weapons. Legends grew around him, particularly one about parachuting from aircraft with a three-foot pet python wrapped around his waist. Not true, he says; it was in his pocket.

Marcos's rule began to falter in 1983 when the opposition leader Ninoy Aquino was shot dead on the steps of his plane at the Manila airport, now named after him. Between then and 1986, Honasan created the Reform the Armed Forces Movement with a group of young officers who became known glamorously as the RAM boys. "We realized that to change things we would have to step out of barracks," Honasan told me, "to attack the very center of power—not to harm the occupants, because Marcos was still our commander-in-chief, but to capture him alive and present him to the people for judgment through due process and the rule of law, something that the nation was deprived off for almost two decades."

In February 1986 Marcos called a snap election, the fading dictator against Corazon Aquino, the widow of the assassinated democracy hero. The result was close and disputed and it was into this acrimonious vacuum that Honasan chose to launch his military operation against Marcos with a plan to seize the presidential Malacañang Palace and key radio and television stations, military bases, and airports. The plan leaked, causing them to abort, but already prodemocracy protestors were taking to the streets, accusing Marcos of rigging the election to stay in power. They gathered along the wide Epifanio de los Santos Avenue, which ran through Metro Manila, in what became known as the EDSA revolution. From all walks of life and supported by the powerful Catholic Church, people stretched through city streets as far as the eye could see. It was into this massive gathering that Honasan, a handful of rebel officers, and Marcos's defense minister walked amid scenes of flowers in gun barrels, soldiers embracing nuns, and military men linking arms with activists, similar to what we would see twenty-five years later in Cairo's Tahrir Square.

"When we made that crossing of a sea of a million people, my greatest fear was that the people would not understand what we were trying to do," said Honasan.

In a whirlwind of shifting loyalties, Marcos's power was being shredded minute by minute by defecting figures from politics, business and the armed forces. When he finally pleaded for support from the United States, he was told instead that it was time to go. One of the more dramatic moments came when a fleet of military helicopters flew low over Manila toward the main army base, creating uncertainty as to whether the pilots were defecting or about to attack. The lead pilot, Red Kapunan, a friend of Honasan's, later explained how he honed his helicopter formation skills on the movie set of *Apocalypse Now*, which had been filmed in the Philippines. Kapunan and his colleagues flew helicopters in the famous scene showing an attack on a Vietnamese village with Richard Wagner's *Ride of the Valkyries* blaring out from Kapunan's cockpit.

On the morning of February 25, with the streets filled with protestors and troops on the same side, Marcos and Aquino were both sworn in as president in rival ceremonies. Marcos's was thinly attended at Malacañang Palace, and Aquino's took place at the exclusive Club Filipino, a lavish hideaway for the wealthy elite. But before the day was out, Marcos had gone. At 10:00 p.m. a US military helicopter took the presidential entourage to Clark air base, where they were given two US military passenger jets needed for their cronies, booty, and families to fly to Hawaii. Marcos was so sick and exhausted that he traveled lying down on a stretcher. The protesters breached the presidential palace to discover his wife Imelda's three thousand pairs of shoes, which became the symbol of the couple's misrule.

Although a national hero, Honasan was far from happy. He had planned to create a military-led government that would clean out the system and oversee new elections after about a year. Instead, the cry to recognize Cory Aquino's swearing-in and for her to continue as president became too strong to resist. He was furious that her ceremony had been held at the Club Filipino instead of somewhere more accessible to ordinary families.

"Cory had not been visible in EDSA," he said. "If she had been there with us, it might have been different, but she did not represent the change we needed. The others decided to subordinate themselves to Cory and, for us, that was a problem. We thought that the national mood, the degree of impatience, the demand for real change would continue. Instead, everyone just went home."

"But you didn't give your new president very long, did you?" I asked. "What did she do that was so wrong?"

"We expected improvements in the system."

"Sure, but that doesn't happen in months."

"She set free a lot of political detainees, and many of those people went back to their armed insurgencies. She did it with the stroke of her pen, not realizing the cost to our soldiers' lives. Thousands of us had died. It was like the Arab Spring. You get rid of the dictator. The pendulum swings from one end to the other, and you create more problems than solutions."

Within months Honasan was plotting to overthrow the new and inexperienced Aquino. He trained a special force of thirty men to carry out yet another assault on Malacañang Palace with its new president inside. They moved on August 28, 1987, when I was having a drink not far away with a colleague at the laid-back bohemian Cafe Adriatico in Remedios Circle.

We rushed toward the Palace, following an armored car that stopped sharply when a mortar or rocket-propelled grenade exploded just yards in front of it. As the smoke cleared, the body of a young man who had been selling cigarettes lay skewed on the street, lit by our headlights, almost cut in half, his stomach ripped open. The armored car was from the mainstream military. Honasan's men had killed the cigarette vendor. The two sides exchanged small arms fire while we watched. Soon reinforcements came, and Honasan's operation was at risk.

By then he had shot his way into the palace and reached the corridor outside Cory Aquino's bedroom. With the palace surrounded by her troops, he realized that trying to abduct her now would raise the stakes to an unacceptable level.

"I was looking at the bedroom of Cory," he said. "We were willing to die, but we were not willing to do what was necessary. Killing fellow soldiers. If I had pushed on with the assault we would have had to fight our way out and she might have died."

"And you didn't want to kill her?"

"Good God, no. I wasn't willing to harm her. If we had, we could not have weathered opinion from the international community. That was when we withdrew to Camp Aguinaldo."

"When you knew you had lost?"

"Not lost, but the momentum had gone. The longer it takes to finish a coup, the more the advantage shifts to the other side."

There were contradictions and conflicting small details, but it was thirty years ago, and Honasan's central story added up. He was a young soldier who had tasted power, and was unprepared for what followed.

"What did you hope to achieve?" I said. "Did you want to become president?"

"No. No. It wasn't that at all."

"What, then? Was it that you didn't understand the democratic space that was suddenly being allowed?"

"Yes. It takes patience to rebuild a nation after a dictatorship. And there's been proof of that all over the world. I was just a soldier. I had no experience."

Honasan fled underground, was captured, lost his middle ring finger by ripping it on razor wire as he tried to escape, and was imprisoned on an old ship in Manila Bay while all the time stirring up more unrest within the military. He spearheaded a third coup in 1989 when the military took control of Manila's international airport, several air bases, and luxury apartment buildings in the Makati financial district. The threat was so serious that the United States deployed its fighter jets over Manila with instructions to confront rebel aircraft if necessary. Again, among the main casualties were cigarette sellers caught in the cross fire on street corners.

"The innocent people who died," I asked. "Do you have any regrets?"

A defensive aura unfolded across his face. "I'm willing to stand in front of a firing squad as long as they hold responsible the ones that caused the loss of life—" He reeled off numbers of civilians and troops killed by insurgents.

"No," I interrupted. "Let's separate things. Do you have any regrets for the people who died during the coup attempts that you were behind?"

"Let's go by the numbers: 150 in '87. About three hundred in '89."

"And regrets?"

"No regrets, but always a lesson."

He stiffened, hands open, pressing on the table, his severed finger stark against the polished wood, which was when I spotted a small, worn tattoo on his right hand just below his thumb. It turned out to be the faded logo of an organization that symbolized much about the Philippine character and explained why Marcos at his peak and President Rodrigo Duterte now have so much popular appeal.

The marking represents a promilitary, right-wing organization, the Guardian Brotherhood, set up in 1976 at the height of the Muslim and communist insurgencies. Its founders were a unit of noncommissioned officers who wanted to make sure they were watching each other's backs. Honasan joined at the time, and since then its membership has grown into the millions and is now more grassroots-focused, working in villages and slums to ensure basic services. Honasan was its national chairman, and its other more famous member was President Duterte, who wears a similar tattoo in the same place on his right hand.

"The Guardians helped me so much when I was on the run. They hid me. They gave me shelter. Without them I wouldn't have stayed free as long as I had. It could be a political force, but it hasn't yet been exploited to its full potential."

Honasan's life as a fugitive ended in 1992 when Aquino's successor, Fidel Ramos, granted an amnesty in exchange for a pledge to stop inciting military rebellion. Aquino suffered at least seven coup attempts against her; Ramos had none. Three years later, still a popular figure, Honasan ran for the Senate and is now a firm supporter of the president, his fellow Guardian Brotherhood member. "He has a clear sense of direction," said Honasan. "This is what was missing before. Every time an issue comes up, you have a surplus of experts talking their heads off. They ask everybody except those who are dying and being killed and the civilians whose property and lives are being destroyed. You can't have a wimp for a leader. You need someone who is feared more than loved and respected."

There are echoes here of Donald Trump's campaign, of the resurgent right in Europe, Britain's split from the European Union, Narendra Modi's massive mandate in India, and Recep Erdoğan's iron-fist rule in Turkey, the loathing of experts and the embrace of what has become known as "populism."

"A populist leader claims to represent the people and seeks to weaken or destroy institutions such as legislatures, judiciaries, and the press," argue Jeff D. Colgan and Robert O. Keohane in their 2017 *Foreign Affairs* article "The Liberal Order Is Rigged."[42] "Populism is defined not by a particular view of economic distribution but by a faith in strong leaders and a dislike of limits on sovereignty and of powerful institutions. Such institutions are, of course, key features of the liberal order."

The weaker the democratic institutions, therefore, the more challenging populism is proving to be and therefore the more vulnerable the Philippines is when it comes to China.

FOR MANY IN the senior ranks of the Philippine military Duterte and Honasan are role model heroes. "We are still not entirely democratic,"

---

42. Jeff D. Colgan and Robert O. Keohane, "The Liberal Order Is Rigged," *Foreign Affairs*, April 17, 2017, https://www.foreignaffairs.com/articles/world/2017-04-17/liberal-order-rigged.

Deputy Chief of Staff Major General Guillermo A. Molina Jr. told me in an interview at the main military base, Camp Aguinaldo. "The appeal of a strongman is still here. That type of leader is what we're looking for. We are not Thailand, but our military provides a sense of stability and predictability, and given our discipline and organization, we give the impression to our people that we are the defender of the homeland. When everything else is in a state of flux, the military stands in the center."

Seen from Beijing, the Philippines under Duterte would be vulnerable for turning. First China had taught the Philippines a lesson with the attacks on its fishermen and economic boycott, then it befriended it. The voters' decision to put in office an authoritarian strongman played right into Beijing's hands. In one of those strange quirks of history, the ballot box was producing exactly the type of government that suited the interests of an antidemocratic government.

Like the armed forces in several Southeast Asian countries, the Philippine military has historically been deployed against internal insurgencies and not external threats. Duterte has now formalized this by ordering the military to protect the nation's infrastructure against "enemies of the state," which are mainly Islamic and communist fighters. The communist New People's Army ran a militia of about three thousand, and it had once been a Cold War, grassroots insurgency, part of the feared domino impact of Marxism sweeping the world, sharing values with Peru's Shining Path, Fidel Castro's Cuba, and doctrines encircling the globe from Moscow. That beacon dimmed long ago. As with the Islamic insurgency, cease-fires came and went, but the communist insurgency has kept going, and routinely carries out attacks on the police, military, and government officials.

Duterte has courted Chinese investment in the hope that high-speed railways and sweeping highways would give the southern Philippines the employment and facelift needed to deter rebellion. The military's job was to make sure none of the flagship projects, ports, airports, telecommunications, fiber optic cabling, and the rest got sabotaged as they were being built.

"We have to be the vanguard of the economy," explained General Molina. "To make this country strong, it has to have peace. Under the previous administration, our critical infrastructure would get blown up, and the army would be sent in afterward. Now, protection of these projects is part of our mandate."

Molina cut a neat figure in a dark blue uniform with a short-sleeved tunic bedecked with medals. He had spent much of his early career fighting the Moro guerrillas in Mindanao. On the table in Camp Aguinaldo he had laid out maps and books to explain the threats to the Philippines. Molina argued that the mission to protect infrastructure was achievable, whereas if deployed against the China threat, the Philippines was bound to lose. "The current maritime situation does not warrant the deployment of the military. The Philippine Coast Guard is responsible for this," he said with a hint in his expression that he understood the irony. While the military was dealing with homegrown threats, the civilian Coast Guard was tasked with warding off a nuclear naval power against which the United States was deploying its aircraft carriers.

Honasan's Senate committee was looking into all the Philippines' multilateral and bilateral arrangements to determine which ones worked and which did not. "You must clearly define your national interest," he said. "Right now, we know we cannot afford to take sides against China. That is a truth we have to live with."

At the same time, however, can the Philippines afford to distance itself so much from the United States, which has both interfered and watched its back since 1899? After Duterte's declaration in Beijing, US officials stress that the US-Philippines relationship was unchanged and nothing had moved on the ground. But the Philippines is clear that as the South China Sea dispute becomes more polarized, it cannot be seen to be getting too close to America, partly because of China's reaction and partly because of Cold War memories that it needs to retain its own dignity of independence.

"We have been conditioned to think that we are the little brown brother of America," Duterte's first foreign secretary, Perfecto Yasay, told me in Manila. "This has not been good for us. We continue to remain subservient and dependent on the US."

Yasay, who had to step aside because of his dual Philippine-US citizenship, said that Washington had been putting pressure on the Philippines to take a more active role in policing the South China Sea by conducting joint patrols with the US Navy. "We don't feel that would be in our national interest because of the realities on the ground here," he explained. "The joint patrols are based on that old fear that China remains a threat, and we don't like that because it's provocative."

"So, is America's tone toward China a help or a hindrance?" I asked.

"It is a hindrance. America's pursuit of its international policy tries to get us involved in whatever quarrel they have with China. It is not worth our while risking our economy because of sovereignty rights around a fishing reef. If the US feels that Chinese aggression needs to be addressed to protect the trade that goes through these waters, let them do that in their own international interests. That's their concern. They must settle their differences with China by themselves, not with countries like the Philippines that have other national interests to pursue."

The policy of détente with China was bearing fruit up in the fishing village of Masinloc. The men were fishing again, and the Masinloc Fishing Association was skeptically studying the offer from China as a guaranteed buyer for whatever fish the villagers caught. The association's head was Leonard Cuaresma, a fifty-one-year-old, slight, bespectacled man who had been taken to China to see for himself the modern fishing industry. In his house on a busy side street, Cuaresma showed me the glossy brochures of the places he had visited, including a fisheries research vessel and a maritime scientific center. The living room was sparsely decorated, neat, certainly not rich or lavish, and on the wall hung plaques depicting Los Angeles, the Statue of Liberty, and other American landmarks. To supplement his income, he ran a brisk business renting out a pool table that stood on a patch of concrete below the window. Cuaresma said he rarely fished himself now because he had lost his boat in bad weather and couldn't afford another one. There had never been enough money. His son had broken generations of tradition and abandoned the fishing trade to become a motorcycle mechanic. Cuaresma told his story while questioning whether he would be right to accept China's offer. "They say they want to be a close friend to the Filipino, but what else do they want to take from us?" he asked. "Will they use this to build more fish farms that will wreck our environment?"

I pointed to the iconic American plaques on the wall. "Five or ten years from now, might you have plaques of Tiananmen Square or Mao Zedong up on your wall instead?" I asked.

Cuaresma smiled, reached down, and brought out a model he had been given in Beijing of the Forbidden City and the Gate of Heavenly Peace. "I have this," he said. "But I haven't shown it yet. I prefer the American ones."

In 2004 the Philippines and Vietnam, now China's main Southeast Asian antagonists over the South China Sea, worked with Beijing to put together a plan for joint maritime exploration of oil and gas. One of its architects, the former speaker of the Philippines House of Representatives, Jose de Venecia Jr., explained that it had been agreed on by all three governments but then blocked by the Philippine Congress. "That is the problem with our style of democracy," Venecia told me. "There are too many vested interests fighting for a bigger bite of the pie."

Venecia revived the plan for Duterte's trip to Beijing because it had obvious advantages for China. Signing with the Philippines and Vietnam would bring on side its two most threatening antagonists. Once that had been done, a second-tier consortium could be formed with Brunei and Malaysia, the other claimants. China's big energy company, China National Offshore Oil Corporation, would be given first refusal on the project. "The appointment of a Chinese operator and drilling company for the multinational consortium will also be logical," Venecia told Duterte in a private letter. "In the event of oil/gas discovery the most proximate buyer will be Chinese refineries nearby and ensure maximum profitability to the consortium while encouraging China's goodwill."

The Asia-Pacific region has far less oil and gas than either Latin America or the Middle East, and there are wildly differing estimates about the South China Sea. Beijing veers to the high side, believing that there could be 125 billion barrels of oil and 500 trillion cubic feet of natural gas.[43] The US Energy Information Administration estimates much less, about 11 billion barrels of oil, which is not a lot given that

---

43. "Why the South China Sea Has More Oil Than You Think," *Forbes*, May 22, 2016, https://www.forbes.com/sites/timdaiss/2016/05/22/why-the-south-china-sea-has-more-oil-than-you-think/.

Saudi Arabia has 268 billion barrels and Iraq 140 billion.[44] Nor are reserves of natural gas enormous, estimated at 190 trillion cubic feet, which would be enough to keep China supplied for only about thirty years, and it is far from certain how much could actually be recovered from the seabed. The number is dwarfed by Russia's estimated 1,688 trillion cubic feet and little Qatar's 890 trillion. On top of all that—and here's the rub—there are few proven reserves in the key disputed areas of the Spratly and Paracel island groups, and only small amounts detected by Scarborough Shoal.

"In sum, the overall potential for the South China Sea is probably relatively limited," writes Mikkal E. Herberg of the National Bureau of Asian Research. "However, Chinese sources make much higher estimates than the US Geological Survey which could suggest a correspondingly higher level of interest in establishing sovereignty and jurisdiction."[45]

It is exactly on this point that China has made its presence known across the western side of the South China Sea with Vietnam, which has suffered none of the Philippines' democratic growing pains. In its wars against world powers, Vietnam has shown that it is not a country to be messed with. That does not, however, mean it can take on Beijing over the South China Sea.

---

44. Mikkal E. Herberg, *The Role of Energy in Disputes over the South China Sea*, Maritime Awareness Project, June 28, 2016, http://maritimeawarenessproject.org/wp-content/uploads/2016/07/analysis_herberg_062816.pdf, 2.

45. Ibid.

CHAPTER 8

VIETNAM:
DON'T MESS WITH US

VIETNAM IS A NARROW SLICE OF LAND THAT WRAPS LIKE A GLOVE around the bulge of the Southeast Asian land mass on the western side of the South China Sea. In May 2014 China put down a hostile marker against Vietnam, much as it had with the Philippines two years earlier at Scarborough Shoal.

The two countries share an eight-hundred-mile long land border across which they fought a war in 1979, and they have an antagonistic history going back centuries. From 111 BC to 938 AD, China colonized Vietnam, and successive generations have never been allowed to forget it. Vietnam has been run by its Communist Party since 1930 and was founded in its original form by the country's charismatic father figure, Ho Chi Minh. Along with Che Guevara and Mao Zedong, Ho became a poster icon for the left-wing antiwar and free love populism that swept the West in the 1960s. Like China, Vietnam is a one-party state that represses free speech, jails dissidents, and holds power while embracing the Western capitalist model to develop the country. Almost a hundred million people live there, with a per capita income of only sixty-four hundred dollars, far behind China and even less than the Philippines. Vietnam is getting richer more slowly than it might because it spent a half century at war and a couple of decades after that isolated by the United States and the international community.

Beijing's marker came shortly after building began in the Spratly Islands. It targeted waters some five hundred miles to the west, south of the Paracel Islands, which Vietnam claimed were within its two-hundred-mile exclusive economic zone. China countered they were within its Nine-Dash Line. The China National Offshore Oil Corporation brought in a massive nine-thousand-square-meter drilling platform, the thirty-six-thousand-ton *Haiyang Shiyou 981*, and started oil exploration. This was the same company that would have been given preferential treatment had the agreement with China, the Philippines, and Vietnam got through the Philippine senate. Open clashes broke out at sea, involving fishing crews and coast guards from both sides on dozens of boats and the sinking of a Vietnamese vessel. The platform left the area in August 2014 since, China said, it had successfully completed its work. Whatever oil reserves might have been discovered counted for little against the rupture in the Sino-Vietnamese relationship that Beijing had forced to a different level by deliberately throwing down a hostile challenge.

And it did not end there. In July 2017 Repsol, a Spanish oil exploration company under contract to Vietnam, was abruptly told to stop drilling days after confirming the existence of a major gas field. Repsol executives said that China had threatened to attack one of Vietnam's Spratly Island bases if it did not pull out.

China might be bigger, richer, and more powerful, but Vietnam has a stubborn warrior streak that has been employed many times before, not only against China but also against France and the United States. Vietnam is the only country to have taken on these three permanent members of the UN Security Council in open warfare and won. Of all the countries of Southeast Asia, it has a track record of prioritizing national dignity above the economy. This was not Cambodia, Laos, Thailand, or even the Philippines. China had stepped across a line to provoke an ancient enemy. Officials in Beijing explained that they had to ratchet up the pressure when it came to Vietnam because in Southeast Asia it was traditionally "the most difficult country to teach."[46]

In Vietnam itself, the government encouraged anti-Chinese demonstrations that scorched buildings and destroyed factories until the rioting began slipping out of control and became protests against the repressiveness of the Vietnamese one-party state. Three hundred businesses and factories were attacked, but only about two dozen were Chinese. Most were Japanese, South Korean, and Thai, indicating a general pent-up anger. The confrontation also exposed a modern truth: China was now a global power and it was a neighbor breathing hard

46. Interviews with author January 2017.

down Vietnam's neck. Vietnam had put up a plucky fight around the Paracels, but it had not won. Strapped for money, the Vietnamese Coast Guard and military were no match for the Chinese. Therefore, Hanoi needed to bury hatchets and get clever. It began by reaching out for help to the very country that had terrorized its people with helicopter gunships and burned its villages and countryside with napalm. It was a meeting of minds. The United States needed Vietnam's help too. A year after the rig confrontation, Washington, DC, lifted its decades-long arms embargo. It gave Vietnam an $18 million loan for six forty-five-foot US-built coast guard patrol boats. F-16 fighters and P-3C Orion maritime surveillance aircraft were in the pipeline together with other military hardware from the British, French, Indian, Japanese, and other governments. Beijing's show of force in oil exploration led directly to the strengthening of the anti-China pro-Western alliance.

Given Hanoi's system of government, the alliance was in no way ideological and Vietnam found itself once again inside an incomprehensible twist of international diplomacy. Throughout the 1970s and 80s, this was one of the world's most closed countries. Visitors spoke about *going into* Hanoi as they spoke of Pyongyang in North Korea, not *going to* as we would with London or Washington. They needed letters of introduction, visas, money, and flight bookings. The country was so heavily sanctioned that it flew only old Russian planes. Barely a vehicle plied the streets. As journalists, we sent stories via telex, from a central post office smelling of damp, rotting wood and disinfectant down by the Hoàn Kiếm Lake. We often ate supper in an illegal family restaurant in a magnificent, crumbling old house that served eel soup and baguettes, washed down with foul Bulgarian wine procured from one of the many flourishing black markets. A daughter played Chopin and Debussy on an out-of-tune upright piano, and a son kept vigil by a window.

Vietnam was under international sanctions because it had beaten the United States in the war. It faced a running issue of returning the remains of American servicemen missing in action, one of those situations that can be kept going indefinitely. The sticking point then was that the United States wanted to search the countryside with helicopters. "How could we do that?" a senior foreign ministry official had

Vietnamese fisherman, Vo Van Giau, beaten with a mallet by the Chinese coast guard.
(Photo: Poulomi Basu)

Author on assignment on Taiwan's Dongsha Island. (Credit: Simon Smith)

Vietnam lays a trap for Chinese warships in 948 A.D.

(Photo: Vietnam Military History Museum)

Concrete stakes on Kinmen Island to impale invading Chinese paratroopers.
(Photo: Humphrey Hawksley)

A Taiwanese military transport plane approaching Dongsha Island.
(Photo: Humphrey Hawksley)

Isaac Wang on Kinmen Island. In 1978, he was a psychological warfare officer.
(Photo: Isaac Wang)

Old Japanese gun position on Taiwan's Dongsha Island.
(Photo: Humphrey Hawksley)

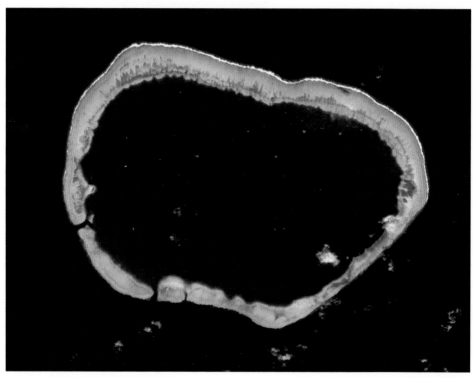

Mischief Reef in January 2012.   *(Credit: CSIS/AMTI/DigitalGlobe)*

Mischief Reef in March 2017 after Chinese military construction.

(Credit: CSIS/AMTI/DigitalGlobe)

Chinese naval officers visit the US Naval War College in June 2017.

told me. "Can you imagine the trauma of our people if they see American helicopters flying above their villages again?"

Inexplicably, Vietnam was also under sanctions for ending the genocide carried out by the Khmer Rouge in neighboring Cambodia, a tragedy made famous in the 1984 film *The Killing Fields*. The Khmer Rouge, which had been loosely allied to the Vietcong during the war, took the Cambodian capital, Phnom Penh, in April 1975, three weeks before the fall of Saigon. While the Vietnamese victors were harsh but disciplined, the Khmer Rouge, under the mercurial ideologue Pol Pot, embarked upon a massacre. Cambodia's population was then 7.5 million, and over the next few years about a quarter of its people were murdered. The first targets were "intellectuals" like schoolteachers and lawyers. When they ran out, Pol Pot targeted anyone not of the Khmer race—Laotians, Thais, and Vietnamese. Then, desperate for more victims, he hunted down the traitors within, Vietnamese "living in Cambodian skins," a case of a ruler looking for someone else to blame. Khmer troops attacked villages across the border in Vietnam, finally prompting Hanoi to invade. On December 25, 1978, it went in with 150,000 troops, and two weeks later ended the genocide and took Phnom Penh.

Beijing had supported the Khmer Rouge, and less than six weeks after Cambodia fell, China invaded Vietnam on what it called a punitive mission, insisting that, like India seventeen years earlier, Vietnam needed to be taught a lesson. But, this time, China miscalculated.

VIETNAM'S ARMY HAD been at war for generations. Skilled and battle-hardened, fighting was in its DNA. China's most recent cross-border military action had been in Korea, though that had ended more than twenty-five years earlier, and it had never imagined the ferocity of the resistance. Vietnam took advantage of a network of tunnels, its long experience of guerrilla warfare, and modern American equipment seized in its victory four years earlier in the south. Chinese troops did eventually reach a string of provincial cities, but with heavy casualties and often in hand-to-hand street combat. By March 6, 1979, Beijing had had enough and announced it had achieved its objectives. As Western military analysts swiftly concluded, Vietnam had given China an unexpected and very bloody nose.

This small war also reflected ongoing antagonism between China and the Soviet Union. Beijing was convinced that Vietnam's move on Cambodia was part of a Soviet plan to control Southeast Asia at China's expense. In many respects its suspicion was justified. Moscow did pass onto Vietnam satellite and signals intelligence used to attack Chinese positions. Later that year, the Soviet Union signed a twenty-five-year lease on the Cam Ranh Bay naval base, giving Moscow a new strategic Cold War advantage in the Asia-Pacific.

What happened next, after the 1979 Sino-Vietnamese War, shows how skewed the global world order can become, resembling some of the arguments surrounding the conflicts in the Middle East and North Africa and the impact on the people in affected areas. Far from being praised for ending the Khmer Rouge genocide, Vietnam was ostracized. Despite the atrocities being well chronicled, the Khmer Rouge kept its seat at the UN and sanctions against Vietnam were ratcheted up. It was as if, after Berlin had fallen in 1945, the Nazis were still recognized as Germany's legitimate government and allowed by the international community to govern large swaths of the country. Those responsible for the Cambodian massacres walked the corridors of the UN head-quarters in New York protected by diplomatic immunity, eating in the finest restaurants, and courted by US politicians playing their next Cold War cards.

One was Republican congressman Stephen Solarz, chair of the Asia-Pacific Affairs Subcommittee. He advocated sending arms to guerilla groups trying to overthrow the Cambodian regime that was now controlled by Vietnam. Solarz tried to argue that no weapons would go to the Khmer Rouge, but there were warnings here of what has evolved in Syria, with the West arming and training guerrilla groups that ultimately merge into one another until it is impossible to tell friend from foe.

In Cambodia, Solarz's aim was to create a coalition of guerrilla groups that would force out the Vietnamese and their strongman, Hun Sen, a young Khmer Rouge guerrilla fighter who had defected. British prime minister Margaret Thatcher was among the world leaders who joined in this argument. "The first thing we need to do is get the Viet-namese out," she told a British television show. "Most people agree that Pol Pot could not go back. . . . There's quite an agreement about that. Some of the Khmer Rouge are very different. There are two parts of the Khmer Rouge. There are those who supported Pol Pot, and there is a much more reasonable grouping within the Khmer Rouge." When the interviewer pressed her on this point, Thatcher said, "That is what I am assured by people who know. So, you will find that the more reasonable ones within the Khmer Rouge will have to play some part in the future government."[47]

Around that time I visited a village on the border with Cambodia and Vietnam. Neak Leung became famous in 1973 when an American bomber mistakenly dropped its payload there, killing 130 people and injuring some 250. It was a tragedy in the fog of war, but one credited with propelling much Cambodian support toward the anti-American Khmer Rouge insurgency.

Clustered in a bamboo shelter with a dirty straw roof, the villagers recounted how their peace had suddenly been shattered by bombing, the village lit up, craters yawning in the road as in an earthquake. They ferried the injured to a makeshift clinic in wooden carts designed to carry rice sacks. Many in the village had been murdered by the Khmer Rouge. One old woman spoke about them bursting into the house, taking her baby granddaughter, and hurling her up in the air to catch the tiny body by impaling her on a bayonet. This practice was also on display in the Tuol Sleng Genocide Museum in Phnom Penh, a former Khmer Rouge prison where many murders took place. As with the Nazis in their concentration camps, the Khmer Rouge kept meticulous records of who was murdered and how.

Both America and the Khmer Rouge had bought unspeakable suffering to Neak Leung while Vietnam had delivered peace. It was far from perfect, but, like Jurrick Oson in Masinloc, the villagers could now get back to their lives. They showed minimal emotion as they told their stories, their eyes expressionless, as if cruelty at this level was part and parcel of their lives. That was, until I asked if they had heard of Congressman Stephen Solarz. They had not. I explained that Solarz was an American politician who wanted to send money and weapons to the Khmer Rouge and other rebel groups. As this was relayed through my

47. British Prime Minister, Margaret Thatcher, BBC Interview, December 1988.

interpreter, faces tightened. One woman let out a scream and put her hand to her mouth. Many looked down at the damp ground, shaking their heads.

"Why?" one asked.

"To overthrow the Hun Sen government," I said.

"Why?" several repeated simultaneously.

I could not explain it. This was a small community. Everyone had lost friends and family to the Khmer Rouge or to the Americans. To them, the suggestion of more weapons and war was incomprehensible, and highly traumatic.

Shortly after that I drove up to the Sino-Vietnamese border, where Chinese tanks had come across in 1979. It was officially closed. There was still cross-border shelling, mostly initiated by the Chinese. That day, however, the border area was a huge market, alive with people—merchants crisscrossing with bicycles, electric fans, motorbikes, cookers, animals, wads of money. It didn't matter if they were Chinese, Vietnamese, or Martians as long as there was something to buy or sell. Someone had strung up a sound system that played an album by the British band Boney M. Hundreds of busy people peeled off bank notes and swapped goods to the rhythm of "Ra-Ra-Rasputin" and "Rivers of Babylon"—a disconnect between politicians with worldly visions in faraway capitals and how people really wanted to live.

A ONCE GRAND French colonial building with faded yellow walls and peeling wooden shutters flung open to the sunlight is home to Vietnam's Military History Museum, where at the front entrance stands a captured American Huey helicopter and a crushed armored car, displayed as symbols of victory. The museum itself is a subtle indicator of how Vietnam deals with its enemies.

In the foyer, huge murals depict Vietnamese victories against China in the distant past. One showed huge wooden stakes cunningly driven into the seabed. At high tide, as Chinese warships approached the Vietnamese coastline, the stakes were hidden under water. When the tide receded, the Chinese found their ships trapped as if in a wooden cage and the Vietnamese moved in for the kill. That was in 948. Other pictures showed a battle in 1077 and another in 1427, when ten thousand Ming dynasty troops were slaughtered by the Vietnamese.

But there was no reference to the wars of the twentieth century: losing half the Paracel Islands in 1956 and the other half in 1974; Johnson Reef in 1988; the 1979 border war and the shelling skirmishes that didn't end until 1987. It was as if Britain's Imperial War Museum had forgotten about Germany, or the United States had thrown a sheet of amnesia over the Iwo Jima Memorial near the Pentagon. And the displays were very different from those I had seen in the 1980s, when the entrance was then marked by three military armored vehicles, one on top of the other, a French one at the bottom, an American in the middle, and a Chinese one on the top with its red star visible on the side. All that had gone. Now, in the forecourt, there was no mention of China being among Vietnam's conquests, a small Asian way of saying Vietnam accepted China's place in the region and would not damage its pride.

The exhibits concentrated on France and America, Western powers much farther away and less relevant in today's regional context: the planning of the 1968 Chinese New Year/Tet Offensive in the south, the taking of Saigon in April 1975, the intricate tunnels used to shelter people from US bombing.

There were scale models and maps showing the tactics that went into surrounding the French garrison in the hilly terrain of Dien Bien Phu in the northwest of the country, commanded by the legendary Vietnamese general Vo Nguyen Giap. Through his experience in leading the resistance against Japanese occupation, Giap had engineered the defeat of French colonialism in Asia. I met Giap in the early 1990s, in Hanoi; he had just turned eighty. He spread maps of the battle area on a huge chart table and spoke quietly, his expression pensive, as if he were planning the battle again. "I am thinking about what I could have done better," he said.

Giap had moved heavy guns up through jungle terrain and dug tunnels so they were hidden, overlooking French positions. In a mix of guerrilla and trench-style warfare, Giap brought his troops forward. Casualties were heavy, progress steady, and the antiaircraft guns took their toll on French aircraft trying to supply the troops. The siege that lasted more than two months, and the French surrender in May 1954, forced a change of government in Paris, the declaration of independence for Vietnam, and the withdrawal of France from Indochina.

The French defeat coincided with an international peace conference in Geneva about the future of the Korean Peninsula. Vietnam was tagged onto the end of it, and the United States remained determined to stop communism gaining a hold over the whole country. It was agreed that Vietnam would be divided along the seventeenth parallel, with Hanoi the capital of North Vietnam and Saigon the capital of the South. Elections were to be held after two years, in 1956, but when the time came, the United States instructed South Vietnam to cancel them. President Dwight D. Eisenhower was convinced that Ho Chi Minh would sweep to power and spread his charismatic communism to Thailand, Indonesia, and beyond. That decision led to an insurgency in the south and, in 1959, Vietcong guerrillas killed the first two American military advisers. Fourteen years and fifty-eight thousand American deaths later, the United States was forced out of Saigon.

Here was an earlier example of what unfolded in the early twenty-first century, where democratic elections produced a winner who did not serve Western interests, such as the Muslim Brotherhood in Egypt in 2012, and the pro-Russian president Viktor Yanukovych in Ukraine in 2010. Each leader was ousted not by elections but by street protests backed by the West.

Vietnam's instability in 1956 gave China an opportunity to make its first move on the South China Sea. It took the Amphitrite Group, in the eastern section of the Paracels. There was no fighting, but South Vietnam responded by sending troops to the Crescent Group in the western section, which China then seized violently in January 1974. Among the museum exhibits, however, there was no mention of the Paracel Islands. These military defeats are airbrushed from Vietnam's history.

On central display was a dog-eared and faded telegram sent from Hanoi in early April 1975 to Vietnamese generals in the field instructing them to move "swiftly" and "not to waste a minute" in taking Saigon. They did exactly that. On April 30, Vietnamese tanks drove into the southern capital, and the United States suffered its biggest defeat of the Cold War. Browsing the exhibits with me were American Vietnam veterans, shaking their heads and asking what it had all been about.

"We called these guys monsters and murderers," said one named Mike, striking up a conversation. "But they were soldiers, just like I was, conscripted and following orders of the North Vietnamese government. I understand now what was going on in Charlie's head. But I've no idea what's going on in the heads of these Islamic groups, executing people on camera, blowing up women and children."

"But did you understand the Vietcong back then?" I asked.

"I didn't have a fucking clue. They were evil terrorists; that's all I knew. And now they're my best fucking friends."

After the displays on the fall of Saigon, there is nothing on the Cambodian war that followed and which lasted more than ten years from the late 1970s to the troop withdrawal in 1988, nor on the short border war in 1979.

The Vietnamese call their campaign against the French the Colonial War. With the Americans, it was the Necessary War. But in Cambodia and with China, at least within the museum, no modern war has taken place. "We don't have any exhibits on this," said a young museum guide, Dinh Thi Phuong. "We don't want any more wars. But we do keep one room empty just in case."

Yet confrontation was routine, with a high risk of violence breaking out, not least around the Paracel Islands in the South China Sea where Vietnamese fishing crews were being assaulted by the China Coast Guard and the maritime militia just as the Filipino fisherman, Jurrick Oson, was around Scarborough Shoal.

IN THE OFFICE of the chairman of Vietnam's Ly Son District, I opened a map of Southeast Asia and asked him to draw on it the Nine-Dash Line. Ly Son comprises three islands in the South China Sea about twenty miles from the Vietnamese mainland and is the home base for most fishermen heading out to the Paracel Islands. Tran Ngoc Nguyen was a neat precise man in his forties, casually dressed in a white and black striped shirt, working in a 1950s-style office. Dark wooden glass-fronted cabinets behind his desk held documents tied together with string. Other papers, secured by black metal clips, were spread out on either side. Tran had lined up his laptop and iPhone neatly next to him. Apart from those, there was no means of communication.

Tran examined the map, cleared more space on his desk, placed his spectacles next to his iPhone, and brought out a red pen. Slowly he traced China's claim, pausing to think, doing it in a single line and not the dashes that Beijing used, moving upward from the island of Borneo, through the Spratly Islands and Scarborough Shoal, hugging coastlines, across and through the Paracels. Then, hardening the pressure, he drew the line right across Ly Son Island, where we were.

"You mean China is claiming even your island?" I asked.

"Yes. They have no coordinates for this line. No one knows exactly where it is, so for defensive purposes we must assume we are at risk."

Vietnamese sovereign waters stretch twelve miles off the coastline, and we were twenty miles out. Technically, Vietnam also controlled a twelve-mile radius around us, but all of that was under dispute.

While Scarborough Shoal is a sea-washed reef, Ly Son is a jumping place filled with the strident sounds of a little metropolis, with a spanking new hotel built right on the harbor. The ferry ride across had been chaotic and crowded: huge packages were handed from jetty to boat across the water, people somehow crammed into the cabin and on deck, and on the bow was an arrangement of yellow flowers, a tribute to someone who had drowned—though how, exactly, was not made clear. Deep sea fishing boats were anchored in the small harbor. Children played in the water on floating rubber tires.

Lined up on shore were yellow taxis, one of which took us up to a map museum on windy high ground overlooking the sea that smelled of mustiness and insects. Moths flitted around the ceiling. The main exhibits were historical maps published in America, Britain, France, and pre-Mao China, all showing Chinese territory stopping on the southern tip of Hainan Island with no reference to the Nine-Dash Line.

There were also photographs and maps of Trường Sa, the biggest of the twenty-nine islands that Vietnam occupied in the Spratly Islands. Trường Sa was 290 miles from the Vietnamese mainland and garrisoned with about two hundred troops. One photograph showed an arrowhead-shaped piece of land with a runway running right through it. Gregory B. Poling's satellite images at the Asia Maritime Transparency Initiative had been tracking how Vietnam was responding to China's island building with new construction of its own. There was work in progress on ten of the twenty-nine islands, mainly to extend existing jetties and shelters, although minimal compared to what China had been doing. Vietnam had reclaimed 120 acres of land compared to China's more than three thousand.

Outside this small museum stood a tall statue that paid tribute to Ly Son fishermen who over the centuries had worked around the Paracel and Spratly Islands. "In ancient times, Ly Son fishermen acted as coast guards to rescue those in trouble at sea and to protect our sovereignty," read a translation of the inscription. "These statues are a monument to them. Now the coast guard safeguards these islands and helps our fishermen fish there in peace."

Except it's too big a job for the coast guard. After finishing drawing the Nine-Dash Line, Tran produced a file that listed attacks by China on fishermen from Ly Son. "There are more and more incidents," he said. "Almost half the boats that go to our traditional fishing grounds now get attacked—at least twenty every year. Of course, we are worried about the Chinese military, their safety, and the damage to their boats. But Vietnamese fishermen do not scare easily."

The next day, in the early morning darkness, we went out on a Ly Son fishing boat.

The Vietnamese vessel was much sturdier than Jurrick Oson's Philippine *banca* with its bamboo outriggers. Even so, there was nothing modern about it. It was cramped and cluttered. A faded Vietnamese flag flew on a mast at the front, and another above the wheelhouse. Inside there was no state-of-the-art marine equipment—just a radio, a compass, and old rusting dials.

"All of us are threatened every time we go out," said Vo Van Chuc, the sixty-two-year-old owner, as he started up the motor with a belch of black smoke out of the funnel next to the wheelhouse. He had been fishing since he was a child. Only in recent years had he experienced serious danger. With him was Vo Van Giau, (no relative) age forty-two, who in July 2015 was beaten up by China Coast Guard crews using his own fishing equipment as weapons.

As Vo Van Chuc steered us out of the small harbor, the breaking dawn cast a red-orange rim around the horizon and Vo Van Giau told his story. He was skippering a fishing boat, like the one we were on.

They were working near the Paracel Islands when a China Coast Guard vessel sped up and rammed into them. The Chinese boarded. They were armed. They dragged Vo Van Giau out of the wheelhouse, kicked him, and made him lie on the deck while they smashed up the wheelhouse. They beat his crew using fishing equipment like hammers and iron rods. Then they took Vo Van Giau across to their vessel. "They forced me to kneel down with my hands on my head. I couldn't see anything around me. They beat me on my shoulders, my neck, and my back. They kept kicking me in the side." To illustrate, he pulled a heavy wooden mallet from a bundle of fishing equipment and struck himself softly on his shoulders and against his sides. He continued, his voice breaking at times. "My father fished these waters, my grandfather and my great-grandfather. From ancient times, they have belonged to Vietnam. Now China has claimed them and invaded them illegally."

He showed photographs of his injuries on his phone—huge swelling bruises and cuts. The attack lasted well over an hour. The Chinese left, telling them not to come back. Vo Van Giau's boat was so badly damaged that it had to be towed back to Ly Son.

Back on the island, we congregated in skipper Vo Van Chuc's spotless but sparsely furnished house with his neighbors and generations of their extended families. These were the foot soldiers of Vietnam's current conflict with China, and there was a feeling of defiance, that they shouldn't give up. Among us was eighty-one-year-old Phan Din, who still crewed on Vo Van Chuc's boat. He had lived through all the troubles of Vietnam's modern history and fully intended to keep working. "We are used to having enemies," he said jovially. "But we are clever people. I began work under the French colonialists as a driver for their officers. I had to take them to the beach with their mistresses and make sure their wives didn't find out. That's how I started being clever. If we think harder, we can beat the Chinese."

As the conversation played out, two things became clear. First, as in Masinloc, few of the younger generation wanted to follow their parents into the fishing industry. Vo Van Chuc's thirty-six-year-old son, Phan Thi Hue, began work as a fisherman but had now gone into tourism while his wife ran a shoe shop. Vo Van Giau had a seventeen-year-old son and two daughters, ages thirteen and eight. They used to go on short fishing trips with him. After seeing his injuries, neither has stepped on a boat. The second point was that if they were going to fish around the Paracels they needed their government to protect them, and that wasn't happening. "Fishing is too hard, with very little money," explained Vo Van Chuc. "It is also becoming dangerous."

Vo Van Giau said he planned to keep fishing. "But we want the Chinese to stop attacking us. We need to fish without this threat, and we hope diplomatic negotiations will quickly bring us peace."

Just over a year later, in a flurry of diplomatic activity, China and Vietnam tried to patch things up. Vietnamese defense minister Ngo Xuan Lich visited Beijing in January 2017, followed a week later by Prime Minister Nguyen Xuan Phuc. He stayed six days, an unusually long time, recalling the long-ago era when Vietnamese kings had to journey to China to pay their respects and bring gifts. Vietnam's economy was too dependent on Chinese trade. Soon, China would be overtaking the United States as Vietnam's biggest export market. For that to work, Vietnam needed greater access to China's markets, which would be blocked if it picked a fight over the Paracel Islands and its injured fishermen.

With Cambodia, Laos, and Thailand already under China's sway, Vietnam was hemmed in. If it opposed China outright, it would lose. If it compromised too much, it risked returning to being a vassal state, and it had fought so many wars to escape that. "In our history, they tried to use military power to make us a province of China," Tran Cong Truc, former head of the National Border Committee, told me. "Our kings used to travel to Beijing and brought them gifts so we could keep our independence. We may have to do a little of that again."

On the way to Ly Son, I had stopped by the nearest Vietnamese Coast Guard station at Quang Ngai, where, in a formal meeting room flanked by uniformed officers, the commander Vu Vanh King recited the mission and achievements of his units. "Patrolling Vietnamese territorial waters is the focus of our mission," he said. "As coast guards we always complete our mission." He took us down to a small jetty to show us a twenty-five-hundred-ton patrol vessel, built in the Netherlands, and revealed that his biggest problem was budget. To take on China, he needed more and better-equipped vessels.

Although Hanoi and Beijing have what they call a "comprehensive and strategic cooperation" agreement dating back to 2008, Vietnam has little trust in China. Several officials made clear that they do not believe in the long-term future stability in the spirit of "good neighbors, good friends, good comrades and good partners" that the agreement is supposed to secure.

"You do not haul a drilling oil platform into your neighbor's backyard if you are working toward that," a senior diplomat told me. "You do not hit your neighbor's fishermen with mallets and try to sink their boats."

When I asked for a comment on the attack on Vo Van Giao, the Chinese Foreign Ministry said it would not comment on an individual case, but that it had the right to enforce measures against boats that had illegally entered its waters "China is unswervingly committed to peacefully resolving disputes," it said.

That commitment has cut little ice with the Vietnamese, who have been reaching out for help. Their defense budget has increased to 8 percent of gross domestic product, or five billion dollars a year—still nothing compared to China's $150 billion, a 7 percent increase in 2017. Russia supplies by far the bulk of Vietnam's weaponry, delivering Sukhoi-30 fighter aircraft and Kilo-class diesel electric submarines. But another hand of friendship reaching through the Strait of Malacca to Vietnam has been India, supplying weapons such as the Akash surface-to-air missile system and military training. It has also bought maritime oil exploration leases. One is the twenty-seven-hundred-square-mile Block-128 in the Phu Kanh Basin in the vicinity of Ly Son island. Vietnam angered China in July 2017 by extending the lease for another two years. Because of the diplomatic tension, there is little chance of the site rendering anything of value in the near future. Both Vietnam and India see the venture as being more strategic than commercial, showing an Indian presence in a disputed area of the South China Sea.

India, like Japan, is the bedrock of the US-built coalition aimed at keeping China's rise within the boundaries of international law. There is, however, a question of how suited India might prove to be for this task. Is it big enough to stand on its own, or, like the smaller Asian countries, does it risk falling into China's arc and, in Beijing's eyes, becoming the biggest prize of all in its collection of vassal states?

PART 3

SOUTH ASIA

Although we are not powerful, we are not afraid of another country. Such an attitude on our part offends other countries.

—JAWAHARLAL NEHRU, founding prime minister of India.

CHAPTER 9

INDIA:
THE VIOLENCE
OF POVERTY

ENSION BETWEEN THE UNITED STATES AND CHINA, STEMMING FROM the latter's actions in the South China Sea, has spilled through to the Indian Ocean, with the growing risk that South Asia could once again become enveloped in a wider global struggle. South Asia comprises Afghanistan, Bangladesh, Bhutan, India, the Maldives, Nepal, Pakistan, and Sri Lanka. Under British colonialism, it also included Myanmar, which was governed as part of India but is now firmly categorized as part of Southeast Asia. Thus, to the east South Asia begins along Myanmar's border with Bangladesh and India and to the west along Afghanistan's and Pakistan's borders with Iran. Its northern edges bleed into China and Central Asia, and its southern edges form the coastline of the Indian Ocean where Chinese money has funded a string of new ports stretching from Myanmar to the east coast of Africa.

While East Asia is dominated by China and Japan, South Asia is dominated by India and, in purely material development terms, has fallen far behind. South Asia is one of the world's most densely populated regions with 1.75 billion people living in an area of nearly two million square miles.

I will examine the fragility of South Asia and how it impacts the future of Asian waters through three prisms. The first is its poverty and lack of development. The second is its nuclear weapons, which will be discussed in chapter 10: both India and Pakistan broke international protocol to become nuclear armed states. And third is how it is either embracing or resisting China's influence, which will be discussed in chapter 11.

This chapter will examine poverty, which India's founding father,

Mahatma Gandhi, described as the worst form of violence. A newborn baby in India is more than three times likely to die in its first year than one in China and nine times more likely than one in Taiwan. Indians are more than twice as poor as Chinese and seven times worse off than Taiwanese. India has been a democracy since independence in 1947. Its neighbors in Bangladesh and Pakistan have swung between democracy and dictatorship, and life for the very worst-off is about the same in all of them. Pakistanis are slightly poorer, with a $5,100 gross domestic product per capita against India's $6,700, and Bangladeshis are way down at $3,900, more on a par with Cambodia.[48]

According to a 2011 Indian census, half the population does not have proper shelter. Thirty-five percent of households have no water nearby, let alone in the house. Eighty-five percent of villages do not have a secondary school. There are no roads connecting forty percent of villages, just paths. India is home to ten of the twenty most polluted cities in the world. If it had the will to house its people, it would have to build thirty-five thousand homes every day until 2024 to keep up with demand. But it almost certainly will not, whereas China is addressing similar problems all the time. Between 2012 and 2016, China put down more railway track than India had since its independence in 1947. Seventy percent of Indians have no access to toilets. Millions of men, women, and children have to defecate in the open, giving rise to a raft of diseases. India's average growth since 1950 has been 6.32 percent, almost double America's 3.2 percent. But where has all the money gone, and how has it been shared?

India has high levels of corruption. Far from bringing progress, its democratically elected institutions too often block it. Many officials and elected politicians are corrupt and use bad practices to get to office. A third of the members of the federal parliament elected in 2014 faced criminal charges—186 out of 543 lawmakers. Of those, 112 faced charges that included kidnapping, extortion, causing communal disharmony, and crimes against women. Nine were accused of murder, and seventeen of attempted murder.[49]

---

48. Central Intelligence Agency, *World Fact Book https://www.cia.gov/library/publications/the-world-factbook/.*

49. Charlotte Alfred, "India's New Parliament Has the Most Members Facing Criminal Charges in a Decade," *World Post,* May 23, 2014.

India's development, its leadership in South Asia, its system of government, and the culture that drives its society will have a pivotal impact on the future of the Indian Ocean, the South China Sea, and other maritime territories. India is the world's biggest democracy and a nuclear weapons power, and its history with China makes it a natural ally to those who want to temper Beijing's ambitions. Both the United States and India have invested much in building a stronger, closer relationship that was fractured during the Cold War. Both may well be setting themselves up for disappointments. Despite every incentive, it remains far from clear whether India is up to the job. And if it is not, America's long-laid plans to retain a balance of power in Asia are at risk.

Since the opening up of its economy in the early 1900s, India has created corporate wealth with companies like Airtel, Reliance, the Tata Group, Wipro, and others. But, that wealth has not been spread fairly. The wretched disparity shows as soon as a visitor drives through any major city, raising questions about how India, and much of South Asia, treats its people.

India and China became new nations within two years of each other—one a new democracy in 1947, the other a new dictatorship in 1949. Their relationship has never been easy, partly because of a misunderstanding about each other's vision. In his 2014 book *Implosion: India's Tryst with Reality*, John Elliott describes how Indian prime minister Jawaharlal Nehru had naive misconceptions about the world order. "Nehru idealistically saw India and China as parallel civilizations that could work together," he writes. "He did not realize until too late that this clashed with China's ambition to achieve regional supremacy."[50]

In March 1947, before India's independence from Britain, Nehru hosted the Asian Relations Conference in New Delhi, an attempt to forge a single Asian identity, arguing that such identity had been fragmented by colonialism. He spoke about how all countries should come together with the "mind and spirit" of Asia faced with a common task. Yet, as noted earlier, the name Asia itself comes not from what defined the continent but from what it was not, from the Greek word that referred to the region east of Europe, beginning on the eastern shore of

50. John Elliott, *Implosion: India's Tryst with Reality* (Noida, India: HarperCollins India, 2014.

the Aegean Sea, covering Anatolia and Persia and from there expanding into the Asia we know today. There was no Pan-Asian identity that united Chinese, Indians, Japanese, or Papua New Guineans, and very little in culture, language, food, or religion that gave India and China shared common ground. Instead there was the mistrust of neighbors.

South Asia still tolerates practices like forced marriage or the stoning to death of couples who fall in love and thereby offend family honor;[51] the tradition of Chhaupadi, when a menstruating girl or woman is banned from the home, from touching others, or from going to school;[52] and bonded labor, in which millions of the very poorest live in conditions defined by the UN as slavery.[53] While these practices are technically illegal, the governments of South Asia have been so weak, corrupt, and ineffective that little or nothing has been done to stop them.

Bonded labor affects some ten million Indians, and it works in two ways. The first is when children inherit debt from parents and grandparents and are born into a system structured so they can never earn enough to end the debt. They begin work very young, usually with little or no schooling. The second is when a family is so impoverished it takes a loan from a labor contractor to work in a key industry such as cotton harvesting or brickmaking. Again, the victims are desperate and have little or no education, and the arrangement is structured so they can never pay back the debt.

I first met a bonded laborer family in 1991 when I was in Delhi to cover the assassination of Rajiv Gandhi. It was a piece to run in the lull before the funeral, along with several others aimed at explaining India to our audience. The Mota family, a husband and wife and their two daughters and son, ranging in age between about seven and eleven, worked less than a half hour's drive from Delhi, breaking rocks by the side of the road. They were malnourished, their skin marked with welts, their noses running and eyes red. Bonded labor had been formally banned since 1976, and twenty years earlier had been categorized by

51. Naina Sharma, "Spike in Honour Killings: Need a New Law to Save Young Couples," *Quint*, May 27, 2017.
52. Poloumi Basu and Evelyn Nieves, "In Nepal, a Monthly Exile for Women," *New York Times*, January 5 2017.
53. Humphrey Hawksley, "Why India's Brick Kiln Workers Live Like Slaves," BBC, January 2, 2014.

the UN as slavery. It is just as easy to find a family living in similar conditions in India today.

The UN's International Labour Organization estimates that twenty-one million people are in forced labor worldwide, at least half of them in India. If Bangladesh and Pakistan are taken into account, South Asia is by far the worst regional offender as regards modern-day slavery. This labor black market creates an annual revenue of $150 billion, exceeding the gross domestic product of many developing countries. More than $40 billion has been traced to everyday industries such as construction and agriculture, which feed straight into the global economy.[54] Only in 2011 did the UN introduce guidelines that held responsible any corporation that allowed human rights abuses in its supply chain.

In the sugarcane fields of Central America and the cocoa plantations of West Africa, I have seen improvements over the past twenty years, but very little in India. Returning time and again, I have found substantive progress, or any political will to make it happen, hard to detect. Scrutiny has been met with denial and, recently, there has been a lashing out against Western democracies for even raising the subject.

STORIES TOLD BY those who have escaped from lives of slave or bonded labor are widespread and horrendous. Workers are kept in check by a wall of fear and threats that reach right back to their villages. On one visit, I headed far into the Indian countryside to meet laborers who had been freed from bondage and were being looked after by a charity, the International Justice Mission. They were in a two-year treatment program to rid them of the trauma they had been through. One of the worst cases was that of Dialu Nial, a teenager who had tried to escape from bonded labor, but was caught. His punishment was to be dragged to a forest, made to kneel, shown an axe, and told by his captors to decide if they should sever his neck, his foot, or his hand. Nial chose to lose his right hand. He was seventeen years old and illiterate. What happened to him and how he managed to put his life back together illustrates the suffering of the people of India, its dysfunctional systems and its, at times, uncaring society. It questions, too, whether India could

---

54. International Labour Organization, "Forced Labor, Modern Slavery, and Human Trafficking," http://www.ilo.org/global/topics/forced-labour/lang—en/index.htm.

ever counter China as offering an alternative model as a beacon for the developing world.

Nial's family lived a half day's drive from the small and chaotic city of Raipur, capital of the state of Chhattisgarh. As we drove, the road deteriorated as did everything else: brick buildings became straw shacks; food stalls became sparsely stocked; animals wandered the dirt road and, to our left, there was a range of mountains that marked the beginning of the "red corridor," occupied by left-wing insurgents. Various rebel groups control swaths of central and eastern India where they fight regular battles with the security forces. In the past twenty years Bangladesh, Nepal, Pakistan, and Sri Lanka have been racked by similar rebellions, whether under the banners of Islam, Maoism, or straight ethnic separatism. China has been responsible for encouraging and sometimes arming some of these campaigns.

I visited Dialu Nial as he was trying to relearn the family's trade. They eked out something from it, not enough to live on, and barely enough to eat. "I didn't go to school," he explained through an interpreter. "When I was a child, I tended cattle and harvested rice." He was sitting on the earth outside the cluster of wood and straw huts that made up his family's home. His village, Nauguda, is a three-hour drive from the nearest town, Bwanipatna, and a day's journey by bus. It has no sanitation, electricity, school, clinic or government services of any note.

Those living in communities like this are driven to become bonded laborers because there is no other way to feed their families. They work in key industries that are crucial contributors to India's transformation into an economic powerhouse, fueling profits of global Indian brands and multinationals. None of that wealth was visible in Nauguda, however.

Nial had been deceived into getting a job in the brick kiln industry, grueling work that involves kneading mud by hand and slapping it into a brick mold, then shoulder-carrying hods up the kiln, like climbing a pyramid, where the bricks are baked hard, taken out, and sold to the construction industry. Many kilns operate with child and illegal labor while the bricks are used to build India's new skylines and shopping malls.

In December 2013 Nial was asked by a friend, Bimal, from a neighboring village if he wanted to take a job working in a nearby kiln.

Nial would get ten thousand rupees ($165) up front, which he could pay back as his salary came in. Another neighbor, Nilamber, who was in his early thirties, agreed to go as well, together with ten others from the area. They took a bus to the nearest town, where a labor contractor lived.

In the eyes of many activists, India's labor contractors are the modern-day equivalent of slave traders. In the eyes of others, they are employment agents giving people an opportunity to work. They advance loans, and through black market muscle ensure the workers do their bidding. They calculate interest and payment schedules in sums that rarely add up, thus producing a debt that puts the worker and his or her family into bondage. With illiteracy rampant and education minimal, most have no idea what they are getting into.

Anyone visiting the small railway town of Kantabanji in western Odisha in November can witness this practice at work. Tens of thousands of farmers who have failed to earn enough from their harvest queue up to take loans to work in brick kilns outside faraway big cities in Tamil Nadu and Andhra Pradesh.

Nial immediately recognized his labor contractor. "I knew he was a rich man. He had a motorcycle and wore a tie," he said. The contractor showed them the promised money, but took it straight back. They would not get it up front, as promised, but sometime later. They did not need it because the kiln was only a few miles away and transportation had been arranged. Nial and Nilamber still believed they would be paid. With a fingerprint, they signed a document agreeing to work.

The next day their friend Bimal took the twelve men to the railway station at Raipur, where they boarded a train. Instead of a short journey, they discovered they were heading five hundred miles south to Hyderabad, a huge city and a pillar of India's booming high-tech economy. Some in the group had heard stories of forced labor there and planned an escape. When the train stopped at the next station, they ran. Nial and Nilamber were too slow. They were caught and taken back to Raipur. "The contractor's henchmen were waiting for us," recalled Nial. "They held us and put their hands over our mouths to stop us shouting."

At this point his friend Bimal slipped away. Nial and Nilamber were taken back to the contractor's house and held hostage. "They called our families telling them to pay money for our release," he said. "They beat us hard, so my brother could hear me crying in pain down the phone."

The contractor demanded twenty thousand rupees, about $330. Nial knew his family would be unable to raise the money. He and Nilamber were held for five days and made to work on the contractor's farm. Every evening, he said, they were beaten.

When it became clear that neither Nial nor Nilamber would be able to deliver the money, they were driven to remote woodland to be punished for trying to escape. It would be a lesson to others. First they severed Nilamber's hand and made Nial watch: "They put Nilamber's arm on a rock. One held his neck and two held his arm. Another brought down the axe and cut off his hand just like a chicken's head. Then, they demanded I decide which I should lose—my life, my leg, or my arm. I told them to do the same as Nilamber. They made me kneel and put my arm on the rock."

He stared out stoically, gripping his leg hard with his remaining hand. "The blood was so much. The pain was terrible. I thought I was going to die. They threw my hand into the woods. I wrapped my left hand around my wound and held it tight. I squeezed it to stop the bleeding until the pain became too much and I released it. Then I had to grip it again."

Basic survival instinct took over. Nial and Nilamber found a stream where they washed their wounds, bound them, and covered them with plastic bags. They followed a stream to a village and from there found a hospital.

Nial's face flashed with impatience. He was keen to get on with relearning the family business. Laid out beside him were old plastic sacks. He needed to unravel them and turn the individual threads into binding cord, which the family then sold. Awkwardly, Nial wedged a wooden spool of thread between his toes. He held another in his remaining hand. His brother, Rahaso, sat next to him doing the same. With just one hand, Nial struggled to wind the cord. Rahaso worked quickly, outpacing him. Nial's spool flipped out of his hand. Rahaso gave it back to him. Disappointment and anger flooded through Nial's expression. Briefly he lost his composure. "How will any girl marry me, when I'm like this?" he whispered, his eyes lowered, his fingers clawing into the arid soil.

NIAL'S STORY WAS shocking enough, but the International Justice Mission had given me a pile of forms with photographic identities of bonded laborers they had freed. Several were as young as three, their little faces staring out from an official form entitled "Release Certificate." It carried an official government stamp, referring to the 1976 legislation banning bonded labor. Alongside that was the photograph, the age, the home village, and the place where the victim was made to work. Most were brick kilns. There is something very wrong with a system that needs an official government stamp to free a child from forced labor.

On the long drive to see Nial, we had met by chance a local member of the state assembly, Rajendra Dhulakia, who was having tea at a roadside stall. We pulled up behind his black sedan with its tinted windows. He was dressed in the politician's traditional garb of a white cotton, loose-fitting dhoti and was friendly at first, speaking about how well the local economy was doing. His mood changed when I showed him copies of the bonded laborers' release certificates. His expression became half bored, a common reaction when I mentioned human rights to people in Delhi, and half irritated that he was being put on the spot.

He said the documents were fake. "But right here," I countered, showing a specific sentence. "It is written clearly, 'bonded labor.'"

"I am not accepting this as bonded labor." He swatted a fly away from his face. "Bonded labor has been illegal by law since 1976."

"On these documents, there is an official government stamp." I pointed to it. "That can't be fake."

He gave his teacup to a staff member and turned to leave. "I am not accepting these documents."

"You recognize this document, but you don't accept it?"

"Yes, I am telling you, I don't accept it." One of the staff members opened the car door. Another moved to step between me and Dhulakia.

"Just to confirm," I pressed. "You say there is no problem with organized crime, people getting beaten up and enslaved by bonded labor."

"Yes, sir. As I have told you, sir." And with that, with limousine tires throwing up a cloud of dust, the member of Parliament was gone. Dhulakia was not alone in his world of denial, and his response was, sadly, unsurprising.

We drove to a series of buildings in a compound just over an hour's drive from Nial's village where he and two hundred others were going through trauma therapy. We arrived to an almost biblical scene. Groups of freed workers had just finished a session sitting under the shade of a tree on an arid grass slope stretching back from the compound. They were walking down for lunch, the bright reds, greens, and blues of their saris blowing back and forth in the wind. From a distance, here was the India we see in the movies, dignified, elegant, filled with humanity. When the line reached us, a dispiriting silence hit us. No one was speaking. Eyes were locked ahead, no expressions, nothing to indicate surprise, relief, fear, security, love, hope, that melee of emotions that dart about our minds all the time.

"There are no words to explain how it feels when you see a human being not being treated as a human being but as a machine," said their counselor, Rosean Rajan. For the 150 people there, Rajan was the matriarchal rock who defined their new security and eased the transition back into an independent life. She explained that the human mind was conditioned to protect itself against abuse by sealing itself off from everyday emotions. The first year of the program concentrated solely on releasing these basic human feelings. "They have been bought and traded as property, and that is how they see themselves," she said. "They don't know how to show emotions. They can't smile or frown or express grief because when they are enslaved, they work on muscle memory. We have social and psychological programs to move them out. But it takes at least two years"

Each had a release certificate to prove that he or she was debt free and not obligated to any labor contractor. One was a three-year-old boy holding a sheet of photocopied paper in both hands that had his photograph in the top right-hand corner. It stated that he had worked in the brick kiln and must not be sent back. Next to him was a seven-year-old girl who had been at a kiln near Hyderabad. She had been released on February 26, 2014. Once freed, the International Justice Mission took the workers' documents to a local government office to get an official stamp put on them.

Rajan introduced us to adult victims. One was a young pregnant wife who had tried to intervene when her husband was being beaten up. She was dragged away, repeatedly kicked in the stomach, and lost her baby as a result. Another had to watch as her husband was thrown off a moving train and killed. When she tried to stop the murder she, too, was kicked in the stomach. Her baby survived.

One family had to endure an unspeakable horror. A woman was repeatedly raped in front of her husband and two children. Rajan explained that this was a common mechanism of instilling fear and obedience, which was why so many labor contractors preferred to recruit an intact nuclear family: it was easier to control.

The International Justice Mission's work was separate from any government service, even though millions of Indians live in a similar illegal predicament. Andy Griffiths, the regional coordinator, explained that slavery in India is not regarded as a serious human rights violation. "No political party includes human rights in its manifesto," he said. "Even if a labor contractor or brick kiln owner is charged, it will take four to six years to go through the courts, usually resulting in a $30 fine."

The system, therefore, gave those involved in bonded labor a sense of immunity. "There is an ownership mentality," said Griffiths. "In our work, we see rape, we see all kinds of sexual violence and murder. Unfortunately, if you believe you can own somebody, that's the kind of mentality you have."

The seven-year-old girl being looked after by Rajan had been a worker at a brick kiln area outside Hyderabad called Ranga Reddy which I had filmed some months earlier. My guide then, Aeshalla Krishna, was an activist with a labor rights group, Prayas Center for Labor Research and Action. In the first brick kiln we visited, there was a mound of coal just inside the entrance, where women and children squatted, breaking up chunks with bare hands. Farther along, men churned mud to mix the clay and water that was slapped into brick molds. In front stood the furnace itself, a huge smoldering, cube-like monument about two stories high. Smoke seeped out of its edges, making the air so acrid that it caught the throat and tightened the lungs. Workers carried hods across their shoulders and then, with the strain of the weight creasing across their faces, climbed the steps to the top to deliver them for baking. Beyond the furnace lay piles and piles of bricks ready to go to construction sites.

"All of this is against the law," said Krishna, reeling off a list of legislation. "The Minimum Wage Act, 1948. The Bonded Labor Act, 1976. The interstate Migrant Workers Act, 1979. Child labor. Sexual harassment. Physical abuse. It's all happening. Every day."

Children were everywhere, sick and hungry. There was no safety equipment. Stories of illness and withheld wages were commonplace. In a squalid mud hut we found Madhiri Mallik, who was only five. Her hair was matted and filthy, her face streaked with dirt, her eyes expressionless, with no evidence of laughter or childhood. Her only clothing was a pair of shorts. She had come from Odisha with her parents and two-year-old brother, the nuclear family unit preferred by labor traffickers because it was easier to control. Krishna crouched down to check her eyes. "She is suffering from an eye problem because of the smoke," he said. "See how the eye is white? The hemoglobin is very low. She would have a headache from the smoking bricks and her stomach would be bad because of the water." He was guessing because Madhiri, like her parents, was operating on the muscle memory that Rajan had explained. There was no expression of pain, of fear, of hope.

Through contacts in the Andhra Pradesh Labour Department, Krishna got us in to interview the labor commissioner, A. A. Ashok, who worked from a vast room ballasted by a wide, dark wooden desk at one end, in front of which stood rows of upright chairs for visiting delegations. On the wall hung photographs and award certificates, several issued by various UN agencies, on how well Andhra Pradesh was doing in tackling poverty and human rights abuse. Ashok was a bear of a man with a huge presence and a big smile, at home with power and his senior government job in an Indian state of fifty million people. He was a snappy dresser too, with thick black hair swept back and slightly tinted glasses that gave him the look of a middle-aged rock star. I began by asking, "What's the problem you're facing in the brick kilns—you know, child labor, bonded labor, minimum wages?"

"No. No," he said quickly. "There is no such thing. I'm very happy to share with you that everyone is paid the minimum wage and the conditions are fine—housing, drinking water, health care system, and so on. Go see for yourself. Ranga Reddy is our model scheme. There are no bonded laborers there."

I told Ashok we had just been to Ranga Reddy. He said I must be mistaken. He showed me a certificate on his wall from the United Nations Development Programme praising his department's work in the Hyderabad brick kilns. It was not unusual in the aid industry for agencies to tour model projects and proclaim what good work was being done. "Tell your big companies that Andhra Pradesh is a perfect investment climate for them," said Ashok enthusiastically. "We will take them on a trip and they can see for themselves that there will not be any exploitative conditions. I give a hundred percent guarantee."

With Prayas and other groups, I had looked at human rights violations in other parts of India. One was the cotton industry in the home state of Prime Minister Narendra Modi, which stood as a model example of India's economic growth.[55] In the cotton factories we easily found children trafficked in from far away. The air was so thick with dust that by their late teens or early twenties many contract byssinosis, a chronic lung condition; they call it "the horror of the white cloud." I had also examined the Indian tea industry in Northeast India, where workers lived on tea plantations made to look so idyllic in the brochures. They are not. The UN had found that these were among the most marginalized communities in India, illiterate and suffering from anemia, malnutrition, and a range of poverty-linked diseases. Private companies controlled them under a cradle-to-grave system left over from British colonialism. Like bonded workers, their salaries vanished in levies for food, accommodation, and health care that they barely understood. In many ways they were even more disadvantaged than the bonded workers because the system cocooned them from the outside world. Issues like child trafficking, forced marriage, domestic violence, and ill health went unchecked.

---

55. "The Gujarat Model," *Economist*, January 8, 2015.

I had tried to get comments from big multinationals like Nestlé, the Indian conglomerate Tata, and Unilever, all of which had huge operations in India and the rest of the world. Nestlé refused to engage, as did Tata. The British supermarket chain Tesco, which uses Indian-sourced products, described the conditions as "shocking" and said it had "the opportunity and responsibility to help make a real difference."

At a lunch in London for Indian industrialists, I raised the issue of bonded labor, but eyes glazed over with irritated boredom. "It is up to the government to handle this. We are just businessmen," said one. I began to counter that his company benefited from the cheap labor, but by then he had moved on.

Peter Frankental, Amnesty International's economic relations program director, summed up the situation. "There are deep-rooted problems of business-related human rights abuse in India," he said. "Much of that involves the way business is conducted, an unwillingness to enforce laws against companies, and fabricated charges and false imprisonment against activists who try to bring these issues to light."

CHAPTER 10

INDIA, PAKISTAN, AND THE BOMB

AFTER PRIME MINISTER NARENDRA MODI CAME TO POWER IN 2014, a more authoritarian atmosphere enveloped India and several activist organizations like Prayas found it more difficult to operate. Some Western multinationals who were donating withdrew funding because of government pressure. These charities and non-governmental organizations are a key element of the developing world because they fill vacuums created by an inadequate state usually for health care, education, and other basic needs. In India, with its corruption and inadequate regulation, they had undoubtedly got out of hand. At a count in 2009, India had a staggering 3.3 million registered—one for every four hundred people. Of those, forty-three thousand were registered as getting money from foreign donors. Yet despite this, India's development figures remained more comparable to Uganda than to its neighbors in Southeast Asia.

Modi planned to change this. To succeed, reform would be needed within government institutions, the police, the judiciary, and health care so they could move in to do the work. And if that were to succeed, he needed not the general muddle through that encapsulated India's development but a strong hand with a clear vision.

A populist leader governing with a large mandate, Modi headed the Bharatiya Janata Party whose roots lay in religious fundamentalism. For many years he had been denied a visa to the United States, which believed that, as chief minister of Gujarat, he had contributed to lethal Hindu-Muslim riots in 2002 during which more than a thousand people—mostly Muslims—died, with twenty thousand homes and businesses destroyed and up to 150,000 people made homeless. The Indian

Supreme Court completely cleared Modi only in 2014, a month before he took office.

India has long suffered communal tension, particularly between Hindus and Muslims, and the election of Modi has exposed more of this fault line. "I do not know when it happened but gradually over the years people around me began to identify me as Muslim," writes Saeed Naqvi in his book *Being the Other: The Muslim in India*. Naqvi describes as a charade the belief that all was well with India's secularism and politics. "As an Indian Muslim who loved his country and was fully invested in it, I felt betrayed," he notes.[56]

Neither of India's two main political parties has succeeded in stepping away from its narrow base. The Indian National Congress has been overshadowed by the ruling dynasty of the first prime minister, Jawaharlal Nehru whose daughter, grandson, granddaughter-in-law, and great-grandson have been party leaders. Drained of ideas and paralyzed by corruption, Congress lost heavily to Modi in 2014.

Founded in the 1950s and claiming to represent all Indians, Modi's Bharatiya Janata Party has been defined over the decades by its support for Hindu nationalism, emboldening grassroots violence against Muslims that has included killings for violating the sacred status of cows and punishing Hindu-Muslim couples for falling in love. In March 2017 Modi put down a marker seen to endorse such behavior by naming a hard-line Hindu priest, Yogi Adityanath, as chief minister of Uttar Pradesh, India's most populous state with more than two hundred million people, 20 percent of whom are Muslim. Adityanath has a number of criminal charges registered against him, including attempted murder. He also controlled a youth organization accused of instigating anti-Muslim violence.

Little of this bodes well for India's future role in global affairs. Since its 1947 independence, the country has mostly been governed either by a party locked in a family dynasty or one defined by religious extremism. Against China's disciplined determination, India—with its corruption, poverty, weak government, human rights abuse, insurgencies, and poor infrastructure—stands little chance. Despite strong ar-

---

56. Saeed Naqvi, *Being the Other: The Muslim in India* (New Delhi: Aleph, 2016.

guments in Washington, DC, advocating the building up of the US-India Strategic Partnership, India's character speaks of it not being able to take on a substantive leadership role either within the region or globally.

Island building in the South China Sea may have been the visible lightning rod, but, as America discovered in the 1970s, South Asia cannot be ignored even though this is where clarity blurs, loyalty shifts, and things get messy and riddled with contradictions.

Through one Asian prism, the strengthening alliance between India, Japan, and the United States upholds international law and democratic values. Therefore, China's solid alliance with India's enemy, Pakistan, is a threat to Western interests. Through another, China's influence in Pakistan has stabilized a nearly failed state torn apart by Islamic extremism and military rule. The collapse of Pakistan would unleash for Islamist terrorism that domino effect so feared with Soviet communism in the 1970s. It would create a swath of unbroken territory—Syria, Iraq, Iran, Afghanistan, Pakistan—only stopping at India which itself is wracked with insurgencies, the most enduring being with the Pakistan-sponsored Islamic unrest in Jammu and Kashmir.

India is the world's third largest Muslim country after Indonesia and Pakistan, with more than 175 million Muslims comprising 15 percent of the population. As a group, Indian Muslims suffer the country's lowest living standards. Would it not be more prudent, an argument goes, for the United States to welcome, even encourage, a stronger Sino-Pakistan alliance? But if so, where else in the world should China's influence be emboldened for the cause of stability and, if there are many more such locations, what is the point of picking a fight with Beijing over the South China Sea?

Tensions within South Asia now stem from the same causes as those in the 1970s. The difference now is that both India and Pakistan have nuclear weapons.

In another world, in Europe or East Asia, the highway that runs between India's Amritsar and Pakistan's Lahore would be flowing with traffic alongside a parallel high-speed rail link. But, the India-Pakistan border crossing at Wagah along the Grand Trunk Road is more famous for its daily ceremony when, in full parade dress, troops from India's Border Security Force and the Pakistan Rangers perform elaborate circus-like dance maneuvers, kicking their boots high, inches from the others' faces, on either side of a thick white line painted across the road. The gates are shut at night and traffic is a trickle. The Wagah border is sold as a tourist attraction. In reality, it is evidence that the threat of war is never far away. Yet a confrontation now in South Asia would directly involve five nuclear powers: China, India, Pakistan, Russia, and the United States.

India conducted its first nuclear weapons test in 1974 using plutonium taken from the Canadian-built reactor at the Bhaba Atomic Research Center, ten miles south of Mumbai. It followed three wars with Pakistan, a war with China, and a standoff with the United States in 1971 over Bangladesh. The UN immediately put it under international sanctions, and the test prompted seven governments, including the Soviet Union and the United States, to form the Nuclear Suppliers Group aimed at preventing nuclear proliferation. Twenty-four years later, in May 1998, less than two months after a Bharatiya Janata Party government came to power, India carried out a series of five tests at the same site. Two weeks after that, Pakistan conducted its first tests and South Asia's nuclear arms race began. While developing its nuclear weapons program, Pakistan had also been breaking all international protocols by selling weapons technology to rogue states around the world.

INDIA'S DECISION TO forge its own nuclear weapons path and its refusal to sign the Treaty on the Non-Proliferation of Nuclear Weapons left it an outcast for more than thirty years. But after 9/11, faced with a new and unpredictable political landscape, the United States moved to change this. It needed India on its side for two reasons, one tacit and one public. First, America was beginning to understand the challenge of China and its alliance with Pakistan. An India with nuclear muscle would be a good counterbalance, and the policy was being crafted long before the South China Sea had become a live issue. Second, India was a democracy, and the administration of President George W. Bush needed to talk up shared values with the developing world as it attempted to install its style of democracy in Afghanistan and Iraq.

"We think it is in America's interests for India to become a great global power," Robert Blackwill, the US ambassador to India, told me at the time. "This is a great democracy. It has our values. Our long-term relationship with India is very stabilizing for Asia."

The United States, therefore, needed to diminish India's image as a rogue nuclear state and prioritize its role as a democracy. To achieve this goal, it had to bend the rules on who could and could not possess nuclear weapons. India agreed, but with conditions. Nuclear sanctions had to be dropped, and it would not sign the Non-Proliferation Treaty. It would also continue to develop its nuclear weapons under its own control, although it agreed to refrain from future nuclear tests.

America's somersault regarding its own policy on nuclear proliferation punched a hole in all that it had been preaching before, but it worked. In October 2008, despite opposition among elected representatives of both countries, a deal was signed. Strategically, it made sense. But it also delivered an unfortunate side-effect in that other governments feeling insecure began to eye the nuclear weapons option. After all, if India could go nuclear and get away with it, what would stop other countries following in its path?

Pakistan's development of nuclear weapons was carried out in a far more dangerous and irresponsible way. Its prompt was after its loss in 1971 of East Pakistan, which became Bangladesh. While India intervened on the side of Bangladesh, the Pakistani president at the time, Zulfikar Ali Bhutto, declared it a matter of the nation's survival that his country should be armed with the bomb. Pakistan ended up not only with its own nuclear weapons, but it also became the world's greatest nuclear proliferator. The man who gave it the bomb was Pakistani scientist and con man A. Q. Khan, who went on to sell nuclear weapons material essentially to whichever government was willing to buy. The Khan story highlights why the frequent attempts by the United States to make a reliable ally out of Pakistan have mostly failed.

Khan was the founder of Pakistan's nuclear research center at Kahuta, thirty miles east of the military cantonment city of Rawalpindi. He had contacts and protection that allowed him to steal and buy the wherewithal for Pakistan to build nuclear weapons. He began in October 1974, six months after India's first nuclear test. While working for a Netherlands company Khan stole classified details on centrifuge technology that enriched uranium. As he gathered more and more nuclear material, he peddled his know-how and information through the global nuclear black market. The Pakistani government allowed Khan to continue until 2003, when US and British intelligence presented evidence that Khan was selling to Iran, Libya, North Korea, and Syria. Without Khan's proliferation, there may have been far fewer of the nuclear threats that have defined so much of US foreign policy in recent years. Dozens of countries hankered after the bomb. Khan sold a few of them the means to begin developing it. But it wasn't Khan alone; India believes that China helped Pakistan with fissile material, missile production facilities, and uranium enrichment equipment.

Khan's international nuclear black market network collapsed, and he was put under house arrest in 2004, but also pardoned by then military leader Pervez Musharraf. When Musharraf was forced to step down in 2008, Khan claimed that he had not been working alone but with the highest levels of the Pakistani government. In his 2008 book *Goodbye Shahzadi: A Political Biography of Benazir Bhutto*, journalist Shyam Bhatia recounts that, before she was assassinated, former Pakistan prime minister Benazir Bhutto told him how she had smuggled data on uranium enrichment into North Korea.[57]

Khan was released from house arrest in 2009 and remained a revered national figure, the Father of the Bomb. Any suggestion that Pakistan should surrender its nuclear weapons has since then been met with ridicule.

From being the world's biggest nuclear proliferator, Pakistan became a key exporter of terrorism. In the post-9/11 period, its own security services were implicated, and the country itself suffered routine terrorist attacks, taking it to a near state of civil war. Pakistan also gave sanctuary to America's most wanted enemy, Osama bin Laden, who was living in a compound in the hill town of Abbottabad, home to the Pakistan Military Academy. After bin Laden's discovery and killing, American support faded and Pakistan tilted even more toward China.

When it comes to reviewing military alliances, India, Pakistan, and Thailand share common ground. The United States has a reputa-

---

57. Shyam Bhatia, *Goodbye Shahzadi: A Political Biography of Benazir Bhutto* (New Delhi, Roli Books, 2008).

tion for turning on and off the arms supply tap according to political winds, whereas China and Russia continue to supply for decade upon decade without interruption.

Until 2010, China and the United States supplied Pakistan's defense industry at equal levels, just under 40 percent each. By 2017 China was responsible for more than 60 percent of the weapons imports and America had dropped to 19 percent.[58]

Despite much debate, India has so far maintained that it has a no-first-use policy regarding nuclear weapons, implying that it would risk a strike on one of its cities before responding. There is, however, a lack of clarity with suggestions that this only applies to nonnuclear weapons states or that it does not include the first use of tactical battlefield weapons.[59] Pakistan has made clear that it would initiate a first strike because in an all-out conventional war its forces would be vastly outnumbered by India's. Its nuclear arsenal, however, may well be bigger than India's.

The Stockholm International Peace Research Institute estimated in 2016 that Pakistan has 110 to 130 warheads compared to India's 100 to 120, and that both countries are expanding their weapon arsenals and improving their delivery mechanisms.[60] Pakistan, with four plutonium reactors against India's one, has the capacity to build more bombs at a faster rate—twenty a year to India's five.[61] One report estimates that by 2025 Pakistan could have as many as 350 warheads, which would make it the third biggest nuclear arsenal after Russia and the United States, which have about 7,000 each. France has 300, China 260, and Britain 215.[62] There are just under 15,400 nuclear warheads in the world shared among nine governments: China, France, India, Israel, North Korea, Pakistan, Russia, the United Kingdom, and the

58. China behind Pak's growing confidence, supplies 63% of Islamabad's arms need," *Hindustan Times*, September 2016.

59. India is not Changings its Policy on No First Use of Nuclear Weapons, Abhijnan Rej, *War on the Rocks*, March 29, 2017.

60. "Global nuclear weapons: downsizing but modernizing," SIPRI, June 2016.

61. "Will Pakistan Soon Have the World's Third-Largest Nuclear Arsenal?" *The Diplomat*, August 2015.

62. A Normal Nuclear Pakistan, Toby Dalton, Michael Krepon, *Stimson Center and Carnegie Endowment for International Peace*, 2015.

United States. More than 90 percent are owned by Russia and the United States, the only two countries that are actually cutting their arsenals. The rest are keeping what they have or making more.

Only Britain, France, Russia, and the United States have weapons deployed with warheads on missiles or on bases ready to be operational. India and Pakistan keep their warheads, with the trigger and the delivery mechanism in separate locations, meaning they would take several hours to prepare for launch.

One of India's apparent storage places lies amid the lush tropical greenery of the Bhaba Atomic Research Center (BARC) compound near Mumbai. I was invited there in 2003 when India was beginning its rapprochement with the United States and the government was keen to show that it was a responsible nuclear player. There are two nuclear reactors, one British built, one Canadian, flanked by sea and mountains, underneath which huge laboratories have been hewn. Five thousand nuclear scientists and ten thousand technicians work there. It was from here that India gathered the means to challenge the world order that mandated that only the five big nations on the winning side in the Second World War should possess nuclear weapons. They became the five permanent members of the UN Security Council, the ultimate arbiter of international law, thus leaving India with its sense of vulnerability.

The BARC director, B. Bhattacharjee, an expert in gas centrifuge technology for uranium enrichment, made no secret that he was heading up a nuclear weapons site when I met with him. "The government asks at any time, 'Can you help us?' Our answer should be 'yes,'" he said. "That's from any sector—either the navy or the army or the air force. We are always prepared to meet any needs for the country."

"And the weapons," I asked. "They are here, now?"

"Yes. The nuclear weapons are designed here, manufactured here, and we keep them here."

The nuclear bomb itself is known as the pit. It would have to be transferred from this nuclear weapons facility or others around the country to an aircraft, missile, or submarine for delivery. The process to prepare a weapon for launch would take from six to eight hours. There would then be another eleven minutes for it to impact on Pakistan. If India adhered to its no-first-use policy and absorbed a first strike, sacrificing one city, it would hit back with everything it had. Within twenty-four hours cities in both countries would be in ruins.

CHAPTER 11

WHERE IS INDIA'S MONROE DOCTRINE?

A HISTORICAL COMPARISON TO BEIJING'S SOUTH CHINA SEA CLAIM is America's nineteenth-century Monroe Doctrine, aimed at deterring European powers from interfering in the Caribbean and Latin America. The United States was then starting out in its role as a regional power, arguing that its style of modernization and governance was more effective and fairer than the systems practiced by the backward-looking, colonial-minded governments of Europe. They were yesterday's powers. America was the future and, in 1823, President James Monroe announced that America would consider any attempt by Europe to influence the western hemisphere as "dangerous to our peace and safety."

In a similar but less aggressive manner, China has declared South China Sea its backyard and stated that it will not brook interference from foreign powers. India has no such doctrine, even though it has comparable interests in the Indian Ocean that are already being diluted because of a Chinese presence.

The American policy came to the fore when the United States invoked the Monroe Doctrine in the 1898 war against Spain, intervening to stabilize an insurrection in Cuba, just over a hundred miles from the Florida coastline. An equivalent for India is Sri Lanka, only fifty miles from India's southern coastline. Both Cuba and Sri Lanka are small island nations, Cuba's population twelve million against Sri Lanka's twenty-two million, and both are on strategic trade routes. Each has posed a threat over the years to its regional power.

The United States intervened in Cuba again in 1961 with an abortive operation to overthrow Fidel Castro, and in 1962 with the Cuban Missile Crisis. Diplomatic relations were only restored in July

2015, but even then, as of 2018, the economic embargo against Cuba remained in place. India's policy toward Sri Lanka follows a more opaque path and is telling as much for when it chose not to intervene as for when it did. One result is that Beijing's influence is now imbedded in many of Sri Lanka's institutions.

The most controversial project is at the coastal port city of Hambantota, 130 miles southeast of Colombo, where Chinese companies are in the process of creating a new trade area around a large modern port with an airport, power station, and oil refinery. To pay off the financing, Sri Lanka is selling 85 percent of the operation back to Chinese Companies. Hambantota is well placed near the major shipping lanes of the Indian Ocean to be a refining center for crude oil from the Middle East, heading up through the South China Sea to East Asia. It is a pivotal Chinese foothold in the Indian Ocean. The Sri Lankan government insists there will be no access for Chinese naval vessels, but few defense analysts believe this pledge will hold.

China also runs much of the Port of Colombo, where, nearby, a skyline of cranes points to a square mile of construction site for apartments, offices, hotels, a marina, and a golf course—all the branding of a modern Asian city. Among China's many other projects in Sri Lanka is a $270 million railway, the first new track to be laid in the country for more than a hundred years.[64]

In September 2014 Beijing deliberately showed its military presence when a submarine docked there on exactly the same day that Shinzo Abe, prime minister of China's regional rival, Japan, was visiting. It was the first such submarine port call, and the unannounced arrival of the *Changzheng* 2, a type 091 Han-class nuclear-powered submarine, broke a long-standing agreement with India about notifying Delhi of foreign military ship visits. Delhi made its views known to Sri Lanka, with officials describing the submarine's port call as a threat to India's national security.

Its objections were ignored. A few weeks later, Sri Lanka hosted another Chinese submarine, this time coinciding with a high-level Indian visit to Vietnam, that key antagonist in Beijing's South China Sea ex-

---

64. "The String of Pearls and the Maritime Silk Road," *China-U.S. Focus*, February 2014.

pansion. On both occasions the submarines broke protocol by docking at the Chinese-owned terminal and not at berths controlled by the Sri Lankan Port Authority. Sri Lanka played down the visits by saying the Chinese terminal had a deeper berth and the submarines had been on antipiracy operations.

"Any warship with permission can come to Sri Lankan ports," said Sri Lanka Ports Authority Chairman Priyath B. Wickrama. "Many ships have come. American ships have come. Nobody is worried about those ships."[65]

The submarine visits signaled a return to Cold War–era divisions when India and Sri Lanka took opposing sides, India veering toward the Soviet Union and Sri Lanka being wooed by the United States. This time Sri Lanka is heading for the Chinese camp and India into the American one. The origins of mistrust between India and Sri Lanka go back to India's role in fueling Sri Lanka's crippling quarter-century-long war with its Tamil minority, which Sri Lanka only defeated, with China's help, in 2009.

The mainly Hindu Tamil community makes up 12 percent of Sri Lanka's population and is congregated in the north of the country. The civil war was about Sri Lankan Tamils being granted an independent homeland. The majority Buddhist Sinhalese community comprises more than 75 percent of the population. During the 1970s and 1980s the treatment of the Tamils by the Sinhalese-dominated government became repressive and discriminatory, leading to disturbance and eventually armed rebellion. India was concerned first about unrest spreading to its own large Tamil population in Tamil Nadu. Mixed up in that was a concern that Sri Lanka was becoming too much of a Cold War ally of America. India stepped in by supplying weapons and training to Sri Lankan Tamil insurgents.

The plan backfired. After infighting between Tamil groups, the Liberation Tigers of Tamil Eelam became the lone predominant force and evolved into one of the most sophisticated and feared terrorist groups anywhere. The Tigers invented the suicide vest, used child soldiers, ran a near totalitarian state in the north of the country, carried

---

65. "Beijing's nuclear subs coming again, India concerned," *The Sunday Times* (India), October 2014.

out civilian massacres of women and children, and made a godlike figure of their leader Velupillai Prabhakaran. The Indian policy was initiated by Jawaharlal Nehru's daughter Indira Gandhi and inherited by
her son Rajiv, who in 1987 changed tack. He sent in peacekeeping
troops, but they were no match for the Tigers' kill-and-run attacks.
India withdrew two years later, defeated, with the war still raging. In
May 1991, the Tigers went as far as assassinating Rajiv Gandhi while
he was election campaigning in Tamil Nadu.

India's reaction, or lack of it, told much about its character. It did
not pursue the Tiger leader Prabhakaran who had ordered Gandhi's
murder. It showed no determination to end the threat to its national security posed by Sri Lanka and its civil war. All it did was put in a formal
request for Prabhakaran's extradition and tracked down the Tiger foot
soldiers in India that carried out the attack. This was not the action of
a regional power avenging the murder of a former Indian prime minister on his home soil.

The war continued until 2009 when China moved in and enabled
Sri Lanka to defeat the Tigers.[66] The end result wasn't pretty, but it
worked. Beijing provided military equipment needed to launch a decisive campaign that cut off the Tigers, along with many civilians being
held as hostages or human shields. With its UN Security Council seat,
Beijing was able to protect Sri Lanka from international condemnation
accusing it of war crimes. The war had been a dead weight hanging
around Sri Lanka's neck. Both sides behaved appallingly. But now that
the government had won, Sri Lanka could move on, and China could
come in. It arrived with confidence, panache, and a panoply of loans,
infrastructure projects, and new business.

In its rush for postwar construction Sri Lanka took on so much
unmanageable debt that in 2016 it had to secure a $1.5 billion bailout
from the International Monetary Fund to handle the repayment sched-
ule. In all it owed $65 billion, $8 billion of which is due to China.
The borrowing reached a stage where 95 percent of government revenue was going toward debt repayment. China's checkbook diplomacy followed a time-honored path of trading aid for influence. There
are shades here of the debt that poorer countries ran up with Western

66. How Sri Lanka Won the War, Peter Layton, *The Diplomat*, April 9, 2015

lenders before China came onto the scene, leading to demands, particularly in Africa, that the debts be canceled so the countries could develop.

On one level, China's Sri Lanka operation differed little from what it was doing all over the world. On another level, Sri Lanka's strategic location made it pivotal in changing the balance of power in the Indian Ocean. Time and again India had an opportunity to stake its ground and failed to do so. "China is bent on domination of the entire Asian continent, and only India can stop it," writes William H. Avery in *India: China's Nightmare, America's Dream.* "China is playing the long game in Asia, and India is still watching from the sidelines."[67]

A map published by the Council on Foreign Relations contains a line showing a regional area of the Indian Ocean. Chinese influence runs from Iran, north into the Russian Far East, across to the Korean Peninsula, looping round Indonesia and back. Within it, India is the only country described as "resisting Chinese influence."[68]

In January 2015, the pro-China Sri Lankan president Mahinda Rajapaksa lost power in elections that brought in the Sino-skeptical Maithripala Sirisena, who campaigned on accusations that Sri Lanka was being turned into a Chinese client state. Several India commentators claimed it was a victory for their intelligence services, which had interfered in the election and Indian foreign policy.[69]

But soon Sirisena was on a plane to Beijing reviving many of the suspended projects. In May 2017, however, he did block the visit of a Chinese submarine, a red line that India had laid down and with which Sri Lanka had complied.

EVEN SO, SRI LANKA has given Beijing a bridgehead right onto the doorstep of India. In military terms, the consequences are clear, and in the terms of pure defense strategy it could be argued as unthinkable that India even allowed China to get this far. But today's military-

67. William H. Avery, *China's Nightmare, America's Dream: India as the Next Global Power,* Amaryllis, New Delhi, 2012.

68. "China and Sri Lanka: Between a Dream and a Nightmare," *The Diplomat,* November 2016.

69. Indian spy's role alleged in Sri Lankan president's election defeat, Reuters, January 17, 2015.

political-economic mix is a quagmire. China was also cutting a 173-mile-long sea lane through Nicaragua in Central America, linking the Atlantic and Pacific Oceans. It was costed out at $40 billion, and at ninety feet deep and 1,706 feet across, would be wider and deeper than, and a direct rival to, the Panama Canal. But then, the Panama Canal is now run by the Hong Kong–based conglomerate Hutchison Whampoa, which has close ties to Beijing.

Nicaragua highlights a circle of history. America's Cold War conflicts included its intervention in Nicaragua to overthrow the left-wing president, Daniel Ortega. Ortega became president again in 2007 and gave permission for Chinese companies to build the new canal. Why, then, should anyone raise a murmur about China's presence in Sri Lanka—or, for that matter, anywhere else?

Beijing's Sri Lankan achievements have been replicated along coastlines throughout the Indian Ocean region. There is Chinese port construction at Kyaukpyu in Bagamoyo, in Tanzania; Chittagong, in Bangladesh; Gaadhoo Island, in the Maldives, where China and Saudi Arabia are working closely together; Gwadar, in Pakistan; Lamu, in Kenya; Port Lucas, in Mauritius; Rakhine State, in western Myanmar; Tamatave, in Madagascar; Techobanine, in Mozambique; and elsewhere.

In 2011 China's Xinhua news agency announced the government's plans to set up a permanent naval base in the Seychelles, the Indian Ocean archipelago better known for its luxury resorts, beaches, and rain forests. As of 2018, nothing had been confirmed, but in 2015 the Seychelles government allocated India land to build one there too, an indication of Delhi's attempt to balance some of China's Indian Ocean military reach.[70]

By then China was building its first permanent overseas military base in Djibouti on the Horn of Africa, a tiny former French colony bordering Ethiopia, Eritrea, and Somalia. The Americans had beaten them to it and moved in after 9/11. Four thousand US military personnel are based at Camp Lemonnier and used for classified antiterrorism operations in the Middle East and North Africa. American and Chinese warships will be docked next to each other, in closer proximity than anywhere in the world.

---

70. "Seychelles committed to Indian naval base," *The Hindu*, March 2016.

"China has only two purposes in the Indian Ocean," explained Zhou Bou of the Academy of Military Science of the People's Liberation Army. "Economic gains and the security of sea lines of communication. The first objective is achieved through commercial interactions with littoral states. For the second purpose, the Chinese Navy has, since the end of 2008, joined international military efforts in combating piracy in the waters off the coast of Somalia. . . . [China is] a country standing tall in the center of the world, strong yet benign, and friendly to all."[71]

There is credibility to this argument. China has been working closely with the European Union, NATO, and the United States on antipiracy operations. It has twenty-five hundred troops in six African UN peacekeeping missions and, in recent years, the Chinese Air Force and Navy have been deployed to rescue civilians, from Libya in 2011 and Yemen in 2015. There are an estimated five million Chinese citizens living and working outside the country for some thirty thousand Chinese businesses, with more than a hundred million traveling abroad every year. The modern Chinese Navy is being designed to have a central role in protecting both the country's citizens and its supply routes.[72]

Chinese naval crews in Djibouti can also safeguard free passage along the narrow Bab al-Mandeb Strait, the choke point that runs between Djibouti and Yemen, through which China gets half its oil supplies.

Peter Dutton, who heads the China Maritime Studies Institute at the US Naval War College, described the Djibouti base to me as a huge strategic development. "It is naval power expansion for protecting commerce and China's regional interests in the Horn of Africa," he explained. "This is what expansionary powers do."

A similar power expansion has been carried out in southern Pakistan, where China has taken out a forty-three-year lease and invested $1.62 billion to modernize the western port of Gwadar near the mouth of the Persian Gulf. China's warships dock at Gwadar, partly to protect Indian Ocean supply lines and partly to watch over a $50 billion project called the China-Pakistan Economic Corridor aimed at linking Central

---

71. The String of Pearls and the Maritime Silk Road, *China Org.Cn* February 12, 2014.

72. "Li vows to protect rights of Chinese working abroad," *China Daily*, May 5, 2014.

Asia, China, and South Asia. From Gwadar, China plans to build a new highway to Kashgar in its Xinjiang region, part of the Belt and Road Initiative's network of roads and railways modernizing Pakistan and its neighbors but not India. An oil pipeline from Gwadar to China is due to open in 2021. It would carry a million barrels a day, meeting 8 percent of China's needs, giving it some hedge against disruption to sea traffic by a hostile power.

The Indian Ocean is a different theater from the South and East China Seas, but it carries similar stakes. In the South China Sea, China is seizing territory against the wishes of its neighbors. In the Indian Ocean, it is being invited in by all countries except the one that gives the ocean its name. In the space of a few years, China has succeeded in setting up military cordons within the South China Sea and forging trade routes across impoverished swaths of Asia, all aimed at diversifying its trade routes. Having set in motion the Gwadar-to-Xinjiang pipeline, it opened a Myanmar pipeline in 2017 from the port of Kyaukpyu to Yunnan Province in the southwest, thus giving China more ways to bypass the Strait of Malacca and South China Sea. There have, of course, been problems with the Belt and Road Initiative: projects that have failed, and continuing allegations of Chinese imperialism. As the Economist stated, "The belt-and-road express has left the station. China is merely trying to improve the on-board service."[73]

India refuses to join the Belt and Road Initiative, of which almost all this infrastructure building is part. Instead, as Xi Jinping was hosting the May 2017 summit in Beijing, the Indian Foreign Ministry released a fractious announcement: "No country can accept a project that ignores its core concerns on sovereignty and territorial integrity."[74]

But if that were the case, most countries around the world would still be in the same hostile state as India and Pakistan, and they are not.

Delhi tried to match China's ambitions by referring to little-known projects such as the Bangladesh, Bhutan, India, Nepal Initiative and the Trilateral Highway Project between India, Myanmar, and Thai-

---

73. "The belt-and-road express: China faces resistance to a cherished theme of its foreign policy," *The Economist*, May 2017.

74. Ministry of External Affairs, India, *Official Spokesperson's response to a query on participation of India in OBOR/BRI Forum*, May 13, 2017.

land without explaining what these programs actually did or making any effort to capture the public imagination. The Belt and Road Initiative is now absorbing the precursor of Indian Ocean port construction known as the String of Pearls, giving China an abundant presence in South Asia. India is dwarfed economically and encircled in a way that even now is beginning to make Delhi a subordinate of Beijing.

Crucially, while China has single-mindedly committed to military expansion, India has muddled along and, as with its overall development, has been left behind. Its defense industry operates like much else in government with parliamentary blockages, protected vested interests, executive indecision, and high levels of corruption. Over the past thirty years, scandals involving bribes and corrupt procurement include German submarines, Israeli missiles, Italian helicopters, Singaporean small arms, and Swedish artillery. The bigger contracts with America and Russia go more smoothly. The United States has strict antibribery laws, and most defense contracts are carried out under its Foreign Military Sales program whereby the buyer does not deal directly with a defense contractor. The system for buying from Russia is well oiled and less prone to revelations of scandal.

The upshot is that China outmatches India in just about every area of conventional warfare. As of mid-2016, India had nineteen attack helicopters against China's two hundred; fourteen submarines against China's sixty-eight; fourteen frigates against forty-eight; 1,488 fighter aircraft against 2,615; and so on. Defense analysts argue that Indian spending needs to double to at least 3 percent of gross domestic product for the country to even start to catch up. Even then, that would not be enough because, in any all-out conflict, India would probably face simultaneous assaults from both China and Pakistan.

India may have fared better in its economic relationship with China, but not enough yet to give it political leverage. Delhi has joined the Beijing-based Asian Infrastructure Investment Bank and the Shanghai-based New Development Bank led by Brazil, Russia, India, China, and South Africa, collectively known as BRICS. An Indian banker holds the presidency. Trade between China and India has been on a rapid increase but is still much in China's favor. In 2000, trade was worth just $2 billion. By 2016, it measured more than $100 billion, but with a

$46 billion surplus to China, which is India's biggest export market. Even now, there are very few direct flights between Beijing and Delhi, the capital cities of these Asian powers.

John Elliot describes China as playing India, alternately confronting and befriending it.[75] One stark example came in September 2014, when Chinese troops entered and set up positions in Indian-controlled Ladakh just as President Xi Jinping was visiting Delhi, ostensibly to drum up business. Less than three years later, in July 2017, China and India were challenging each other again on the Doklam Plateau claimed both by China and the tiny kingdom of Bhutan which traditionally fell under India's arc of control. Like the submarine visits to Sri Lanka, these were public reminders as to who was ultimately the big power in Asia: China.

Delhi's indecision and lack of initiative has left it with impossible choices. Either it does nothing and watches as influence continues to melt away, or it tries to compete with China, which it cannot realistically do alone, either economically or militarily. Or it supports China's aspirations, but to do that it would have to concede that it is a junior partner on its own patch, and China would have succeeded in creating a string of vassal states beholden to its power, and India would be by far its biggest prize.

THE WAY IN which Asia's alliances are falling into place in the early twenty-first century had been on the cards since the 1960s, when the United States backed Delhi against the Chinese incursion and used India as a staging ground to sponsor a secret insurgency in Tibet. Beijing's closeness to Pakistan has been long held. Pakistan backed China in the 1962 conflict, and since then it has eased Beijing's path into the Islamic world. In return, Beijing has condoned the Pakistan-sponsored insurgency in Kashmir. Historically there has sometimes been a correlation between an upsurge in the Kashmir conflict and Chinese troop operations on its disputed border with India. For much of the 1980s and 1990s Pakistan helped China keep an Islamic insurgency at bay in its restless Muslim region of Xinjiang by stopping terrorist traffic into Xinjiang

---

75. John Elliott, *Implosion: India's Tryst with Reality* (Noida, India: HarperCollins India, 2014).

from Pakistan. The arrangement held pretty much until it was over-taken by social media and transnational movements like the Islamic State. Xinjiang is now under threat, with routine insurgent attacks.

Modi's 2014 election came a year after China began its island building in the South China Sea. Coincidentally, Modi sought a more proactive relationship with the United States which inevitably included talks about the rise of China. By 2016 India and the United States were discussing joint naval patrols in the South China Sea. In May 2016 India deployed four warships on a two-and-a-half-month operation into the South China Sea and northwestern Pacific, describing it as a demon-stration of its "operational reach and commitment to the government's *Act East* policy."[76] The vessels called at Busan in South Korea, Cam Ranh Bay naval base in Vietnam, Port Klang in Malaysia, Sasebo in Japan, Subic Bay in the Philippines, and Vladivostok in Russia. In late June they took part in joint exercises with Japan and the United States involving antisubmarine and air defense training off the coast of Okinawa, which hosts large American bases. There had been similar exercises in 2015, with Japan joining for the first time, thereby underpinning a new Asian defense alliance.[77]

The Sino-Indian relationship ebbed and flowed. It hit a low point in June 2016 when India wanted to seal its nuclear deal with member-ship of the Nuclear Suppliers Group, the antiproliferation organization set up after India's 1974 test. There were now forty-eight members, all of which had pledged only to supply nuclear fuel to another country if satisfied it would not go toward making a nuclear weapon. The United States and most other members favored India joining, but China blocked India's application, insisting that Pakistan should be allowed to join as well. Given Pakistan's proliferation history this would have been unacceptable. Beijing also blocked Delhi's attempt to get an Islamist leader living in Pakistan branded by the UN as a terrorist. Masood Azar had led the Jaish-e-Mohammed group blamed for the 2001 attack on the Indian Parliament and a raft of other operations. Delhi also raised objections to construction work for the China-Pakistan Economic Cor-

---

76. "India's Act East Policy: Strategic Implications for the Indian Ocean Region," *The Journal of the Indian Ocean Region*, October 2016.

77. "India Sends Stealth Warships to South China Sea," *The Diplomat*, May 2016.

ridor inside the Pakistan-controlled area of Kashmir. As these tensions unfolded, a movement in India to block Chinese goods gathered speed.

The Dalai Lama and Tibet remains a point of friction between the Chinese leadership and Delhi as well as for many Western democracies that regard Tibet as a showcase for China's heavy-handed rule and violation of human rights. Now in his eighties, the Dalai Lama has watched from exile as Han Chinese flooded into Tibet as colonizers, repressing the Buddhist way of life, imposing Beijing-style communism, building infrastructure, and banning any mention of him.

China and India continue to test each other's defenses along the still disputed border, just as they had in 1962. Like Nehru before him, Prime Minister Modi is reaching out to bolster India's bond with the United States, talking up the symbolism of the world's two biggest democracies and their shared values.

"As the US seeks to build on its new strategic partnership with India, one of its greatest challenges has been overcoming lingering doubts about its reliability as an ally," explains Jeff M. Smith of the American Foreign Policy Council. "It need not shy away from its record of defending India in its darkest hour. New Delhi and Beijing are unclear about where America would stand in the event of any future Sino-Indian hostilities. A precedent was set in 1962, even if it's been largely forgotten."[78]

Today, in that fragile part of the Himalayas, the Indian military faces both Chinese and Pakistani troops. A de facto border known as the Line of Control runs between the Indians and Pakistanis. Shelling and cross-border skirmishes leading to loss of life are common. Kashmir has become a breeding ground for Islamic extremism, and insurgents have links with global franchises such as al-Qaeda and the Islamic State. The border dispute, Tibet, and the 1962 war overshadow attempts by China and India to use trade as a healer. More than a half century on, those same issues keep appearing.

In October 2016, in a show of unity with India, the US ambassador to Delhi, Richard Verma, visited Tawang in the disputed border area of Arunachal Pradesh, which China had captured during its 1962

---

78. Jeff M. Smith, *Cold Peace: Sino-Indian Rivalry in the 21st Century* (Lexington Books, Maryland, 2014.

offensive and then handed back. China still refers to Tawang as being in Southern Tibet. In April 2017 India infuriated China more by allowing the Dalai Lama to visit Tawang. He was welcomed by crowds waiving prayer scarfs and the Tibetan flag with its distinctive red and blue diagonal stripes and splayed rising yellow sun.

In July 2017, troops from both sides were deployed against each other in new tension, this time over the tiny landlocked buffer kingdom of Bhutan, where China was building a road along the Doklam Plateau toward India. Bhutan, a mountain nation of only 750,000 people, is traditionally under Delhi's protection, and the road threatened to give China strategic access directly into the Indian state of Sikkim. At its peak, the crisis involved thousands of soldiers facing each other down and the Chinese government–controlled *Global Times* introduced alarmist echoes from 1962 warning that India faced "the consequences of an all-out confrontation."[79]

The editorial, published with the full support of the Chinese authorities, was significant in the public lambasting it gave to India, shifting quickly from India's military weakness on land to its vulnerability at sea: "If India fancies the idea that it has a strategic card to play in the Indian Ocean, it could not be more naïve. China does hold a lot of cards and can hit India's Achilles' heel, but India has no leverage at all to have a strategic showdown with China."[80]

After a ten-week standoff, China withdrew and, while the diplomatic talk was muted, Indian defense analysts claimed victory, directly linking Beijing's advance on the Doklam Plateau with its island building in the South China Sea. "For the first time since China's success in expanding its control in the South China Sea by artificially creating seven islands and militarizing them, a rival power has stalled Chinese construction activity to change the status quo on a disputed territory," writes Brahma Chellaney of India's Center for Policy Research. "India's refusal to bend while talking peace offers other Asia-Pacific nations an example of how to manage Chinese coercion. Doklam also raises a broader question: Had US President Barack Obama's administration

---

79. Duo Mo, Global Times *India's provocation will trigger all-out confrontation on LAC,* July 2017.
80. Ibid.

stood up to China in the South China Sea, would the seven artificial and now-militarized islands have been created?"[81]

Yet China's incursion also posed questions from the other side. Beijing had openly challenged India's regional influence and called on Bhutan to make a choice: would its future be better served by China or India? Here was another Beijing salami slice, one of many.

India, meanwhile, had been bolstering its alliance with Japan. In November 2016 Modi went to Tokyo, where he signed a civilian nuclear deal with Japan that would give India access to state-of-the-art nuclear technology. He and Japanese prime minister Shinzo Abe issued an unprecedented joint statement about China's actions in the South China Sea. They warned that the parties involved must not resort to "threat and the use of force" and that Japan and India were committed to "respect freedom of navigation and unimpeded lawful commerce based on the UN Convention of the Law of the Sea." After a troublesome year, when issue after issue had stacked up, India reached across the Strait of Malacca to reaffirm and consolidate its public support for the pro-Western alliance in Asia.

China's fury was immediate and loud. "India should beware of the possibility that by becoming embroiled in the disputes it might end up being a pawn of the US and suffer great losses, especially in terms of business and trade from China," warned the Chinese routinely hawkish *Global Times*. "India, however, seems to have overestimated its leverage in the region. Although China's major rivals in the dispute, such as the US and Japan, have been trying to draw India into their camp, the country will be likely regarded as having a token role."[82]

India brushed off this warning and sent its air crews and submariners to train the Vietnamese military on their newly acquired Kilo-class submarines and Sukhoi-30 aircraft.

As China had encircled India to the west, so had India now become part of the defense cordon cast around China to the east. The

---

81. Brahma Chellaney, "India's Refusal to Bend Showed the World How to Deal with Chinese Coercion," *Daily Mail India*, September 1, 2017, http://www.dailymail.co.uk/indiahome/indianews/article-4845618/India-s-refusal-bend-Doklam-standoff-China.html.

82. Liu Zhun, *India overestimates its South China Sea leverage*, Global Times, November 8, 2016.

United States had succeeded in bookending its Asian defense policy with two major powers with shared democratic values. Although the term Indo-Pacific has long been used in diplomatic circles, it became popularized by Trump during his November 2017 tour of Asia. He repeatedly called for a "free and open Indo-Pacific," where independent nations could "thrive in freedom and peace".

What this meant was that India had thrown its cards in with Japan and the US and that "free and open" referred to an Indo-Pacific not controlled or overly influenced by China. It was also an indication that China's three-thousand-year-old formula of using rewards and punishment to create a supplicant state might have failed with India. Its siding with America might have been acceptable in Beijing if it had not led to such a warming of ties with Japan. But, when it came to regional friction with China, Japan stood on a platform all its own. China was neither able nor willing to forgive the atrocities carried out by Japan during the Century of Humiliation. Nor would it allow Japan to challenge Chinese supremacy in Asia. But underneath all that, China understood that it was now what Japan had once been—a new and confident industrial power, facing down America in Asia.

China was determined to succeed where its rival had failed. The question was how.

PART 4

EAST ASIA

In view of history, I sincerely wish that the ravages of war will never be repeated.

—EMPEROR AKIHITO of Japan

CHAPTER 12

JAPAN:
ASIA'S FIRST
INDUSTRIAL POWER

A S WITH THE SOUTH CHINA SEA, THE LIGHTNING ROD OF MISTRUST
in East Asia lies in remote, disputed islands. There are eight of
them. Three barely break the surface; the others are inhospitable
clumps of rock where no one lives and nothing useful grows. The best
use the Americans could find for them at the end of the Second World
War was as a place for bombing practice. The closest landfall is the
northern coast of Taiwan and the Japanese tourist island of Ishigaki,
both a hundred miles away. China's nearest coastline is more than two
hundred miles away. In Chinese, they are known as the Diaoyu Islands
and in Japanese as the Senkaku, meaning "sharp pavilions," and for
many years most of the islands had been in private hands, bought and
sold between families. China claimed them, but since last century had
been too busy with its civil war and with India, Korea, Taiwan and
Tibet, to care much or do anything about them.

That ended in 2012 when the hawkish governor of Tokyo, Shin-
taro Ishihara, offered to buy the islands from the Kurihara family,
which had owned them since the 1970s. Ishihara, a populist politician
who never shied away from provoking China, was feeding on a growing
nationalist sentiment that was winning support in many parts of Japanese society. Later in the year, the same patriotic mood brought Prime
Minister Shinzo Abe to power. Memories of Chinese and Japanese commercial success were eclipsed by long-standing regional rivalry. Ishihara
used the disputed islands precisely to show up divisions in the Sino-
Japanese relationship.

The Japanese government stepped in and purchased the islands
itself, paying $20 million. China reacted angrily, setting off a chain of

events that turned the Diaoyu/Senkaku Islands into another global flashpoint. It brings to mind an image of two well-heeled billionaires fighting over a cigarette butt in a trash can. The thought that these desolate blots of maritime nothingness could be the cause of such disagreement between two of the world's biggest economies beggars belief. Yet, that is what has happened because, even while riding the crest of a wave of wealth, an uneasiness deep inside each country has refreshed old hostilities that have yet to be dealt with.

Japan's announcement that it was taking ownership of the islands prompted protests in China. Claiming the anger was spontaneous, Beijing called for calm while doing little to stop the spread of riots. The protests lasted through September 2012, with crowds breaching a security cordon at the Japanese embassy in Beijing and trashing and burning factories owned by Honda, Panasonic, Toyota, and other Japanese companies.

"Return our islands! Japanese devils get out!" was a chant of the rioters. One placard read, "For the respect of the motherland, we must go to war with Japan."

In public, Japan tried to play down the schism, but a senior official told me without nuance, "China has exploited the goodwill of the Japanese people. It needs Japan as an enemy because they have exchanged communism for nationalism."

The uncovering of that fault line in 2012 threw a spotlight on others. Cracks appeared; first one, then another, as in an earth tremor. They tangled and then merged into a question about the future of Asia: What would the rise of China hold, and how should Asia and the United States, its protector, deal with it? The economic relationship between the two countries was entwined and strong. What reason on Earth would there be to damage it? Yet, if Beijing were willing to risk its economic relationship with Japan over these islands, what else was it prepared to do and from where was it drawing its confidence?

Thirty-four years earlier, in 1978, China's new reformist leader Deng Xiaoping had traveled to Japan to sign the Sino-Japanese Treaty of Peace and Friendship. It was a brave, pragmatic move. China had neither forgiven nor forgotten Japan's invasion, including its 1937 massacre of up to three hundred thousand Chinese in the old capital of Nanjing. There was no love lost between China—indeed, the whole of East Asia—and Japan. But Deng needed Japan's trade and money. He visited the global giant Panasonic and asked if it would help in China's modernization. Panasonic said it would, and began building factories there. Other Japanese companies followed; today twenty thousand Japanese companies have factories in China, employing ten million workers.[83]

"Deng came to us and pleaded for Japanese companies to invest in his country," the Japanese official told me, showing a photograph of the Panasonic factory when it was first built and another of it in ruins. "In the spirit of friendship, we did that and this is what we get in return." After the riots, Japanese investment fell by more than 40 percent.

The economic relationship between China and Japan was—and still is—entwined and strong. There is no pragmatic reason to damage it. It is another fault line that has been bandaged up for the past half century or so, and it needs to be healed or bandaged again until a cure can be found.

Japan's population is 128 million, against China's 1.4 billion. Japan's economy in 2016 was $4.41 trillion against China's $11.3 trillion. On a map Japan looks like a thin, curved crooked finger of an archipelago, slightly bigger than the Philippines but smaller than Indonesia. It could fit into China many times over. But, unlike much of the region, Japan has never submitted to the concept that all power emanates from Beijing, that China is a big country and all others are small countries, or that it needs to journey there with gifts, humility, and tributes in order to survive. China and Japan have swapped ideas and cultural practices, but Japan has always seen itself as at least equal to, if not better than, China and this is a challenge that East Asia has yet to resolve.

Japan was the first Asian country to develop the strengths and economy of the West. It was also the first and only country to suffer a nuclear attack. "We were destroyed because we were too strong," a Japanese diplomat told me. "We could not control our strength. China was defeated because it was too weak. But always, China thinks it is a

---

83. "More than twenty thousand Japanese enterprises invest in China," *XinhuaNet*, April 11, 2017.

big country and that it lies at the center of the world. Everyone else is on the periphery of its power. The Chinese system runs down from a high pinnacle, which makes it inward looking and intolerant. The leaders are secluded from the real world. China is now where we were in the 1930s. Then look what happened. China's strength may end up destroying it. Everyone thinks China is too big to fail. That is what we thought in Japan in the 1930s. But believe me, China is not too big to fail, and when it does, everything will burn down."

THE HIROSHIMA PEACE Memorial Museum is built on the site where the world's first nuclear bomb exploded at 8:15 a.m. on April 6, 1945. Its purpose is not to expose the United States for inflicting such horror on the city. Nor does it explain why Japan deserved such a horrific attack. The museum's mission statement is to "continuously appeal for the elimination of nuclear armaments and the realization of permanent world peace." The exhibits do not pull any punches with their graphic displays that include the shriveled, torn, and blackened uniforms of schoolgirls killed in the blast.

"Nobuko Shoda (then 14) was a second-year student at Yamanaka Girls High school, attached to Hiroshima Women's Higher School of Education," reads one inscription. "She suffered burns over her entire body . . . . Her face and both legs swelled up and the skin on her hands peeled off . . . . She passed away on 10 August." With it is Nobuko's torn and singed school uniform and a note saying she was twelve hundred meters from the center of the explosion.

"The blast also threw people across distances of several meters," the museum tells us. "Countless shards of glass penetrated the victims' bodies. Even today, fragments of glass are discovered and removed from atomic bomb survivors who complain of bodily pains."

What actually happened is relayed in a chillingly measured manner: "The surrounding air expanded enormously, creating a tremendous blast. The blast pressure was immense, 19 tons per square meter as far away as 500 meters from the hypocenter. Nearly all buildings were crushed; people were lifted and thrown through the air."

Japan's defeat after the destruction of Hiroshima and, three days later, Nagasaki led to occupation by the United States for seven years and resulted in the creation of Japan's democratic system and a pacifist constitution, which banned the nation from going to war again or even keeping a defense force that had "war potential."

But that changed in December 2012 when in the wake of the islands dispute and China's anti-Japanese riots, the forthright and telegenic Abe became the Liberal Democratic Party's prime minister for the second time in a landslide election win. Abe's reputation was as a right-wing hawk, and his platform was for economic reform and increased nationalism. As Japan's war crimes and colonial record were once again being put in a hostile spotlight, Abe fought back. He questioned whether women in occupied territories were forced to have sex with Japanese troops during the Second World War, promoting a furious reaction in China, South Korea, and elsewhere. He visited the controversial Yasukuni Shrine, which commemorates Japan's war dead—including those accused of war crimes. He refused to offer his own apology for Japan's war record, instead saying, "We must not let our children, grandchildren, and even further generations to come, who have nothing to do with that war, be predestined to apologize." When pressed, he only reaffirmed his support for previous official apologies, saying his country had inflicted "immeasurable damage and suffering."[84]

Relations that had been difficult with China got even worse and once again focused on the Diaoyu/Senkaku Islands. In December 2013, Beijing declared an Air Defense Identification Zone around the islands, requiring all aircraft crew to report when they entered it. Such zones are not new, and there were several already across East Asia, put in place after the Second World War. But China's was introduced without consultation or notice and overlapped with zones run by Japan and South Korea. At the same time, Chinese warships repeatedly entered the contested area around the Diaoyu/Senkaku Islands. One even locked its missiles system onto a Japanese vessel, a move from China that could have quickly upped the stakes.[85]

Japan's only outside military protection came from its 1952 security treaty with the United States; thus, by threatening Japan with a ship-

---

84. Prime Minister of Japan, Shinzo Abe, in a speech marking marking the 70th anniversary of the end of World War Two, August 14, 2015.

85. "Chinese Warships Prepared To Fire On The Japanese Navy Twice," *Business Insider*, February 2013.

to-ship missile, Beijing sent a direct message directly to the Pentagon. Drawing America into even a skirmish with China was a dangerous move. Abe's view was that Japan needed the wherewithal to handle China itself, but to achieve that he would have to amend the country's pacifist constitution. He led a parliamentary coalition, which meant horse-trading with the New Komeito Party, his Buddhist-based, pacifist-minded coalition partner. In July 2014, after much bargaining, Abe succeeded in winning cabinet approval for constitutional changes. Japan would be able to engage in "collective self-defense" and come to the aid of an ally under attack. Japanese troops could also serve overseas, although only in peacekeeping operations.

"The global situation surrounding Japan is becoming ever more difficult," Abe explained. "Being fully prepared is effective in discouraging any attempt to wage a war on Japan. The cabinet decision today will further lessen the chance of Japan being engaged in war. That is my conviction."[86]

The United States and Western allies supported the changes. Beijing reacted harshly. The government news agency, Xinhua, accused Abe of "leading his country down a dangerous path. . . . No matter how Abe glosses over it, he is dallying with the specter of war through a cheap scam."[87]

Then, amid the hostile rhetoric, in November 2014 Prime Minister Abe flew to Beijing for a regional conference and met China's president Xi Jinping. The discussion between the two leaders took place behind closed doors. Japanese officials painted a picture of a bland, formal discussion lasting thirty minutes, but the photographs afterward told all: an awkward handshake; unsmiling, dour expressions; and a reluctance, almost an inability, to look each other in the eye. Images of this frozen relationship were beamed around the world, and a week later Abe called a snap election, won easily, and consolidated his grip on power.

Three years later, however, Abe and Xi adopted a more pragmatic and mature approach toward each other as if accepting that that the

---

86. "Japan's pacifist constitution: After 70 years, nation changes the rules so it can go to war," *Independent*, July 2014.

87. Abe's Faustian flirtation with specter of war, *China Daily*, July 1, 2014.

region's key democratic and autocratic governments could not operate fruitfully if they are stayed at loggerheads with each other. At the November 2017 Asia Pacific Economic Cooperation Summit in Danang, Vietnam, they hailed a 'fresh start' Abe said that stable relations were in the interests of both countries. Xi corroborated by stating that China and Japan 'must take constructive steps to appropriately manage and control disputes.'

Much impetus came from the joint recognition by China and Japan of the regional unease created by the unpredictable Trump administration. Japan was suspicious of Trump's excessive praise of Xi and what he stood for. China realized that if it were to expand its influence securely, it should start looking at Japan not as a rival, but an ally. How that might work could never be sealed in a warmed handshake on the sidelines of a regional summit, but there was soon a cooling of tensions around the disputed Senkaku-Diaoyu island.

Shortly after the summit the Asia Maritime Transparency Initiative published photographs showing a marked contrast between Chinese fishing boats testing the contested waters around the islands. A year earlier, in August 2016, days after China's annual fishing ban ended, up to 300 Chinese fishing boats accompanied by sixteen Coast Guard vessels worked near the Senkaku-Diaoyu islands and many repeatedly entered the twelve-nautical mile sovereign maritime territory there, causing stand-offs with the Japanese Coast Guard. In 2017, however, in the lead up to the summit and the announcement of the 'fresh start', the Chinese fishing boats stayed away, and did not test Japan's claimed sovereign waters.

"With China holding the 19th Party Congress and Japan organizing a snap election in late October, an incident around the Senkakus could have introduced unwelcome and difficult to control dynamics at a politically sensitive time for both countries," concluded AMTI report. "Instead, Beijing and Tokyo seemed intent on advancing a tentative rapprochement."

A not unconnected element is that Japan and ten other Pacific governments began to push ahead with the Trans-Pacific Partnership from which the US had withdrawn and signed a deal in March 2018. The Obama-administration had put long hours into negotiating a rules-based trading system aimed at achieving much more for the region than simply transactional trade. The plan was to eliminate tariffs on ninety-five per cent of goods covering half a billion people, but China was not included.

American analysts on Asia created a spectrum of scenarios on how things might unfold, bearing in mind that the Trump presidency is finite and the Sino-Japanese relationship stretches back for centuries. James Manicom in his 2014 book Bridging Troubled Waters: China, Japan, and Maritime Order in the East China Sea argued that while the relationship was difficult, it had a good track record in sensible management. China needed a stable region to push its own economic growth. Japan's military treaty with the United States remained a powerful deterrent.

Scott Warren Harold of the Rand Center for Asia Policy, writing almost two years later, believed that economics may not be the most important factor in China's mind: "Chinese policymakers are likely to ask themselves three questions: Do we need to fight? If we fight, can we win? And third, what will the costs be? Disturbingly, none of the answers to these questions are currently trending in a positive direction. . . . Moreover, the two countries' economic links are trending downwards, suggesting a potential further erosion of the economic constraints on war."[88]

Lyle J. Goldstein of the US Naval War College went a step further in describing the East China Sea as "the most dangerous place on the entire planet." The trigger could be a "bumping incident" between rival vessels as happened routinely in the South China Sea. "In such circumstances, the steps from gun fire to exchanging volleys of anti-ship missiles between the fleets, to theater wide attacks on major bases, to all out global war could be all too abrupt."[89]

His colleague, James Kelly, a former US carrier group commander and now a Naval College dean, was concerned about the risk of miscalculation. The Chinese, Japanese and US navies were all operating in the same theater. "When you get the mix of all those things going on,

---

88. "Do Economic Ties Limit the Prospect of Conflict?" The Rand Blog, August 2016.

89. "The World's Most Dangerous Rivalry: China and Japan," The National Interest, September 2014.

you have to walk the dog pretty carefully when you're a mariner out at sea, particularly when you're the captain of the big guns out there," Kelly told me. "If the leaders of the forces are in close proximity to each other and if they're not talking to each other bridge to bridge by whatever means necessary, you could have something go on that's not going to make people happy."

The Sino-Japanese tension revived a sense throughout East Asia that although Japan had apologized time and again, its expressions of regret were not enough. The difference with how Germany had behaved was subtle and almost impossible to quantify. It was as if German politicians regularly visited the graves of Nazi war criminals in order to bolster their poll ratings. In Asia there was a sentiment that Japan did not yet understand how brutal its colonization had been, nor what it needed to do to move on. As the Diaoyu/Senkaku Islands were the symbol of the current Sino-Japanese power play, so the war heroes in the Yasukuni Shrine were that of Japan's failure to understand its past.

AN EQUIVALENT IN China to the Hiroshima Peace Memorial Museum is the Massacre Memorial Hall in Nanjing, which pays tribute to victims of the Japanese slaughter that took place in the city in December 1937. Unlike the nuclear attack, the brutality was personal, with at least twenty thousand women raped, killing competitions among Japanese soldiers against Chinese prisoners, buildings burned, homes looted, bodies left unburied, and more than three hundred thousand killed. All of this is meticulously chronicled in halls specially lit to maximize the impact of the exhibits. One enlarged photograph shows a procession of Japanese imperial troops on horseback, with crowds by the side of the road. Another is of an old man about to be beheaded, and another shows corpses strewn about the landscape. They are images of conquest and cruelty. Outside are sculptures of civilians fleeing, tranquil water features, and, at the exit, a portrait of President Xi Jinping, who led an anniversary commemoration there in December 2014 just as Abe was being reelected. "History will not be altered as time changes," Xi told the crowd. "And facts will not disappear because of any chicanery or denials."[90]

---

90. Xi Jinping blasts Japan's wartime atrocities at high-profile Nanking massacre memorial, *South China Morning Post*, December 13, 2014.

These deepening, competing sentiments underpin a realization that while East Asia had seemed united through trade, it had so far failed to create a collective sense of a future or drawn up a system of common values. Europe achieved a sense of a future after the 1945 defeat of Germany and again when absorbing the countries of Soviet-controlled Eastern Europe after 1991. Yet, even in Europe, nationalist sentiment is rising again. As in Asia, economic integration is proving not to be enough. With no mechanism in place to take things further, old enemies were falling back on bad history. This was Japan's Sun Goddess pitted against China's Mandate of Heaven. Historically, Japan had outpaced China in its development, much as China was now outpacing India. Part of Japan's success had been in its subtler and results-oriented way of dealing with the encroaching West in the nineteenth century, with the result that Japan had been the first Asian country to become a modern industrialized society.

"Beijing has sought to convince the world that Japan is reassuming its militaristic past," says Richard Javad Heydarian of Ateneo de Manila University in the Philippines. "Any sober analysis, however, would suggest that the real bone of contention is an emerging Chinese-Japanese contest for regional leadership."

In at least three earlier contests between the two, the winner had been Japan.

For centuries, Chinese and Japanese traveled freely between their countries, but they lived in near isolation from the wider world outside Asia. Japan's initial taste of foreign interference came in the 1550s, when Portuguese Jesuit missionaries' enthusiasm to convert people to Catholicism led to insurrection. They were expelled in 1639 and Christian converts were executed. Only the Dutch, who avoided evangelism, were allowed to set up a trading post in Nagasaki and from that Japan was able to glimpse Western modernization in the form of books and scientific inventions.

The early nineteenth century brought an insistence from the West that both China and Japan open up for trade. Both countries were against a foreign presence, with China confining traders to its southern port of Canton, and Japan allowing only the Dutch their one post. In 1825, as the European threat widened, and European and American vessels kept encroaching in Japanese waters, Japan issued a command to "expel foreigners at all costs."

The change came in 1842, with Britain's victory against China in the First Opium War. Japan took note of British brutality and how better guns, bigger ships, more sophisticated technology, and disciplined soldiers had defeated China. Twelve years later, an American naval commander, Commodore Matthew Perry, led a flotilla of ships to Japan and, under threat of military action, insisted Japan open its ports for American whalers to resupply. Japan quickly complied, prompting Perry to expand his brief and insist that Japanese ports open for American trade. In March 1854 Perry signed the Kanagawa Treaty, which ended Japan's isolation and allocated a handful of ports for international trade.

The treaty sparked a civil war between those who supported the existing militaristic system of shogunates that had controlled Japan pretty much from the end of the twelfth century and those who wanted reform. By now, Britain and France were hovering behind America to get a slice of Japanese trade and took different sides in the conflict. Britain armed the reformists, while France supported forces loyal to the shogunate. Fighting continued on and off for fifteen years, but by 1869 shogunate rule ended and Japan began the era of the Meiji Restoration.

The direct translation of *Meiji* is "enlightened," and the Meiji Era was one of modernization during which Japan tried to take the best of the West, its advanced technology and thinking, while retaining its own Asian way of life. During the same period, Beijing's lingering feudal system tried to resist Western infiltration, but was unable to defeat it. In the 1850s the British took the Second Opium War deep inside the country, humiliating China by marching into Beijing, destroying the summer palace, and taking control of large coastal areas for Western powers that acted as a colonizing, occupying force.

Japan, on the other hand, after signing the Kanagawa Treaty with the United States in 1854, went on to embrace all the West had to offer. Restaurants with chandeliers and orchestras offered European cuisine and fine wines. Men wore Sherlock Holmes capes, had western haircuts, and danced the waltz and quadrille at the Rokumeikan, the Hall of the Baying Stag, in central Tokyo where they ate French food prepared by French chefs and played billiards. The first motor cars, barely seen even in the West, appeared on Tokyo's streets. Japan lapped up science, engineering, politics, and lifestyles. It acted not as if it had been forced into accepting Western doctrines but as if it had actively adopted the concepts of international law, trade, learning, and even political debate, convinced that by cooperating with Western powers it would become stronger itself.

Foreign visitors experienced impeccable politeness, order, and efficiency, while Japan acquired muscle and knowledge. Its own businessmen set up operations throughout East Asia. The first test came in 1894, forty years after the Kanagawa Treaty, when China and Japan were vying for influence in Korea, traditionally a Chinese vassal state. Their armies fought. Japan won, seizing from China its historical sway over Korea and taking the mantle of the dominant regional power.

Japan did not stop with Korea. Nor had it finished with China. Its Western-inspired military colonized Taiwan, swiftly and brutally putting down any Chinese resistance, in what was later to become an official policy of the Southern Expansion Doctrine (Nanshin-ron). Japan's view that Southeast Asia and the western Pacific lay in its sphere of national interest was its equivalent of the Monroe Doctrine, also borrowed from the United States. It also planned the Northern Expansion Doctrine (Hokushin-ron), which, although only on the drawing board at the time, brought Japan into head-to-head conflict with another European power, Russia. Having won on the Korean Peninsula, Japan now eyed northeast China, referred to as Manchuria, where Russia kept its warships at the all-weather Port Arthur.

In a style that would be repeated at Pearl Harbor thirty-seven years later, Japan carried out a lightning preemptive strike on Port Arthur and put it under siege. It fought a stream of battles with Russia, which surrendered in September 1905 with a peace agreement brokered by the United States; for that, President Theodore Roosevelt won the Nobel Peace Prize. Japan's decisive defeat of a European country stunned the international defense community and catapulted Japan from a regional to a world power. But inside Japan there was a sense of having been cheated, that even now it was not being treated as an equal but as an inferior Asian power, and that the United States in its intervention, had denied Japan the legitimate spoils of war.

China's president, Sun Yat-sen, sounded a note of warning even then. In a speech in Japan in 1924, he praised Japan's victory over Russia as a defeat of the West by the East. "We regarded the Japanese victory as our own victory. It was indeed a happy event," he said, adding, "Now the question remains whether Japan will be the hawk of the Western civilization of the rule of Might, or the tower of strength of the Orient. This is the choice which lies before the people of Japan."[91]

At the time Japan was colonizing Korea, where it conducted a program of deliberate cruelty. Thousands died as Japan suppressed uprisings. Hundreds of thousands were sent to labor camps, and women were forced into sex as "comfort women," which remains a point of anger in the Japanese-Korean relationship today. Japanese occupiers tried to eradicate the Korean language and cultural identity, smashing artifacts and destroying historical buildings. Korea gave the world a glimpse of what was to come from Japan. By then European powers were becoming embroiled in their own power struggles. When the First World War broke out, Britain and France were only too appreciative of Japan joining them in moving against German interests in Asia.

It was at this time that the United States realized that in helping to industrialize Japan it might have created the makings of a modern, capable enemy that could cause trouble. At the Naval War College, on Roosevelt's instruction, military analysts began formulating a road map to use against a rising Asian power that threatened US interests. It was called War Plan Orange.

91. Sun Yat-sen, President Republic of China, speech on Pan-Asianism in Kobe, Japan November 28, 1924.

CHAPTER 13

THE UNITED STATES: WAR GAMES AND BLACK SWANS

I N 1890 THE UNITED STATES REALIZED THAT IF IT WAS TO PROTECT THE homeland and its national interests it would have to become a Pacific power. This was eight years before it got an Asian foothold by taking the Philippines off Spain and a generation before it sent troops across the Atlantic to fight in a European war. The Atlantic Ocean acts as a bridge that links America and Europe with the shared values of Western democracy and many Americans—particularly on the East Coast—see their country through that prism, keeping Russia at bay through NATO and sharing so much heritage with Europe. The view from the newer cities on the West Coast runs across the Pacific, where the heritage of Los Angeles, San Francisco, and Seattle is as much entwined with China, Japan and Korea as the heritage of Boston and New York is with Dublin and Naples.

The 1890 threat from the Pacific percolated when Japanese ships were spotted near Hawaii, which was not yet US territory but run by American businessmen. The United States annexed Hawaii in 1898 with its victory in the Spanish-American War, but that did not end the Japanese threat, and US war planners began looking at how to contain a rising Japan. Five years later, Japan stunned the world with the victory over Russia at Port Arthur in northwest China. It was then that the US Naval War College initiated War Plan Orange, examining both containment scenarios and, if necessary, a strategy to defeat Japan.[92]

In barely fifty years, this once backward Asian country had listened, watched, and learned and molded itself into a European style industrial

---

92. Edward S. Miller, *War Plan Orange: The U.S. Strategy to Defeat Japan, 1897–1945*, Naval Institute Press, 2007.

and military power, putting itself head-to-head first with Russia and then with the United States. It is little wonder that President Theodore Roosevelt was anxious.

Since its foundation in the late nineteenth century, the US Naval War College has designed and advised on America's long-term military strategy war gaming in which scenarios are played out between imaginary combatants. The outcome is fed back to the Pentagon, which draws on it for naval contingency plans and strategies.

The war college students are midcareer officers on the way up the ladder; most are from the United States, but dozens come from other countries that train and exercise with the American military. The words of its founder, Commodore Stephen B. Luce, are recited during the convocation of new students, often by an actor decked out with bushy sideburns, a deep blue uniform, and a gravelly voice, offering unpalatable truths. Luce described war as a "dreadful scourge," then went on to say, "But after all has been said no student of history however superficial can deny that through that same dreadful scourge ultimate good has been brought about." He finished his argument by explaining how war could be averted: "In one way and one way only, and that way is to be fully prepared for it. That is the meaning of this college."[93]

To underpin how layered both the Japanese-American relationship was early last century and the Sino-American relationship is now, the commander of the Japanese Fleet, Isoroku Yamamoto, visited the college in 1924 and went on to serve as naval attaché at the Japanese embassy in Washington, DC. Ninety years later, in 2006, Wu Shengli, then head of the Chinese Navy, was also a guest at the college. Yamamoto went on to mastermind the 1941 Pearl Harbor attack, and Wu oversaw the growth of the Chinese navy to become a sea power that is now keeping American admirals up at night. He stepped down in 2016.

War gamers allocate each country a color; the United States, blue; Britain, red; China, yellow; Germany, black; the Korean Peninsula, brown; Mexico, green; and Japan orange—hence, War Plan Orange. This game involving Japan was the most complex and long-running in

---

93. *The Writings of Stephen B. Luce*, Edited with Commentary by John D. Hayes and John B. Hattendorf, Naval War College Press, Newport, Rhode Island, 1975.

US military history and fundamental to securing the US position as an Asia-Pacific power.

The first version of War Plan Orange was developed against the backdrop of Japan's war with Russia, and it included detailed operations for a naval war in the Pacific. The expectation was that Japan would first go for the Philippines, which, if the United States chose to fight, would take at least two years to win back.

So, more than a hundred years ago, the United States was faced with the option of fighting a strong-minded Asian country or withdrawing from the Pacific altogether. Today China is determined to become the regional power and the United States is equally determined to retain its position of predominance. In many respects, therefore, its position as a Pacific power has been far longer embedded within the American psyche than that of being a European one.

Like Japan before it, China argues that it holds a natural position of predominance in Asia. America continues to attach an altruistic motive, just as President William McKinley did when the Philippines' conundrum first landed on his desk, partly for national interest and partly to uphold international law and prevent big power hegemony.

In the First World War, Japan incrementally increased its territory, island by island, taking German-controlled places like the Caroline, Mariana, and Marshall Islands and Palau. During the 1920s it continued building up its forces with the advantage that it only had one region on which to concentrate, while the United States was by then divided between the Atlantic and the Pacific. In today's scenario, America has commitments in Africa, Europe, and Latin America, while focusing on Islamist terrorism and the Middle East. China can choose where it concentrates it resources and planning.

What also became apparent in Japan's rise was that any war involving an Asian power would principally be a maritime conflict, while the wars in Europe involving Germany and Russia had been fought village by village, trench by muddy trench. As planners switched from Europe to the Pacific, they had to adapt their mind-sets from the fixed bayonet to the warship torpedo. Another comparative change now underway is shifting expertise from the handmade roadside bomb to the science of the precision ship-busting missile.

One element factored into War Plan Orange was that, unlike European navies, the United States had never been in battle against a modern fleet; this meant training up for whatever Japan might throw at it. The short war against weak and unmotivated Spain was not counted.

"So, what they did is they gamed what war in the Pacific would look like at an operational and strategic level," Naval College dean Tom Culora explained to me. "If you had a rising Japan that had started taking territory in the Pacific, and the US found itself in conflict with Japan, how would you manage it?"

There was an added domestic political issue to this military planning. Thousands of Japanese were arriving to set up home in California, creating a racist backlash that spilled over into local and congressional politics. Anti-Japanese organizations mushroomed, demanding that measures be taken to contain the immigration, including legislation to stop the "yellow peril" from buying property. That sentiment worsened over the years, spiking when Japan invaded northeast China in 1931. The anger became horror in 1937 with news of the Nanjing Massacre reaching American shores. But the United States did not take action directly until 1940, when Japan went into Indochina with the aim of stopping oil and other supplies from reaching China. By then Nazi Germany controlled France, and Japan struck a deal with the pro-Nazi Vichy government, which governed Indochina, to seal off China's supply routes. In response, President Roosevelt froze Japanese assets in America and slapped an embargo on its oil supplies. Britain and the Netherlands, two allied powers with Southeast Asian territory, followed suit, cutting off three quarters of Japan's oil supplies. Japan now had a choice of abandoning its ambition to be the primary Pacific power or fighting America. It chose to fight. The catalyst to war was not anything high-minded like competing ideology, but Japan's need to protect energy supplies and access to raw materials, the same motivation that drives China today.

Isoroku Yamamoto, who seventeen years earlier had been a guest of the Naval War College, planned the Pearl Harbor attack with two ideas in mind. One was that success would be decided by aircraft carriers. The other was that if Japan could not defeat the United States within a year, it was likely to lose. He was right on both counts.

One original plan was to carry out a single sweeping attack on the whole of Southeast Asia, including the US-colonized Philippines. But, Yamamoto argued, if Japan was going to confront America via the Philippines it should also directly hit the naval fleet in Hawaii. Once that was crippled, Japan would have a free hand in Asia. He struck on the morning of December 7, 1941, with 353 planes from six aircraft carriers, hitting eight battleships, three cruisers, three destroyers, and a training ship. Japanese casualties of sixty-four dead and the loss of twenty-nine aircraft were light against the 2,403 Americans killed and 188 aircraft destroyed. Almost simultaneously, Japan attacked Hong Kong, Malaya, the Philippines, and Singapore. In the United States, War Plan Orange swung into action.

In his 2007 book *War Plan Orange* Edward Miller neatly lays out the cause of the war, and try reading this passage substituting China for Japan:

> The geopolitical premises of the plan held that, in spite of historically friendly relations, a war would erupt someday between the United States and Japan, a war in which neither could rely on the help of allies. The root cause would be Japan's quest for national greatness by attempting to dominate the land, people, and resources of the Far East. America regarded itself as the guardian of Western influence in the Orient. Its popular dogma favored self-determination of peoples and open international trade. To achieve its goal, Japan would feel it necessary to expunge American power from its sea flank.[94]

From 1905 to 1941, War Plan Orange had undergone countless dogged revisions and scenarios, and it is widely credited with giving the United States the road map it needed to defeat Japan. The surprise Pearl Harbor attack, of course, had not been factored in and was categorized as a black swan, a hard-to-predict, unexpected and rare event that happens regardless of how much planning has been done. A second omission was the nuclear weapon that led to Japan's surrender, which had not

---

94. Edward S. Miller, War Plan Orange: The U.S. Strategy to Defeat Japan, 1897–1945, Naval Institute Press, 2007.

been invented in 1941. A third was the kamikaze suicide pilots deployed at the end of the war to crash Japanese planes into American ships.

"The war with Japan had been reenacted in the game rooms by so many people and in so many different ways that nothing that happened during the war was a surprise," Fleet Admiral Chester W. Nimitz said when giving a guest lecture to the War College in 1960. "Absolutely nothing except the kamikaze tactics toward the end of the war."[95]

Nimitz, who had an aircraft carrier class named after him, attended the War College as a student in 1923 when he submitted a paper simply entitled "Policy." In it he made an observation that could again be read today by substituting China for Japan. "Policy, to be effective, must be founded on right and justice and must be backed by public opinion, particularly in a democratic country like the United States. In a highly centralized, militaristic government like Japan the public opinion of the masses is relatively unimportant as the government through its control of the press can readily mold public opinion."[96]

The 2016 RAND Corporation report *War with China: Thinking Through the Unthinkable* expands on Nimitz's point by arguing that should it come to conflict between the United States and China, domestic opposition could jeopardize America's ability to fight: "The ability of the president to be an effective commander-in-chief could be impaired by politicization; opposition could come from peace factions, war factions, or both. Unless the country's security is directly threatened, the wholehearted support of the general public and the elite cannot be assumed." That would give China an advantage, the report adds: "Public opinion in China, though an important source of pressure and potential cradle of dissent, is not critical to the regime's survival: The middle class is mainly patriotic in sentiment, the rural poor are voiceless, migrant factory workers are formless, and dissidents are a small minority and more concerned with political or religious freedom than foreign policy."[97]

---

95. John W. Lillard, *Playing War: Wargaming and U.S. Navy Preparations for World War II*, Potomac Books, 2016.

96. Commander C. W Nimitz, "Policy," US Naval War College, Class of 1923.

97. RAND Corporation, *War with China: Thinking Through the Unthinkable* (Santa Monica, CA: RAND Corporation, 2016).

Tom Culora explained how all these factors—political pressure, economic impact, legal questions on dealing with the maritime militia—are being tested and retested in different scenarios to avoid another black swan and to ensure that regardless of whatever unfolds, with whatever enemy, the United States would win. "In the interwar years, we were looking at this new technology, for example, how would you deploy with this technology of the airplane?" he told me. "How would that fold into what warfare would look like in the Pacific? If you fast-forward today with the rise of precision strike missiles, the ability to target at a long range very accurately, the implications of cyberspace and electronic warfare and how does that look in the Pacific region, this is very similar to what we did in the interwar years."

The tapestry of Asia has changed slightly, and the technology that might define its future is very different. But much is the same. The 1940s Pacific war is defined by two images, mushroom clouds over Japanese cities and US Marines raising a flag on an uninhabited island. Nuclear weapons and remote islands still define Asian regional tension.[98]

---

98. RAND Corporation, *War with China: Thinking Through the Unthinkable* (Santa Monica, CA: RAND Corporation, 2016).

CHAPTER 14

NORTH KOREA:
THE MOON LANDING
AND THE BEATLES

I N 2017 THE US NEED TO REMAIN A PACIFIC POWER BECAME STARKLY illustrated by open threats from a nuclear-armed North Korea not only on other Asian countries, but also on American territory. Military treaties demand the United States protects Japan, the Philippines, and South Korea, and to contain danger to US territory it is best to tackle it at source. The North Korean crisis has drawn in China, Japan, Russia, South Korea, and the United States. During 2017 North Korea carried out a series of long-range missile tests that it claimed were designed for a nuclear strike on the American mainland. Three US aircraft carrier groups were deployed to the Pacific. The UN imposed yet more sanctions on North Korea, backed by the nation's traditional allies China and Russia, indicating further isolation of the regime.

Yes, much of this was bluster and rhetoric. Comparisons with the 1962 Cuban Missile Crisis were misplaced because Cuba is just over a hundred miles from Florida, while North Korea is fifty-five hundred miles from the American West Coast and two thousand miles from Guam, the US Pacific island with military bases, threatened by Pyongyang. So far North Korea has only proven that it had some kind of nuclear weapon and a missile that in August 2017 flew for forty-five minutes, reaching a height of twenty-three hundred miles and traveling for a distance of more than six hundred miles. Without a doubt, North Korea is working hard and fast on improving its arsenal. But it knows that if it ever did directly threaten Japan, South Korea, or the United States, the Kim family regime would be unlikely to survive.

"One would hope that the North Korean crisis is moving away from bluster and counter-bluster, and toward realism," writes Anthony

H. Cordesman of the Center for Strategic and International Studies. "The risk is not today's potential North Korean nuclear threat. It is what can so easily evolve over the coming decade: An open-ended nuclear arms race in northeast Asia with players whose actions and level of restraint in any given crisis is far harder to predict than the impact of mutual assured destruction in the Cold War."

North Korea is controlled by an outdated, insular, Stalinist-style family dynasty, currently run by Kim Jong-un, who is only in his thirties. He inherited the mantle from his father, Kim Jong-il, son of the country's revered and canny founder, Kim Il-sung, who started the Korean War. In the strange way in which North Korea operates, Kim Il-sung's 105th birthday was celebrated in April 2017 because, within its mythology, the Great Leader, as he was known, was named after his death as the "eternal president"—meaning he is, in the mind of the nation, still alive.

The country is flanked to the north by its ally China, and to the south by its enemy South Korea, across the demilitarized zone agreed upon in 1953 to stop the fighting. Technically, the two sides remain at war. To the east North Korea shares a short border with Russia. On the map, the country resembles an upside-down ankle and shoe. The Kim family has maintained a skillful grip over North Korea's twenty-five million people by repressing, threatening, and isolating them. Borders are kept closed. Martial music, slogans, and worship of the regime are embedded in citizens from birth. Television, radio, and the Internet are highly restricted. Some 150,000 labor camp prisoners live in a Soviet-style gulag system, facing starvation, torture, rape, and execution, and the threat of being sent to such a camp hangs over every citizen. No one is exempt. To strengthen his grip on power, Kim Jong-un executed his own uncle in 2014, together with an aunt and many other relatives. During a visit in 1994, I interviewed a deputy minister who handled energy and nuclear issues. I tried to contact him later, and was told he had "moved job." I later learned he had been executed by firing squad.

By sealing itself off and instilling in people the idea that they lead perfect lives, the Kim family has created a bizarre social laboratory. North Koreans are motivated, bright, and disciplined. They have to be to outfox the regime and survive. Those I have met are funny, clever, and quick-thinking. The minders allocated to me during two visits in the mid-1990s—when the United States was drawing up plans for air and missile strikes in order to stop North Korea from developing nuclear weapons—had been educated at the best universities in Beijing and Moscow. Conversation flowed, jokes were cracked, beer was drunk, and stories were told of wild times, difficult spouses, and sexual infidelities. Nothing, it seemed, was off the table—except, of course, scrutiny of the regime.

On my first visit, posing as tourists, we filmed lunchtime airstrike drills with sirens wailing and crowds rushing toward the metro stations. That evening, we were taken to the monument celebrating the North Korean ideology known as Juche; there a fake red flame symbolizing the self-reliance that glues the country together flared up from a tall, thin tower. It was devised by Kim Il-sung as an image of absolute loyalty, a nation blessed with happiness under the guidance of the Great Leader. We were there at dusk, and a full moon appeared in a clear sky, untainted by city lights because in Pyongyang there weren't many.

One guide said, "The moon is so big and beautiful and it's so close, I feel I could touch it."

"Yes," I answered. "And to think people have walked on it."

The guide stiffened and said, "You are wrong. No man has ever walked on the moon. Under the guidance of our Great Leader, Kim Il-sung, the Democratic People's Republic of Korea will be the first nation to send a man to the moon."

You could cut the dusk atmosphere with a knife, so I said, "Oh. Maybe I'm wrong. I thought people had." The next day we toured Pyongyang's main maternity hospital, which had only one baby and not a pregnant woman in sight, and a disabled center with no one who was disabled.

My second visit, a few months later, came in the summer of 1994 after Kim Il-sung had died. I led an official BBC film crew, or delegation as they called it, bearing a gift from the chairman with the BBC coat of arms and the inscription "Nation shall speak peace unto Nation," and got into a similarly confused conversation again. This time we were in the dreary and soul-stripping Koryo Hotel, where everything was gray or dirty maroon. We were laughing over beers, and in the background came piped-in music, the North Korean version of Wagneresque jingoistic songs. We had a different set of guides from another department, but they had an equally sharp wit, this time ripping into South Korean men for being ugly and impotent, which was why all the beautiful women sought sanctuary in the North. Gradually, seeping into the background noise came the Beatles song "Hey Jude," wafting over from another group. Bulgarian engineers, sick of the patriotic music, had turned on a CD player.

Our guides were both called Kim. They knew the song, and had even sung it in karaoke in Beijing. I said, "I wonder what music the Beatles would be doing now if they hadn't split up."

Suddenly we were back in a moon-landing situation. Silence ensued as they took in the apparent enormity of what I had said and processed what to do. Frowns. Nervousness. Laser-like glares. Whispered discussion. Eventually one stood up; he was thin, bespectacled, in his early thirties, wearing a tight, badly fitting dark blue suit. "Mr. Humphrey, could I have a private word?"

We walked to the edge of the bar area, round the table where the Bulgarians were tapping their feet to "So let it out and let it in, hey Jude, begin. . . ." We stopped on steps leading down to the main foyer. "Mr. Humphrey, I must correct you. The Beatles have not split up. They are coming here to perform for our Great Leader Kim Il-sung—" He hesitated, adjusting his spectacles, his face creased with the contradiction of what he had just said. The country was in mourning for the Great Leader who had just died, while a rock band that no longer existed was on its way to perform for him. The man fixed me with an even harsher gaze. But his tone changed completely. "Listen, we don't know which fuckers are watching us. You've got to help us, okay? We let you in as a test, and if that test fails it's kaput for us."

"Moon landing, Beatles, anything else?" I said quietly.

"Too much with those fuckers. Too much. You never fucking know. No-one does." He put a shaking hand on my elbow to guide me back.

By mid-2017 Kim Jong-un was intensifying his missile tests, and US president Donald Trump declared his patience had run out and that the only good outcome would be North Korea's capitulation. Air strikes could lead to a nuclear war. At another level, the sudden collapse of the regime, advocated by many in the West, could be catastrophic. Similar scenarios had unfolded in the early twenty-first century in Egypt, Iraq, Libya, and Ukraine: a familiar pattern of false jubilation from the West, then reality, then bloodshed and division. North Korea had brought the world to the brink of war before, most seriously in 1994, when President Bill Clinton drew up detailed strike plans. Since then, however, none of the major regional powers could agree on how to handle the disintegration of the North Korean regime.

Before the invasion of Iraq in 2003 many believed that Britain, the United States, and others had drawn up a plan on how to rebuild Iraq and had anticipated scenarios so as not to be caught by surprise. But they had not, and there is little evidence of lessons learned should Trump carry out his threat to destroy the regime. North Korea not only threatens US interests in the Asia-Pacific but now, with its missiles, has openly warned that it intends to attack the homeland.. This is far too dangerous a place for us not to have a plan.

With numerous weapons tests dating back to 2006, North Korea has been slowly acquiring the ability to deliver a nuclear warhead over long distances. The United States has been caught like a rabbit in headlights, uncertain how to stop it. While America could intervene in Afghanistan, Iraq, Iran, and Syria, similar action in North Korea would be fraught with danger, risking an attack on the South Korean capital, Seoul. There is a fear that any strike would be met with a barrage on Seoul from the hundreds of artillery guns that North Korea keeps across the border. Estimates of their firing ability vary from half a million shells in an hour, destroying Seoul, to only obliterating an area that reaches the northern suburbs. There would be a high risk, too, of shells carrying the chemical nerve agents VX and sarin, of which North Korea has plentiful stockpiles. Much of North Korea's equipment would not work; in fact, military estimates believe that up to one-fourth of its weaponry would fail. But it could still cause a high level of civilian casualties.

"North Korea is a failing state," Bruce W. Bennett, who has been advocating that a detailed plan be drawn up, told me. "Its government could collapse in the coming months or years, causing an immense humanitarian disaster and potentially other, even more serious consequences. This is not a stable government. The more I researched, the more frightened I became."

One scenario Bennett examined in his 2014 RAND Corporation report *Preparing for the Possibility of a North Korean Collapse* was the assassination of Kim Jong-un by a rival faction, which could propel North Korea toward civil war. Within hours of trouble breaking out, four emergency elements would need to be handled by international powers.

First, Bennett expected refugees to head both north and south. To prevent a human flood, humanitarian aid would have to be delivered swiftly and in plentiful supply throughout the country. The second emergency measure would be to neutralize North Korea's air defense system; this would require military intervention agreed upon by China, South Korea, and the United States. Each hour taken to arrange it would worsen the humanitarian crisis. The third measure would be Beijing insisting on a buffer zone inside North Korea's northern border, perhaps as deep as thirty miles, where its troops would be deployed. South Korea, which views the North as Korean sovereign territory, would have to agree. And finally, North Korea's weapons of mass destruction would have to be secured quickly to prevent them falling into the hands of a terrorist organization or a North Korean faction that might use them.

In April 2013 the US Naval War College war-gamed a North Korean scenario, some results of which have been declassified. The game was conducted in a theater resembling the Korean Peninsula with the rivals code-named North and South Brown Lands. It involved three hundred people who played out a collapse of North Korea, either through intervention (as in Iraq in 2003) or through internal regime overthrow (as in Egypt in 2011). Among the participants were Army chief of staff Ray Odierno and his vice chief, John Campbell, both veterans of the Afghanistan and Iraq campaigns, knowledgeable about hostile occupation and insurgencies. The scenario rapidly brought opposing Asian powers head-to-head because of North Korea's geographical position bordering China, Russia, and South Korea, with US bases in Japan just across the sea to its east. It was worrying that the four governments had no agreed-upon formula for how to contain any collapse.

"There is not a great deal of planning on this," the college's North Korea expert, Terence Roehrig, told me. "It's a delicate issue because planning for a collapse means you may be interested in encouraging one, and that could be diplomatically problematic."

What the war game found made for uncomfortable reading. It would take ninety thousand troops fifty-six days to secure North Korea's nuclear materials. In that time, Kim's fracturing regime could distribute weapons-grade material to terrorist groups and rogue states around the world. The North Korean military would be expected to fight to keep control of their regions, status, salaries, and pensions, because the officers and party elite would be aware of the punitive measures the United States took against the Iraqi Army by summarily dissolving it. Rivalry in North Korea would be regional because it does not suffer the same ethnic and religious divisions as Iraq, and South Korea, not the United States, would most likely be the leading military force.

A prevailing view in Washington, DC, has been that China could be allowed to secure the nuclear weapons, given that the key North Korean nuclear installation at Yongbyon is only eighty miles from the Chinese border. Even so, there would need to be agreement. The fractious US political establishment would be divided. Japan would be tense and suspicious. South Korea would feel vulnerable.

There would be an emotionally charged reaction from Western democracies as revelations about concentration camps, starvation, and state cruelty emerged on twenty-four-hour news networks, creating a clash of interests between what would be needed for stability and a popular demand for instant action. As North Korea's ally, China would not come out of this well, and there would be demands that it should be held accountable for supporting such a barbaric regime. Similar responses would feed out toward other governments, such as Pakistan and Russia, that have aided and abetted North Korea.

Even if the immediate crisis were handled as well as could be, China, South Korea, and the United States would jointly have to settle on a new government framework for the Korean Peninsula. Beijing and Washington would project their competing national interests, while Seoul would decide if it wanted full German-style unification and, if so, how to pay for it. There would also be the question of who in North Korea should be punished, and which officials should keep their jobs to hold institutions together. Who should lead the transition? Neither

Beijing nor Washington has a good track record in this area. China remains stained by Cambodia's Pol Pot and North Korea itself; The United States is bruised by Iraq. And the European Union has become too weak to have any impact.

A temporary arrangement could be a new partition of the North, in which Seoul would control the southern area of Kim Jong-un's old territory while Beijing handled the area closer to its border. Pyongyang would become a shared administrative center, and there would be a timetable for Chinese withdrawal. Candidates for government would be drawn from factions within the North, who would bring to the new government their networks and knowledge of power, and from the diaspora in the South, who would deliver an understanding of good governance and trade. Far from perfect, such a partition would usher in a transitional era during which everyone could get used to the new landscape.

Bennett published another RAND Corporation report in 2017 pointing out that a key number of military and party officials in the North would have to be won over if Korean unification was to work. "North Korean elites likely need to feel that unification will be good for them, or at least not unacceptably bad," he explains.[99] The measures would include maintaining status, wealth, and security for families—exactly what the United States failed to do in Iraq, where the disbanding of the army and excluding elites from the ruling Baath Party fueled the insurgency.

The psychology itself would be challenging enough, taking people embedded in North Korea's warped ideology and switching their mindset to one of understanding and trusting South Korea and the United States. But it may be more acceptable to China, which categorizes such a tactic as " nonpeaceful measures" whereby sanctions or a state of siege prompt high-level defections. This is how Beijing eventually fell to Mao Zedong's communist army in 1949, and an option that it retains for eventual unification with Taiwan.

Scenarios on the Korean Peninsula pose far more danger than Beijing's operations in the South China Sea, raising a familiar question: Why would the United States object to the Chinese military oc-

---

99. Bruce W. Bennett, *Preparing North Korean Elites for Unification* (Santa Monica, CA: RAND, 2017), ix.

cupying a handful of remote uninhabited islands when Beijing and Washington need to work together on the Korean Peninsula and a myriad of other issues? In his January 2017 handover, President Barack Obama warned Trump that North Korea and its missiles would be his top national security threat. North Korea's missile program first became a threat in the 1990s, and there were even reports (never confirmed) that it was being designed by a team of rogue Soviet scientists laid off after the collapse of communism.[100] Pakistani involvement is well-documented.[101]

In its more than twenty missile tests during 2017, North Korea claimed to have achieved its aim of designing a missile and nuclear warhead that could reach Washington D.C. It even hinted at carrying out an atmospheric nuclear missile test over the Pacific Ocean. US attempts to pressure China into stopping North Korea had yielded little during this period of heightened tension, and North Korea appeared determined to keep going until it had the nuclear deterrent it thought it needed. North Korean officials frequently cited the examples of Iraq, Libya and Ukraine as countries that had forfeited their nuclear weapons programs only to be invaded by foreign powers.

BY EARLY 2018, exasperated at the stalled diplomatic process, the US had drawn up detailed plans for special forces operations against nuclear facilities in North Korea. Against the Dystopian option of nuclear war and/or the destruction of Seoul in the first hours of any war, the Pentagon was beginning to accept that a forensic strike might be the least worst option available. If it were fast, it might also persuade Kim Jung-un to surrender his nuclear weapons.

By September 2017, with the increased North Korean missile testing, South Korea deployed the US anti-missile defense system, Terminal High Altitude Area Defense. The weapons system is designed to intercept and destroy a missile on its descent to a target. This went some way to allay domestic fears about a North Korean missile strike, but it caused friction with China that viewed it as an unnecessary hostile act.

100. "N. Korean Missiles Have Russian Roots, Explosive Theory Suggests," *Los Angeles Times*, September 2000.

101. "The Long History of the Pakistan-North Korea Nexus," *The Diplomat*, August 2016.

More significantly, defense analysts had concluded there was a real possibility that it might not work. The Obama administration had concluded that the traditional system of the destruction of one missile by another missile in midair, like a bullet hitting a bullet, gave no security guarantee.[102] Some tests had shown a more than fifty percent failure rate, and that was in noncombat conditions.[103] Three years earlier, Obama had ordered the stepping up of countermeasures against Pyongyang's missile program by using cyberstrikes with the aim of causing a launch to fail in its opening seconds.[104]

In April 2017 a much-heralded North Korean missile test failed. The occasion was the 105th birthday of Kim Il-sung, and the test came at the end of an extravagant display of weaponry and warplane flybys. If there was one test North Korea needed to get right, it would have been this one. An American carrier group was only three hundred miles off the coast, and China warned that conflict could break out at any moment. The missile blew up seconds after leaving the ground amid speculation that the cause was a US cyberattack. Some defense analysts argued that even the threat of cyberattacks crippling North Korea's missile and nuclear programs would be enough to bring it to the negotiating table.

Two military threats of modern warfare are missile attacks and cyberattacks, which move the Asian waters contest over reefs and islands into unknown territory. Cyberwarfare is a great equalizer and North Korea, together with China, Iran, and Russia, has some of the most skilled military units working on it.

"Cyber is a new domain we have to research and think through that, and we're trying to posit as broad a number of scenarios on the effect of that, and long-range precision strike missile," Tom Culora told me. "We're not sure how to deal with that, although it's a little easier because there are kinetics and you can tell where a missile had been launched from. It's harder to tell a cyberattack and where it's coming from."

---

102. "Trump Inherits a Secret Cyberwar Against North Korean Missiles," *New York Times*, March 4, 2017.

103. "Ballistic Missile Defense Intercept Flight Test Record" Missile Defense Agency," February 28, 2017.

104. "Barack Obama Warns Donald Trump on North Korea Threat," *Wall Street Journal*, November 22, 2016.

CHAPTER 15

THE TECHNOLOGY RACE: CYBERWARFARE AND WARFARE IN SPACE

THE FIRST SIGNIFICANT CYBERWARFARE STRIKE WAS CARRIED OUT BY Israel and the United States in 2009, targeting Iran's nuclear program at its Natanz complex 150 miles south of Tehran. Computer engineers developed malicious software, known as Stuxnet, that invaded the Natanz computer system. Centrifuges used for uranium enrichment failed and computers crashed, showing that even without direct military strikes Iran's program was vulnerable to attack. Stuxnet may well have confused Iran enough to bring it to the negotiating table to strike the 2015 deal with the United States and other governments. It is planned that a similar strategy could work with North Korea. Kim Jong-un ordered an investigation as to the reach of the US cyberwarfare operations against him, and analysts believed the result may have been the execution of some of his officials.

Cyberattacks and counterattacks revolve around playing catch-up with your opponent. With Stuxnet, Israel and the United States were at the forefront, but that prompted China, Iran, North Korea, and Russia to up their own games. The Iran operation focused on a known and stationary target at the Natanz underground enrichment plant. Practice runs were carried out on a mock-up of the installation whose details were obtained through covert intelligence gathering. It took time, high expertise, and long experimentation to get it right. North Korea is a higher challenge because the regime is far more controlling and the missiles are not at stationary locations, but fired from mobile launchers and from different sites around the country.

---

105. "An Unprecedented Look At Stuxnet, The World's First Digital Weapons," *Wired*, March 11, 2013.

Cyberwarfare and space warfare are entwined in that satellites control much of our connectivity and electronic lives, and China and the United States closely watch each other's space programs. Beijing plans to have its first fully manned space station operational by 2023 and has developed a massive workhorse of a rocket, the Long March 5, to do the heavy lifting of carrying material to the station. Its inaugural 2016 launch broke with the government's traditional policy of secrecy over space. Beijing invited crowds of tourists and VIPs to a lavish ceremony to watch the fifty-seven-meter-high rocket blaze off from a platform emblazoned with the Chinese flag, leaving a streak of yellow flame glowing in south China's night sky.

Beijing boasts that the Long March 5, with its twenty-five-ton payload, matches America's Delta 4 heavy launch rocket, and that as well as servicing the space station it will also be used to carry equipment for a robotic moon landing that will send back samples of moon rock for analysis.

THE UNITED STATES is historically sensitive about space. The Soviet Union's surprise launch of the Sputnik program in 1957 prompted it to set up both the National Aeronautics and Space Administration for its own space program and the Defense Advanced Research Projects Agency (DARPA), whose mission is to ensure that US military technology remains better than anything produced by an enemy. Since then DARPA has given us e-mail, satellite navigation, simultaneous translation, and many other high-tech gadgets.

Beijing spends about $6 billion a year on its space program, a fraction of America's $40 billion annual budget. But China is playing catch-up with such worrying determination and speed that the United States has forbidden its scientists from any collaboration, and China is excluded from the American-led multinational International Space Station put together by Canada, Japan, Russia, the United States, and the European Space Agency. Dozens of astronauts from some twenty countries have visited since it began operation in 1998, but none from China. The long historical rivalry on space exploration is based on two elements. One is that breaking barriers, such as a moon or Mars landing, is seen as a symbol of national pride. The other is that cutting-edge space technology feeds into more sophisticated weaponry.

The United States tested space as a theater of war with the Soviet Union long before China was a global player. Moscow experimented with missiles that could destroy satellites, and the United States developed the Strategic Defense Initiative against Soviet intercontinental ballistic missiles, known as the Star Wars project. In the honeymoon relationship at the end of the Cold War, Russia and the United States sought cooperation in projects like the International Space Station, which continues, despite the later ups and downs of the US-Russian relationship.

China came into the frame as a space rival in 2007 when it used a missile to destroy one of its own weather satellites, proving both the satellite's vulnerability and the ease with which one can be attacked. The next year the United States made a retaliatory point by shooting down one of its own already malfunctioning military satellites. Both attacks showed the possible consequences of a fully-fledged space battle. Satellite navigation; live television; instant phone calls; video chats; crop and market prices; climate change surveillance; tsunami, hurricane, and drought predictions; and much more are all coordinated through space. Space hostilities together with cyberwarfare on Earth could change the world in a more fundamental, if not more devastating, way than a nuclear attack.

In recent years Chinese military cyberwarfare units have carried out repeated attacks on American companies and government departments. Bill Gertz, in his book *i War: War and Peace in the Information Age*, lists numerous Chinese infiltrations, including stealing personal details of 2.7 million federal employees, pilfering eighty million records from a health care provider, and hacking into such companies as Alcoa and Westinghouse as well as the Service Workers International Union. Sensitive information stolen includes air refueling schedules for the US Pacific Command, which would give China details of aircraft capabilities; records of thirty-three thousand officers and 300,000 US Navy user identifications and passwords; missile navigation and tracking systems information; and nuclear submarine and antiaircraft missile designs.[106]

In 2010 China carried out a blitzkrieg-style cyberattack throughout Southeast Asia. A Chinese military cyberwarfare unit operating out

---

106. Bill Gertz, *i War: War and Peace in the Information Age* (New York: Threshold, 2017).

of the Chengdu military region and known as 78020, used 1,236 Internet protocol addresses across twenty-six cities in eight different countries to strike networks in Cambodia, Indonesia, Laos, Malaysia, Myanmar, Nepal, the Philippines, Singapore, Thailand, and Vietnam.[107]

Gertz writes that China is accused of stealing fifty terabytes of data in all, or the equivalent of five times the information contained in the nearly 161 million books and other printed materials held by the Library of Congress. The response from Washington, DC, has been to set up the US Computer Emergency Readiness Team in 2003 as part of the Department of Homeland Security, and the US Cyber Command, a new unit within the National Security Agency (NSA) at Fort Meade in 2009, together with other government and military units. Britain set up its National Cyber Security Centre in 2016, which covers both commercial and government protection and is run out of Britain's NSA counterpart, the Government Communications Headquarters, in the western city of Cheltenham.[108]

In 2014 a grand jury indicted five Chinese military hackers from the People's Liberation Army based in Shanghai and known as Unit 61398. Even though there would be little chance of ever bringing them to justice, cyberattacks dropped off for a brief time, then resumed with extra energy and damage. The next year, records of twenty-two million current and former US federal employees were stolen from the Office of Personnel Management, including fingerprints, background checks, and other personal details. Many worked in security and defense areas. US intelligence traced the cybertheft back to Unit 61398, where the indicted hackers allegedly worked.

"China already has infiltrated US information networks on a grand scale," writes Gertz, "and is believed to be preparing for future warfare that will involve computer-based attacks capable of shutting down US electrical power grids, or destroying the networks used by financial institutions, thus crippling our ability to function as a nation and disrupting civil society in ways we have yet to fully fathom."[109]

In 2014 China's ally North Korea was identified as a cyber enemy

---

107. Ibid.,
108. Ibid.,
109. Ibid.,

when its computer experts broke into the database of Sony Pictures Entertainment just as it was about to release a movie making fun of the podgy young leader Kim Jong-un. *The Interview* was a satirical comedy in which Kim is assassinated and North Korea gives up its nuclear weapons and becomes a democracy. Even before the release, complaints came in from North Korea, prompting Sony to reedit the end and try to make it more acceptable. "I would be horrified if anyone got hurt over this," the movie's screenwriter, Dan Sterling, told *Creative Screenwriting*.[110] But that wasn't enough. Hackers calling themselves Guardians of Peace broke into the Sony system, released personal details of staff including pictures of them with their families, and threatened attacks against any movie theater that showed the film. The release was curtailed to a handful of theaters, but its digital release grossed $40 million, a new record for Sony.

Citing intelligence and open sources, Gertz tells how the attack was orchestrated by Unit 121 from North Korea's Cyber Warfare Guidance Bureau, which was headquartered in northern Pyongyang but carried out this attack from a hotel in Thailand. The same unit is held responsible for striking three television stations and a bank in South Korea in 2013. South Korean and US intelligence believes Unit 121 has twelve hundred cyberwarfare specialists and a total hacking force of about six thousand.[111]

North Korea was also high on the suspects list for an international cyberstrike in May 2017 that demanded ransom. It froze some 300,000 computers in 150 countries, affecting FedEx, Russia's Interior Ministry, and Britain's National Health Service, where medical operations had to be canceled and ambulance services were disrupted. Significantly, this attack followed the failure of the April 2017 North Korean missile test, about which the United States refused to confirm or deny if it had used cyberwarfare to infiltrate the software and cause the missile to crash on launch.

Each of the past US presidents Bill Clinton, George W. Bush, and Barack Obama had signed a deal with North Korea, in 1994, 2007,

---

110. How 'The Interview' screenwriter Dan Sterling became 'the guy that brought down Sony', The Frame, December 15, 2014.

111. Gertz, Bill. *iWar: War and Peace in the Information Age.* New York: Threshold, 2017.

and 2012, respectively. None worked. The most significant was the 1994 Agreed Framework, which had come about precisely because North Korea had been close to building a nuclear weapon. The United States had drawn up detailed plans for a military strike, and war was close. There is much debate as to why the Agreed Framework collapsed and whether the United States should have done more to keep it alive. Under the deal, North Korea would shut down its two nuclear reactors used for making weapons material. The United States and its allies would build two new ones that could not produce weapons material and, in the interim, supply oil for its energy. It worked well for a time, but was then torn up not by the North Korean regime but by the administration of President Bush. At precisely the time that it was preparing to invade Iraq, the United States declared that North Korea was violating the agreement. In October 2002 US assistant secretary of state for East Asian and Pacific Affairs James Kelly had visited Pyongyang and accused the regime of running a uranium enrichment project. The United States cut off the promised oil shipment, after which North Korea removed UN nuclear monitoring equipment and started up its Yongbyon nuclear reactor. The regime broke seals on eight thousand rods of spent fuel, which could be used to make weapons-grade plutonium. The Agreed Framework was dead.

"North Korea feels emboldened because of the world's interest in Iraq," said Defense Secretary Donald Rumsfeld in 2002, as the Pentagon was planning the Iraq invasion. "If they do, it would be a mistake. . . . We are capable of winning decisively in one and swiftly defeating in the case of the other. Let there be no doubt about it."[112]

But the United States neither solved the North Korean problem nor destroyed its nuclear weapons plants. Instead it became bogged down in Iraq, while Pyongyang built the bomb. Over the years of this seesawing US policy, North Korea took its technology from the Soviet Union, China and Pakistan and sold it to Libya and Syria, and possibly some elements back to Pakistan. By 2017, North Korea was estimated to have about ten basic nuclear bombs of about five kilotons each. Its nuclear test in September 2017, heralded as a hydrogen bomb, measured

---

112. Reuters, December 22, 2002.

well over a hundred kilotons, more than three times more powerful than a test carried out a year earlier.

The 2002 allegation against North Korea coincided with the false US claim that Iraq had weapons of mass destruction. Therefore, questions are now being asked about how much the evidence against North Korea was exaggerated, fabricated and politicized.

The argument against the Bush administration's North Korea policy was put forward in detail by an Asia specialist, the late Selig Harrison, who had a good deal of experience in reporting on North Korea. As Harrison wrote in *Foreign Affairs* magazine, "Relying on sketchy data, the Bush administration presented a worst-case scenario as an incontrovertible truth and distorted its intelligence on North Korea (much as it did on Iraq), seriously exaggerating the danger that Pyongyang is secretly making uranium-based nuclear weapons."[113]

Harrison detailed the complexities, including the need for reliable electricity flows, technically sophisticated centrifuges, and a long list of related equipment. He concluded, "Washington must not once more become embroiled in a military conflict on the basis of a worst-case assessment built on limited, inconclusive intelligence. There is a real danger that military and other pressures on North Korea, designed to bolster a failing diplomatic process, could escalate into a full-scale war that none of North Korea's neighbors would support."[114]

Some nuclear experts dismissed Harrison's argument, saying that North Korea had been violating the Agreed Framework all along and that by 1998 already had one or two crude nuclear weapons.[115]

Even so, at that stage, it had been a far lesser threat than in 2017. Long before North Korea conducted its first nuclear weapons test in 2006, Harrison points out, "The US confronts the disturbing immediate reality that the breakdown of the 1994 freeze agreement has made the United States less secure."[116]

---

113. Selig S Harrison, "Did North Korea Cheat?" *Foreign Affairs*, January/February 2005.

114. Ibid.,

115. "Q&A: Richard L. Garwin, Expert on Nuclear Weapons," *IEEE Spectrum*, October 2006.

116. Selig S Harrison, "Did North Korea Cheat?" *Foreign Affairs*, January/February 2005.

When Donald Trump moved into the White House in January 2017, North Korea was at the top of his foreign policy challenges and he quickly announced that he would be changing policy. But North Korean aggression and its incrementally advancing nuclear weapons program were nothing new. In 2010, four years after its first nuclear test, relations had become particularly tense. In March, the South Korean naval vessel *Cheonan* sank off the west coast of the Korean Peninsula, killing forty-six seamen. A team of international experts found it had been hit by a North Korean torpedo. Eight months later, in November, North Korea reacted to South Korean military exercises by shelling the South's Yeongpyeong Island, killing four civilians and injuring nineteen in one of the most dangerous confrontations since the 1953 armistice. The increased tension coincided with the then leader, Kim Jong-il, consolidating a power base for his son, Kim Jong-un, who was due to succeed him. Analysts believe the younger Kim was involved in both the *Cheonan* sinking and the shelling. His father died the next year. Kim took power, violently cleaned out those who opposed him, and continued to build missiles and nuclear weapons.

"Diplomacy has failed because Pyongyang remains determined to build its nuclear arsenal," write North Korean experts Joshua Stanton, Sung-Yoon Lee, and Bruce Klingner in the May–June 2017 issue of *Foreign Affairs*. "The only remaining hope for denuclearizing North Korea peacefully lies in convincing it that it must disarm and reform or perish."[117]

Stanton, Lee, and Klingner chronicle the history of failed agreements with North Korea since the early 1990s and argue that the policy of engagement had seen money pour into the regime, which had given nothing in return and had continued developing its nuclear weapons. Tellingly, they expose how Pyongyang had successfully dodged sanctions to use the US banking system as a source of dollars. Compared to the treatment of other rogue governments, the sanctions against North Korea were lenient and favorable.

"By July 2014, the Treasury Department had frozen the assets of just 43 (mostly low-ranking) people and entities in North Korea," they

---

117. "Getting Tough on North Korea: How to Hit Pyongyang Where It Hurts," *Foreign Affairs*, May/June 2017.

write, "compared with about 50 in Belarus (including its president and his cabinet), 161 in Zimbabwe, 164 in Myanmar (including its junta and its top banks), nearly 400 in Cuba, and more than 800 in Iran. Foreign banks that processed transactions for Cuba, Iran or Myanmar risked getting hit with secondary sanctions and multimillion-dollar fines. The result was that many banks avoided doing business with those countries altogether. But doing business with North Korea posed no such risks."[118]

The US Congress finally put a stop to this practice in February 2017, but Stanton, Lee, and Klingner note that Washington had to make clear that it preferred the regime's chaotic collapse to a nuclear-armed North Korea: "Washington must threaten the one thing that Pyongyang values more than its nuclear weapons: its survival."[119]

By mid-2017, Trump was turning long-standing North Korean policy around. He hosted Chinese president Xi Jinping at his Florida resort, moved a carrier group into the North Korea theater, threatened military action, and promised to end the regime's nuclear weapons program. He also complimented Kim Jong-un on being "a smart cookie," and said that under the right circumstances he would be honored to meet him.[120]

China, too, has become impatient and irritated with North Korea, more so since Kim Jong-un took power, and North Korea has been distancing itself from China. Gone from the official rhetoric is the Chinese view that the two countries were "as close as lips and teeth," or the North Koreans' declaration that their bond with China was "forged in blood in the victorious war to liberate the fatherland."[121]

In a 2016 visit *Financial Times* reporter Jamil Anderlini found that, even in the presence of his North Korean minders, people were venting hostility toward Beijing. "That only made the anger at China more striking," he writes, "since it means such attitudes carry a certain amount of official approval." Anderlini noted that in their condemna-

118. Ibid.,

119. Ibid.,

120. "Trump Says He'd Meet With Kim Jong Un Under Right Circumstances," *Bloomberg News*, May 1, 2017.

121. James Anderlini, "North Korea makes public its paranoia over China", *Financial Times*, May 18, 2016.

tion of Japan and South Korea, North Koreans seemed to be going through the motions. "With China, however, the insults were more spontaneous and the depth of feeling obvious."[122]

A year later, that depth of feeling became official with a blistering commentary against China from the Korean Central News Agency. In short, Pyongyang told Beijing to back off and stop interfering. "China should no longer try to test the limits of the DPRK's patience," the commentary said. "China had better ponder over the grave consequences that would ensue from its reckless act of chopping down the pillar of DPRK-China relations."[123]

Such rhetoric has prompted fresh thinking in Beijing whereby China itself could examine how to engineer regime change in Pyongyang. It would need a shift of mindset not only in China but also in South Korea, Japan and Washington and the process would be fraught with disagreements. The aim would be to install a Beijing-friendly leadership in North Korea and ensure China's continuing influence and the securing of the nuclear weapons. Beijing could move on to initiate a formal peace treaty between the north and south, thus removing the threat of war. A final step would be to persuade South Korea that it no longer needed a US military presence on its soil. If successful, and the American bases close, China would have won a significant strategic victory without out a shot being fired in anger.

"At a fundamental level, China would be acting not to assist the United States but to ensure that a reunified Korea would not include U.S. troops," writes Oriana Skylar Mastro of Georgetown University. "In that case, the end of a permanent U.S. military presence on the peninsula would be a reasonable price to pay to ensure that a second Korean war had the best possible outcome."[124]

In January 2018, as President Trump boasted about the size of the 'nuclear button' he could use against Pyongyang on Twitter, North and South Korea, in contrast, were embarking on unusually concilia-

---

122. James Anderlini, "North Korea Makes Public Its Paranoia Over China," *Financial Times*, May 2016.

123. "North Korean Media, in Rare Critique of China, Says Nuclear Program Will Continue," *New York Times*, May 4, 2017.

124. "Why China Won't Rescue North Korea", *Foreign Affairs,* January/February 2018 Issue.

tory talks about the North's involvement in the winter Olympics in the South, indicating again that with America's depleted reputation. Once again, there are signals here of a diminished American involvement against an increased Chinese one.

In some respects, the China–North Korea relationship can be compared to the US––Saudi Arabia one: they might not like it, but they need each other, and the collapse of either could have a catastrophic global impact. Just as the United States believes it can ill afford to abandon Saudi Arabia in the Middle East, for China to relinquish influence in North Korea would go against Beijing's wider ambition in the Asia-Pacific.

CHAPTER 16

TAIWAN:
A DIVIDED FAMILY

THE EAST CHINA SEA RUNS SOUTH FROM THE KOREAN PENINSULA TO a disputed island controlled by China's rebel province of Taiwan. Dongsha Island lies between the southern Chinese province of Guangzhou and the northern Philippine island of Luzon, on the northern edge of the South China Sea. It is the most strategic of the contested South China Sea islands because aircraft or missiles from Dongsha would easily have the range to target all shipping passing to and from northern China, Japan, and South Korea.

"This is the most important island of them all," a highly placed official told me in Taipei. "This is the one we are really afraid China may try to take."

Dongsha is so remote, hot, and inhospitable that Taiwanese military conscripts once posted there called it the Island of the Dead. In 2000 the Coast Guard replaced Taiwanese troops, and in 2007 the government declared Dongsha a protected national park with a maritime scientific research center. As far as anyone knows, no civilians have ever lived there, and Dongsha is now, technically, a civilian-administered island.

From the air Dongsha looks like a millionaire's private tropical island, with pale yellow beaches, deep green undergrowth, and dark or light blue water depending on whether it is inside or outside the lagoon. Its European name is Pratas Island, from the Portuguese meaning "silver plate." The Chinese Dongsha means "eastern sandy archipelago," to separate it from the western archipelago of the Paracel Islands. By far its most distinguishing feature is its long runway, originally built by the Japanese, who used the island as a military base.

Phan Din, 81, still earns his living fishing. (Photo: Poulomi Basu)

Paracel's Woody Island, December 2012.   *(Credit: CSIS/AMTI/DigitalGlobe)*

Paracel's Woody Island, new military structures, January 2017.
(Credit: CSIS/AMTI/DigitalGlobe)

Paracel's Woody Island modernized airbase, March 2017.
(Credit: CSIS/AMTI/DigitalGlobe)

Author on patrol with Taiwanese Coast Guard. (Photo: Simon Smith)

Filipino fisherman Jurrick Oson, just back from Scarborough Shoal.
(Photo: Humphrey Hawksley)

The former Commander in Chief of the PLA-Navy Admiral Wu Shengli at the US Naval War College in 2014. (Credit: USNWC)

Captured American aircraft at Vietnam's Military History Museum.
(Photo: Humphrey Hawksley)

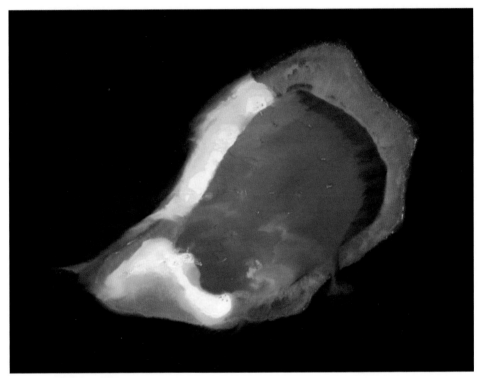

Subi Reef March 2015, no runway.   *(Credit: CSIS/AMTI/DigitalGlobe)*

Subi Reef with runway, June 2016.   (Credit: CSIS/AMTI/DigitalGlobe)

Vietnamese fishing boat heads out from Ly Son Island.   *(Photo: Poulomi Basu)*

In one respect, the South China Sea and East China Sea disputes are separate issues. One is between China and its Southeast Asian neighbors. The other reflects historic rivalry between China and Japan. But both are areas of American interest, and both Japan and Southeast Asia look to the United States for military support. These are dual lightning rods of East Asian tension, and when Taiwan comes into the mix there is a twist in that it upholds Beijing's claims to both the Diaoyu/Senkaku Islands and the South China Sea. Over the years, Taipei has come up with initiatives to demilitarize the islands and create an international center of marine environmental science. But the bottom line is that what Beijing claims, Taipei also claims, although if it came to outright conflict, Taiwan makes clear it would ally itself with Washington, DC, and not Beijing.

"We're determined to defend these islands," Edward Chen, a long-term defense adviser to the Taiwanese government told me. "The US has asked us not to deploy missiles there so as not to escalate tension. But if they did ask, we would be more than happy to."

I traveled to Dongsha in late 2013 on a Taiwanese military transportation plane with pallets of supplies for the two hundred people garrisoned there: members of the coast guard, government officials, and marine scientists working on coral restoration. The coast guard commander, Lee Su-ching, was a leathery and lean man who came from a special forces unit within the guard, as did most of his men. They got around on bicycles and electric carts along concrete paths that wound past low-rise, whitewashed buildings. On the rooftops were heavy weapons covered with green tarpaulins. The island carried an outward air of tropical tranquility blended with the underlying threat of what these men were actually doing there. While cycling alone, I stopped outside an oblong, windowless building. Two highly alert men leapt out, weapons ready, and firmly told me to move on. The tallest building was the radar tower used for tracking aircraft and shipping over a wide radius. The south Chinese coast was at least two hundred miles away, and the Philippines almost five hundred miles in the other direction.

Commander Lee's main threat came in the form of Chinese fishing crews who either tested his defenses or asked for help and came ashore. Many were part of what US defense analysts refer to as China's Maritime Militia, fishing crew who report directly up through a military command structure. These civilian-military crews have been used numerous times to stake China's maritime claims. One of the most notable in recent years was during the 2014 standoff against Vietnam over the oil drilling rig and the various encounters with the Philippines at Scarborough Shoal.

"This is a third sea force after its navy and its coast guard, composed of maritime industry professionals," Andrew Erickson, professor of strategy at the US Naval War College, told me. "It is militarily controlled and state sponsored, an irregular paramilitary organization that can be tasked to engage in specific operations in support of Chinese state objectives. The maritime militia is used in a manner designed to be covert and confusing."

The size of the maritime militia is unknown. More than fifteen million people work in the Chinese fishing industry, which is responsible for 18 percent of global fishing production. Those who could be deployed as maritime militia, therefore, run into the millions, and the available vessels into the thousands.

On average, Commander Lee dealt with one Chinese fishing boat intrusion every couple of days; the majority would be part of the Maritime Militia. Most came from the southern island of Hainan and have for many years been part of Chinese military operations, whether harassing vessels at sea or gathering intelligence by sailing close to Dongsha.

Erickson tracked the Chinese Maritime Militia vessels involved in the first 2012 Scarborough Shoal confrontation when the Philippine Coast Guard found eight Chinese fishing boats making off with cargoes of giant clams and tried to prevent them from leaving. Soon the coast guard was facing down Chinese paramilitary ships. Erickson discovered that two were crewed by unit squad leaders Chen Zebo and Xu Detan from the fishing village of Tanmen, Qionghai County, in Hainan, which Xi Jinping visited in 2013. The Tanmen Militia was formed in 1995 to support the building of platforms on bamboo stilts on Mischief Reef; China claimed the platforms were bad weather havens for fishermen. One militia crew member, Yu Ning, from a fishing boat named after the county, *Qionghai 02096*, transmitted messages to alert the Chinese military that the Philippines was sending in a naval vessel. In a later message, Yu accurately identified it as the BRP *Gregorio del Pilar*. Even though this was the Philippines' biggest warship, it was merely an old US Coast Guard cutter and would have been no match for the Chinese. By then a typhoon was approaching and the Philippine and Chinese governments agreed they would both withdraw. But only the Filipinos left; the Chinese stayed and took control of Scarborough Shoal, and the giant clam cargoes made their way back to the mainland for processing. That incident alone showed the almost invisible divide between the China Coast Guard, the Maritime Militia, and racketeers tearing up the seabed for clams.

Another unit, the Danzhou Militia, dated back to 1974, when it was the key element in China's violent takeover of the Paracel Islands from Vietnam. A sister unit, the Sanya City Militia, went into action against the US Navy ocean surveillance ship USNS *Impeccable* in 2009. Five civilian Chinese fishing boats grouped around the American ship and tried to snag its trailing acoustic sonars. The confrontation happened shortly after President Barack Obama had taken office, testing the new presidency and warning the United States to stop spying near China's coastline.[125] The Sanya City Militia, operating out of the Chinese-occupied Paracel Islands, is also tasked with deterring Vietnamese fishing boats. These militia crews were most likely involved in the attack on Vo Van Giau from Ly Son Island (see chapter 8).[126]

Thus far Chinese fishing crews had avoided friction with Lee's highly trained men on Dongsha, and confrontation there would be a game changer because of the strategic importance of the island. China could take Dongsha in a half hour if it chose to; the closest Taiwanese fighter jets are an hour's flying time away. At present, Chinese Maritime Militia crews would be under instructions to avoid an incident unless told otherwise by Beijing.

There was a wall map in the entrance to Lee's coast guard building that pointed out the distances from Dongsha: 740 miles to the Spratly Islands; 160 miles to the closest Chinese landfall; 416 miles to

---

125. Navy Visual News Service, March 2009 https://www.youtube.com/watch?v=hQvQjwAE4w4.

126. Conor M. Kennedy and Andrew S. Erickson, China Maritime Report, March 1, 2017.

Hainan; and 485 miles to the Philippines. Lee took us out on patrol, and it was disappointingly quiet. Dongsha faded into the horizon, and we were left in a slightly choppy, deep blue South China Sea. There was not a Chinese fishing boat in sight, nor one on the radar—or at least not one that Lee wanted to show us.

"We are always ready, but we never provoke," he said, holding onto the strut across the central cabin for balance. "If this boat isn't enough, we can call in bigger vessels and we will only use force as a last resort. But we will, because we are determined to defend this island."

Lee kept check, too, on fishing practices. Chinese and crews from other countries use explosives to kill shoals of fish at a time. They also swim underwater with canisters of cyanide, which they squirt either directly at the fish or onto the coral and habitat where the fish are. The poison stuns the fish so they can be easily caught.

In recent years, evidence has emerged of how the China Coast Guard, the Maritime Militia, and Chinese organized crime gangs work together to destroy the marine environment in the South China Sea for profit. After clearing the Filipino fishermen out of Scarborough Shoal in 2014, China opened up the lagoon for the farming of giant clams, to be sold on the Asian culinary black market. Measuring as much as four feet across, with an intricately decorated shell in black and yellow, the giant clam is an expensive delicacy. Its muscle inside the shell is sold to restaurants, and the shell itself is carved into an ornamental accessory. Some can be a hundred years old and fetch a thousand dollars or more apiece in an industry that is worth up to a half billion dollars a year. After exhausting supplies closer to home, the Chinese government subsidized poachers to go farther afield; Scarborough Shoal and China's other freshly acquired maritime territories were perfect harvesting fields. When levering out the clams, the coral around it is torn and shredded, and ecologists estimate that some 10 percent of the total area has been destroyed by clam poachers.

The BBC's Asia correspondent, Rupert Wingfield-Hayes, swimming underwater, filmed clam poachers at work around the Spratly Islands in December 2015. He witnessed a massive clam, at least three feet across, being ripped from an underwater slope and dropped into a boat next to two others. As Wingfield-Hayes describes the scene: "The sea floor is covered in a thick layer of debris, millions of smashed fragments of coral, white and dead like bits of bone. In every direction, the destruction stretched for hundreds of metres, piles and piles of shattered white coral branches." He later saw the mother boat with hundreds of clams piled on the deck.[127]

A satellite image of Scarborough Shoal from January 29, 2015, shows two China Coast Guard and several Maritime Militia vessels nearby and more than forty unidentified vessels, almost certainly clam poachers, inside the lagoon. No coast guard vessel guarded the lagoon entrance. It made sense, if China did plan to build an outpost in the Scarborough Shoal lagoon, to farm the clams first because the marine environment would be ruined anyway by the land reclamation. Ten months later, in November, the poachers had all gone and the China Coast Guard was back guarding the entrance.

On Dongsha, Taiwan runs a maritime research center tasked with tracking environmental damage and reviving decaying or damaged coral. Its founder was Hsu Shao-liang, a lively figure with gold-rimmed glasses who had set up the Dongsha Atoll National Park in 2007; coral grew inside glass tanks that lined Hsu's laboratory. Coral reefs are often referred to as underwater rain forests, and it is easy to think of the beautiful rainbow-colored, curling, spiky stuff we gaze at with admiration while snorkeling as clusters of marine plants. But corals are animal life, living invertebrate beings, albeit without limbs and a brain. They provide a habitat for a quarter of marine species as well as forming barriers around islands like Dongsha to lessen storm and tidal damage. Chinese land reclamation, clam poachers, global warming, and sea pollution are all killing corals in one way or another. Globally their destruction is one of the markers of climate change. In the northern section of Australia's Great Barrier Reef, the warming of the water has killed 70 percent of corals. Some scientists argue that 90 percent of sea corals will be dead by 2050.[128]

---

127. Rupert Wingfield-Hayes, "Chinese Poachers Destroying Coral Reefs", *BBC News Magazine*, December 15, 2015 http://www.bbc.co.uk/news/av/magazine-35101121/chinese-poachers-destroying-coral-reefs

128. More than 90 percent of world's coral reefs will die by 2050," *Independent*, March 2017.

Hsu's mission here was to reverse all that by experimentally growing corals and rehousing them in the seas around Dongsha. "This one here"—he pointed to gray brown coral splayed out like fingers, sitting on a thick bed of sand—"this is a fast grower, about ten centimeters a year."

"And this one?" I hovered my hand over a much smaller maroon and yellow mound in another tank.

"This is very, very slow," Hsu said, shaking his head. "It grows like a tortoise. Only about one centimeter a year."

He told me how fishermen used to use explosives that ripped corals apart. "We've stopped them doing that now. We are very firm."

"And cyanide?"

He grimaced. "Yes. They still try that. It is more difficult to stop. But some we catch."

"And people really do eat fish killed with cyanide?" It was a chilling prospect, given the crowded street stalls and luxury restaurants around Asia.

"Of course." Hsu was surprised at my incredulity. "How do they know? They can't taste it. In China and Hong Kong restaurants serve up cyanide fish all the time."

Hsu's environmental initiative was aimed at toning down the military element of the South China Sea, emphasizing marine science, and shifting focus from disputed sovereignty to joint development of the environment and resources. Through his rimmed glasses, his eyes danced with excitement as he described his end goal of transforming Dongsha into an international ecotourism destination, like a miniature version of Ecuador's Galapagos Islands in the Pacific. His specialty was turning military installations into tourist sites. His previous job had been to create the Kinmen National Park on Kinmen Island that lay just over a mile from mainland China and remained in the crosshairs of any invasion. "Do you think it might work here?" he asked. "You know, to stop governments arguing?"

"If you did it in Kinmen, I'm sure you can do it here," I said.

"Yes, I am an expert in battlefield tourism."

"But have you asked Chinese scientists here to come and work with you?"

"Not yet," he said wistfully. "Yes. That would be good. But our governments will not allow it. That is the problem." He played his fingers in the water above some coral. Then a smile returned to his face. "But it will happen. Come back soon to my Dongsha National Park, where the whole world will be welcome. We will call it coral diplomacy."

On the flight out from Dongsha, I ended up sitting next to Lee. Halfway out he tapped my shoulder, pointing down to the sea. "That's the *Liaoning*," he said. We were looking down at China's new aircraft carrier, an old Soviet battle cruiser bought nearly twenty years earlier and converted, on one of its first sea trials. Provocatively, it was heading toward the Taiwan Strait. The sun played off the deck of the *Liaoning*, where there were just a couple of fighter planes, and across the gray-blue water four warships flanked the carrier. There may have been more; I could not see. The naval formation said everything about China's mind-set. It takes a rare person to negotiate away an advantage. China was on a roll, and it was staying there. Three years later, naval commanders declared the *Liaoning* combat ready, and what I had seen flying back from Dongsha Island was an image that sat alongside the bullet trains and city skylines, the jigsaw piece that, in the minds of China's leaders, would protect the nation and make it secure enough to return to its rightful place as the richest and most powerful country in the world.

WHILE HE WAS still president-elect, Donald Trump used Taiwan to raise America's stakes with China. On Friday, December 2, 2016, shortly after his election victory, he took a congratulatory phone call from the new Taiwanese president, Tsai Ing-wen. Some of Trump's more hawkish advisers arranged the format and timing, smashing a protocol that had kept peace over Taiwan for more than forty years. Moments later, in one of his famous tweets, Trump questioned the bedrock of the arrangement itself, the One China policy, which had been in place since January 1979.

By telephoning Trump, Tsai was testing both Beijing and Washington and, by taking the call, Trump had, in effect, recognized Tsai as leader of an independent government. Once in the White House, the administration pulled back in what became a familiar characteristic of the presidency. But already Trump had moved the goal posts by even suggesting that the One China policy was up for scrutiny, creating a sense that, if not now, at some stage it might be torn up. Leaders come and go. Power balances swing back and forth.

Taiwan is a modern, practical place. Trains run on time, and it has higher cancer survival rates than much of Europe. It is unconventional, artistic, and slightly wacky. In its first presidential election in 1996, it pioneered Western-style democracy in a Chinese Confucian society, showing that if it could work in Taiwan, it could work anywhere. Without drawing breath, it jailed a former president for corruption and then in 2014 voted in its first female president, fifty-nine-year-old Tsai, an unmarried academic who loved her two cats and supported gay marriage. "When it comes to love, everyone is equal," she said in a campaign video. "I am Tsai Ing-wen, and I support marriage equality. Every person should be able to look for love freely, and freely seek their own happiness."

Tsai was the face not only of modern Taiwan but also of global democracy. Unlike her female counterparts in Myanmar or South Korea, she does not come from a political dynasty, but studied her trade at Cornell University in the United States and the London School of Economics. In the early 1990s there were fistfights in the Taiwanese legislature because politicians were unsure of how democracy worked and how a debate could win the day without violence. They quickly matured and, despite its diplomatic isolation and constant threats from China, Taiwan moved from dictatorship to its energetic democracy without spilling blood. Not many nations have achieved this. As its weapon of choice, Taiwan deployed trade and the semiconductor rather than insurgency and the suicide bomb. Its twenty-four million citizens have done well from it. Taiwan has a lesson or two for other small nations that are impatient with having a bigger and more powerful, not particularly nice, neighbor on their doorstep.

Tsai led the Democratic People's Party that was formed in the 1980s, arguing that Taiwan should be a sovereign, independent nation because it had never really been part of modern China. Taiwan was invaded by the Dutch and the Spanish, and from 1895 to 1945 was run by the Japanese. This is one of the few places in Asia where you hear people speak affectionately about Japanese colonization.

Through voters' eyes the Kuomintang party, derived from the old nationalists, is close to Beijing, continuing to advocate reunification of China. Tsai's Democratic People's Party has shelved its original independence demands, but it still keeps its distance from Beijing. Like in many democracies, opinion swings between these two mainstream parties. Until January 2016, the Kuomintang had enjoyed eight years in office with two presidential terms. Then, with 56 percent of the vote, Tsai won power, immediately putting a question mark over Taiwan's future with the mainland. She had been voted in because people were becoming uneasy with Taiwan's growing pro-China intimacy.

The way China and Taiwan handle each other is choreographed through careful parameters, overseen by the United States. In the 2008 presidential campaign, President George W. Bush felt compelled to intervene when Tsai's party argued strongly for full recognition and a seat at the UN. Bush told them to stay quiet. Eight years later, when Tsai came to power, she refused to commit to a long-standing agreement that Taiwan was part of China, the 1992 Consensus. In the consensus, using opaque language typical of face-saving Chinese techniques, Beijing stated, "Both sides of the Taiwan Strait uphold the One China Principle and strive to seek national unification." Taiwan added its caveat: "Although the two sides uphold the One China Principle in the process of striving for cross-Strait national unification, each side has its own understanding of the meaning of One China."[129]

And there lay the shades of gray in the formula that had kept the two sides from fighting for so many years.

Trump's flirtation with upending US-China policy was short-lived, but it came at a time when Taiwan itself was drawing up plans for a new future. Over the past thirty years it had forged trade with China, particularly in computer and Internet technology. Between them they controlled the world markets. But now, Taiwan felt it had gone as far as it could. Under Xi Jinping, China was becoming more authoritarian and nationalist which put Taiwan and its democracy directly in its crosshairs. In his October 2017 speech to the Communist Party Congress, Xi Jinping emphasized China's "resolve, confidence and ability"

---

129. Edward A. McCord, "One China, Dual Recognition: A Solution to the Taiwan Impasse", *The Diplomat*, June 20, 2017

to defeat any Taiwanese aspiration toward independence, saying, "We will never allow anyone, any organization or any political party, at any time or in any form, to separate any part of Chinese territory from China."[130]

China's hostile policy toward Taiwan comes in three forms: economic, diplomatic and military, the last of which is the black shadow of war that has hovered over the Taiwan Strait since 1949. Unlike India, Japan, or North Korea, Taiwan is a nonnegotiable element of China's long-term plan and it views the former British and Portuguese colonies of Hong Kong and Macau in the same way. Taiwan is feeling squeezed. Its special forces hold regular training exercises in how to organize an insurgency on the remote chance that China would invade. "It is the ultimate deterrent," a former deputy defense minister, Chong-pin Lin, told me. "Beijing might have overwhelming force, but we would give them a war without end, like in Iraq." He didn't think it would happen. In 2004, just after the United States invasion of Iraq, China had issued a defense white paper that outlined a strategy to dominate East Asia without war.[131]

But a year later, in 2005, it introduced an anti-secession law to be implemented should Taiwan veer toward proclaiming independence, a reaction to Democratic People's Party's campaign to get Taiwan's own seat at the UN. The Chinese law went into detail about the need to prevent Taiwan's formal secession but also to protect property, civilians, and foreign nationals, underlining that an all-out Iraq-style invasion was no longer on the table. The law only applied to Taiwan, not to the two recently recovered territories of Macau and Hong Kong, neither of which at the time had a movement for independence. A decade later, in 2016, one did emerge in Hong Kong, but with little impact.

The inner thinking in Beijing, however, is far from clear. In 2013, the Taiwanese Defense Ministry claimed China had drawn up a plan to use overwhelming military force to take back control of Taiwan by 2020, as long as it could keep America out of the conflict. To do that,

---

130. President Xi Jinping of China speaking at the opening ceremony of the 19th Communist Party congress at the Great Hall of the People in Beijing, October 16, 2017.

131. PRC: 2004 White Paper on National Defense, https://fas.org/nuke/guide/china/doctrine/natdef2004.html#1.

Beijing would need to have gathered enough leverage to bring trade reprisals against the US if it intervened on behalf of Taiwan. Taiwan is well aware that should the Sino-US relationship ever reach that stage, its existence would be severely threatened. Already, the reluctance of governments to provoke China by selling Taiwan sophisticated weaponry has led to Taipei's armed forces falling behind.

In a conflict a few years from now, Taiwan would have to pit its 1990s-era F-16 fighter against Beijing's Chengdu J-20 stealth fighter and its ageing early Cold War era submarines against China's fast and lethal state of the art ones. "Taiwan needs to realize that its defense is, ultimately, in its own hands," bluntly sums up the US Naval War College's, Andrew S. Erickson.

In a large Chinese military training ground in Inner Mongolia, Chinese training operations against Taiwan include a full-size replica of the presidential building in Taipei and city neighborhoods, showing that in the mind of the military, at least, war is far from off the table. They do not, according to Chinese military sources, have similar replicas from Tokyo or Hanoi.

"Of all the powder kegs out there, the potential for a war over Taiwan is by far the largest and most explosive," argues China analyst Ian Easton in *The Chinese Invasion Threat: Taiwan's Defense and American Strategy in Asia*. "The People's Liberation Army considers the invasion of Taiwan to be its most critical mission, and it is this envisioned future war that drives China's military buildup. . . . Before the invaders began landing along Taiwan's coast, the PLA would launch wave after wave of missiles, rockets, bombs, and artillery shells, pounding shoreline defenses, while electronic jammers scrambled communications."[132]

The challenge to this scenario is that it goes against the often quoted advocacy of Sun Zhu that wars should be won without a shot being fired. This would not only cause China to face highly trained and motivated Taiwanese insurgents, but would also punch a hole in its plan to sit at the top table and control a new world order. Put simply, China would risk losing international trust. In Beijing, General Xu Guangyu outlined to me an alternative scenario. "We would take Taipei like we

132. Ian Easton, *The Chinese Invasion Threat: Taiwan's Defense and American Strategy in Asia* (Arlington, VA: Project 2049 Institute, 2017.

took Beijing," he said. "The city was surrounded. There was no fighting because we wanted to protect the historical architecture, so we laid siege and persuaded some generals to come over to our side. Taiwan would benefit from this internal revolution. It is not exactly war. We call it nonpeaceful measures."

At many levels this scenario feeds into the current Chinese threat to Taiwan which is not military but economic and ranged on two fronts. First, some 40 percent of Taiwan's trade relies on mainland trade. Second, it has had difficulty in becoming more self-sufficient because China blocks its attempts to win independent trade deals by threatening reprisals against governments that attempt it. In 2013, after a painstaking wait, China allowed Taiwan a free trade agreement with Singapore and New Zealand. But it blocked similar ones with Malaysia and Chile. If Chile had signed with Taiwan, for example, it would have found Chinese investment abruptly halted. Beijing refers to this strategy as the three warfares—economic, legal, and psychological—to bring a country under its control, similar to the tactics it has been using against the Philippines, Vietnam, and other Southeast Asian governments over the South China Sea.

"Every time Taiwan tries to expand its trade with other countries, Beijing swoops in with its economic warfare to squash any deals," explains Peter Navarro, a business professor at the University of California. "Indeed, it is precisely in this area, where Taiwan's economic fortunes seem so despairing, that Beijing's bullying has often been its most intense and effective."[133]

After a quarter century of building up a China-based economy, Taiwan now needs to break away. Its biggest trade has been in semiconductors, a key element of any electronic gadget, accounting for 20 to 25 percent of Taiwan's total exports to mainland China worth about $20 billion a year. Starting in 2015, China launched its own official semiconductor industry development plan with the aim of having 35 percent of its needs met by local producers. At one level, this is a natural development of any economy. But in Taiwan's case it is damaging, because China tries to influence to whom else Taiwan can and cannot sell.

---

133. Peter Navarro, "Chinese Bullying is Drying up Sources of Trade," *National Interest*, July 2016.

China has also been targeting specific economic areas in Taiwan, such as banning tour groups from constituencies loyal to the ruling Democratic People's Party and encouraging visits to those held by the more pro-China Kuomintang. The message from Beijing is that Taiwan must toe the line or face the consequences.

"Even without military confrontation, we face a very serious challenge from China," Roy Chun Lee of the Chung-Hua Institute for Economic Research told me. "We need to develop in places where we still have a technological advantage over China. We will create an Asian Silicon Valley, like America has in California. We will develop alternative energy, and smart machinery like robots, biotech, and pharmaceuticals. We want to become less reliant on the US for defense, so we will move into that area too."

The United States is the sole provider of sophisticated weapons systems to Taipei, and there is a growing impatience within the Taiwanese defense community of being a captive customer and therefore being charged too high a price. European defense sales are minuscule in comparison because few European governments want to risk losing bigger contracts with Beijing.

"Taiwan is rich," said Chong-pin Lin. "It is natural for the US to milk the cow for as much as it can. But we don't like it."

Shortly after President Tsai took office, Taiwan set up a submarine development center with the aim of building diesel-powered electric attack submarines. A year later, at a ceremony attended by Tsai herself, it announced a billion-dollar investment in its own advanced jet trainer aircraft.

There are shades of Israel and the Middle East here. Israel has a flourishing economy despite having next to no trade with its Arab neighbors, several of whom do not recognize it as an independent nation. Partly because neither side has much to lose economically by fighting, the Israeli-Arab conflict has continued. In Taiwan, the reverse has unfolded; trade with China gave incentives to keep the peace. Now, however, Taiwan believes it has passed a tipping point and that its survival may be at risk precisely because it is doing too much business with the enemy.

President Tsai is playing much harder ball against China than her

Kuomintang predecessor, and China is in turn ramping up the pressure. As of 2017, under the One China policy, Taiwan only had official diplomatic relations with twenty governments: two in Africa, five in the Caribbean, six in Latin America, six in the Pacific, and one in the Vatican. Year by year, dozens of others have switched from Taipei to Beijing. Taiwan's latest loss was Panama in June 2017.

"If Taiwan is totally deprived of any diplomatic recognition, if Beijing continues to pressure other countries not to recognize this island, that is a diplomatic red line for us," the highly-placed official told me. He went on to suggest that, after Trump's December 2016 phone conversation with Tsai, the United States could do more to promote its recognition of the Taipei government. At present, Taiwan has "representative offices' in major capital cities whose staff work as professional diplomats but do not have official diplomatic recognition. He suggested switching titles: "For example, if the US sends an ambassador to be stationed in Taipei and one in Beijing, the US government would be taking an approach of dual representation. One is the People's Republic of China and one is the Republic of China."

"If the US offered you that, would you accept it?" I asked.

He hesitated for some seconds, the professional politician weighing up the impact of a direct answer. "If you ask the common people on this island, they believe Taiwan has long been treated as—"

"But would the government?" I interrupted.

"It's a very good question." His face became drawn, his eyes lowered in thought. "But it's hypothetical."

"So you haven't decided? It would be risky, wouldn't—"

"Sure, it would be risky," he shot back, this time interrupting me. "We do need to have all kinds of preparation, but if there was some kind of offer, the government here would not reject that proposal."

"*Would not reject?*" I needed to be sure.

"We would not reject that proposal." His tone was tight and clear. The atmosphere chilled among the dozen or so of us in the room who understood the implications of what he had just said. Taiwan would welcome the United States recognizing it as an independent nation. Trump's offer hadn't happened. It had only been suggested, and swiftly withdrawn. But, with Trump, it could bounce back again at any time.

Half of Taiwan wanted the security of its giant neighbor; half wanted the freedom of being independent. On the surface, right now, everything was fine. There was no need for change, except that human nature craved it and Taiwan was no longer feeling safe. The skyscrapers kept getting taller, the bullet trains faster; the money rolled in. But, psychologically, the system strained, with a growing sense that the abeyance in which Taiwan lived could not go on forever. Something would have to give.

ON KINMEN ISLAND, gunmetal gray water lapped rhythmically onto a yellow sand beach. Light-brown camouflage netting shrouded a line of tanks on the beach, gun turrets facing out to sea, part of the long-ago military campaign to defend the island. On the walls of an old machine gun bunker nearby were now posters of rare birds—brightly colored kingfishers, cormorants, and tiny blue-helmeted sunbirds that found sanctuary in this unspoiled place. This was the work of Hsu Shao-liang, the battlefield tourism expert now at work on Dongsha Island.

Inland, old concrete poles rise out of fields growing sorghum, peanuts, and sweet potatoes. On the top of some, like twisted coat hangers, are three-pronged spikes pointing skyward to impale descending Chinese paratroopers. Just off a narrow winding road, shielded only by a steel gate with peeling blue paint and secured by a single rusting padlock, is a yard of mothballed artillery guns. As the wind roars across this stark, flat coastline, there is a sense of a slow island pace, of isolation and natural wildness.

From there, across a narrow stretch of sea, spreads the futuristic skyline of the Chinese eastern port city of Xiamen, one of a hundred Chinese cities with more than a million people. Xiamen, meaning "Mansion Gate," has four million people. Bold in ambition and determination, the city itself is a statement of intent. Hotels and office blocks have risen at an astonishing pace. In part it evokes the forging of the nineteenth century and the American West and carries a whiff of California, with palm trees, highways, and yachting marinas. In another way it resembles a world of our imaginations—Gotham City from the Batman movies, *Blade Runner*'s dystopian Los Angeles, or the majestic King's Landing from *Game of Thrones*. We haven't seen anything like it before, a ragged history of corruption, crime, cruelty, power, ideology, weakness, insecurity, creativity, optimism, audacity and daring, all underpinned with a laser ambition to escape from a bad past and stamp itself with a new identity. For many in Kinmen, Xiamen is their view of the future, already their first stop for shopping, health care, and real estate investment. Families on both sides try to ignore the divide bequeathed by their ancestors and share food, language, and culture— and above all, to make money together.

I crossed to Kinmen from Xiamen on an early morning commuter ferry. The sun rose over the city's spanking new ferry terminal with its sweeping approach, curved white roof, huge television screens, and shining tiled floors. Friendly Chinese immigration officers stamped papers while travelers chose from a panel of colored buttons, smiling or frowning faces, to say how satisfied they were with the service. I gave mine top marks.

Schoolchildren, sports teams, and duty-free shoppers filled the amiable old ferry that took us across this narrow stretch of water, just thirty minutes from pier to pier, one every hour, crisscrossing back and forth. The only sign that anything might be untoward were frosted windows so one couldn't see out. Passengers were not allowed on deck. Instead they chatted, ate soup noodles, and took selfies and posted them on social media. Most weren't even born when the politics that linger here came into play.

A few of us managed to cluster around a dirty porthole to glimpse what was a disappointingly bland scene, certainly no majestic Antarctica or picturesque South Pacific. The water color stayed gray until the sun broke through when it shifted to bronze and later to a dark shade of blue. Islands were visible in the distance, but it was difficult to know which was which except for the imposing Gulangyu, which I had seen with the breaking dawn from my hotel room.

Gulangyu is easily identified by its commanding statue of a seventeenth-century warlord, Zheng Chenggong. Standing high on the edge of a hillside, this young-faced, armor-clad general cut a figure that brings to mind Brazil's statue of Christ in Rio de Janeiro: solid, tall and commanding. Better known as Koxinga, he had set up a miniature empire along the east coast and used Kinmen as his military training camp.

His soldiers fought off Dutch merchants trying to get onto China's coastline. He captured their women and made them his slaves and concubines. Koxinga was the epitome of a Chinese warlord, a strong and ruthless leader who kept order.

Kinmen itself came into view about fifteen minutes out, a dark low-lying piece of land that resembled a dragon's tongue. Only twenty miles long and fifteen wide, Kinmen is merely a speck on the global landscape, but like many specks around the world it has consumed military minds for decades. In that old jargon of the 1950s, it was the line between communism and capitalism, and it has now emerged as a current division between Chinese-style authoritarianism and American-style democracy, but what that means today is unclear. On the ferry, it was impossible to distinguish a communist from a capitalist, a democrat from an authoritarian. There were no defining logos on the designer sneakers and colorful backpacks. Chinese-made Huawei smartphones were as prevalent as American iPhones, made by a Taiwanese subsidiary with factories on the Chinese mainland. Brand, price, and performance had a stronger pull than patriotism and politics, at least for the moment. Midway, as more of Kinmen came into view, we crossed the unrecognized, invisible frontier that was once, to quote from a 1950s Pathé newsreel, the "hottest spot on Earth." Kinmen, then known as Quemoy, was "shell torn" from "red" Chinese artillery barrages. In the phraseology of the day, it was here that "godless communism" met "God-fearing freedom and capitalism." This frontier was as dangerous as Checkpoint Charlie, which separated East and West Berlin, each a focal point for opposing values and competing moral high ground. The Checkpoint Charlie threat is long gone, but not the Taiwan Strait, even though the gap between living standards and ways of life has narrowed to be almost negligible. The skylines might have changed; the bottom-line politics have not.

When the ferry docked, immigration formalities between these two potential enemies were a breeze compared to, say, moving between two NATO allies, Canada and the United States. I was, though, able to log on to Google, whereas in Xiamen, Internet search engines were blocked. I could also buy a local SIM card for my phone—ten dollars for unlimited data, calls, and texts for a month. In China, I never did because it involved a lengthy registration process and interviews with the police that might have jeopardized those I was meeting.

The difference between the communist state and a freewheeling democracy has narrowed down to these small things: Internet restrictions, press censorship, political controls. The jailing of dissidents is an unpalatable element rubbing against embedded Western values. But in the minds of many they count for little when China's success is measured alongside violence in the Middle East and the insoluble wretchedness in much of Africa and South Asia.

For generations, these poorer regions had put their trust in Western guidance, receiving chunks of aid dollars, holding elections (usually flawed and corrupt), and receiving often unpoliced investment from multinational corporations. China doggedly stuck to its own way forward, building cities from shanty villages and connecting people by road, rail and air. It did so with such determination that in three years, from 2010 to 2013, it used more cement than the United States had in the whole of the twentieth century.[134]

By prioritizing infrastructure and trade over democracy and individual freedom, China turned the West's development formula on its head, and the short ferry ride between Xiamen and Kinmen gave a snapshot of the predicament. Although culture, language, and food are similar on both sides, this frontier represents something much wider and more mystifying. No longer is it about the two sides of the Berlin Wall; for hundreds of millions around the world it is whether you prefer the democracy of the Central African Republic, where you are ridden with malaria and scrambling around for a pair of sandals, or the repression of authoritarian China, where you are filling forms for a loan on your first apartment.

I was met on the jetty by two guides who drove me to the national park that looked back across to Xiamen.

IT WAS HERE, some seventy years earlier, that the pro-American nationalist forces finally repelled the advance of Mao Zedong's troops in the 1949 Battle of Guningtou, the first military clash in Asia of the Cold

---

134. Parag Khanna, *Connectography: Mapping the Global Revolution*, Random House, 2016.

War hot where nationalist tank crews were so low on ammunition that they ended up ramming straight into Chinese soldiers, crushing them under the treads.

Today Xiamen's skyline is an architectural glimpse of a tiny corner of this ambitious Asian century, a confidence that stretches from Beijing to Delhi and beyond. But in 1958 Xiamen was a hair's breadth away from being destroyed in a nuclear strike. The United States faced down both China and the Soviet Union because then a victory on Kinmen could have spread the communist doctrine throughout Asia. Xiamen remains on the Pentagon's target list.

My guide, Isaac Wang, served as psychological warfare officer on Kinmen in the final months before the shelling stopped and the One China policy came into force in 1979. "The communists were shelling us," he said. "You could set your clock by it. Seven-thirty in the evening every Monday, Wednesday, and Friday." He pursed his lips and let out a long, low whistle:

If you heard a very sharp shhchheeew sound, it meant you were okay because the shell would already be over your head. But if you heard a rapid-fire shhchew-shhchew-shhchew, it meant it was coming in and was near you and you'd better hide or get away. The shells exploded in midair. The powder ignited inside the chamber, and pushed out fliers which fell around the island. The shells dropped to the ground headfirst and buried themselves in fields, sometimes eight or ten feet deep. These weren't shrapnel shells. They were for propaganda bombardment. They contained pamphlets, saying crazy things like how China had color televisions and shiny bicycles. They sent over copies of Mao's Little Red Book too. If anybody was found with one, they were arrested. We had martial law then, and it was very strict. The shells came like clockwork and we took shelter automatically. The dogs, too, would scuttle under the tables or down into the cellars. Then on December 31, 1978, the shelling suddenly stopped.

Isaac laughed. "But the dogs, they worked on muscle memory and the next day, seven-thirty sharp, they slunk down and hid."

"And what about now?" I asked. "Has the threat of war gone away?"

"Over here, we think of ourselves as an old used car, and over there is a Ferrari. For sure the Ferrari doesn't want to get into a collision with us. If they attack us here, they'll only hit a national park. If we bomb them, they'll lose a whole city."

Ebullient and silver-haired, Isaac, who was sixty-two, encapsulated many of the contradictions of the Taiwan Strait, of China and America, of the global connectivity through which so many of us now balance our lives. He spent half his time advising San Francisco on its city finances (he once ran for the office of city treasurer), and half running a church charity on Kinmen and, obviously, doing some freelance work on the side for the Taipei government. In many ways, he embodied the new-style rhetoric about patriotism being pumped out of Europe and the United States by nationalist politicians and raising the question of who we are. Where do we belong? Where should our loyalties lie? What is the concept of country? What of freedom?

With one foot in California and one on Kinmen Island, Isaac's family roots stretched back to the Chinese mountain town of Kangding in Sichuan Province, nestled high on the Tibetan Plateau. To the west of Kangding unfolded the world of Tibetan Buddhism: poor, shambolic, religious. To the east stretched Han-dominated China and the atheistic Communist Party. Kangding was where these two communities uneasily met. Centuries ago the Han had moved in to create their wide cordon against invading foreign forces, swallowing up Kangding, which was once the capital of the Tibetan Chakla Kingdom. Isaac, therefore, had an instinct for how China handled its sensitive outer regions. He was the son of a nationalist congressman who had moved to the capital Nanjing, then fled to Taiwan in 1949 when it was struggling, poorer than Africa and propped up with American aid. Isaac was born in 1954. Twenty-four years later he found himself a young conscripted officer posted to Kinmen to help counter China's artillery barrages. He joined an elite unit in which all members were security-checked for their loyalty to the Kuomintang, and his main task was to prevent Maoist propaganda from reaching the Kinmen islanders and converting them to communism. He arrived in June 1978, seven years after President Richard Nixon's historic visit to China and six months before the United States withdrew its recognition of Taiwan in favor of Beijing.

Isaac showed me underground canals hewn out of a mountain to protect Taiwanese supply boats during the artillery siege, a souvenir shop that made knives out of old Chinese shells and sold them back to Chinese tourists, the Kinmen Kaoliang Liquor factory that exported so much to China that its profits paid for the schools, transportation, health care, and other essential services on the island.

"The Taiwanese people were never looking for war," Isaac said. "We are not interested in it."

"That's what they all say," I replied. "In Bosnia, in Syria, in Lebanon the citizens say they are never interested in war, but they ended up fighting it."

Isaac raised his forefinger. "Ah, what was it that Lenin said? No, it was Trotsky. Something like, 'You might not be interested in war. But war is interested in you.'"

Kinmen's Everrich Golden Lake Hotel could represent Taiwan's business confidence in its future with China or it could end up as a victim of politics, a shell of a vision that shatters when governments get things wrong. It resembles a couple of giant shipping containers, one on top of the other, no frills, dull beige in color with a stark name and logo strapped under the roof. Inside the foyer is cavernous, with marble everywhere, sweeping circular staircases, statues, and high ceilings, part Great Hall of the People, part Fifth Avenue excess, a touch even of Trump Tower—except that when Isaac took me there the hotel was pretty much empty.

The adjoining duty-free shopping mall, the biggest in Asia, had barely a soul in it. We glided from store to store—Ferragamo, Gucci, Omega, Prada, Tiffany—with sartorially perfect young shop assistants, so unfamiliar with the sight of customers, it seemed, that their eyes lit up with astonishment when we walked in. Isaac had brought me here because $2.5 billion had been invested in this project, not a small amount of money, and you don't spend it in a place that's likely to have a war. We took the elevator to the top floor and the presidential suite—it was lavish, light, with views over the water. More specifically, it had been designed for formal meetings, with small conference rooms on either side.

Isaac explained that all of Taiwan except for Kinmen was organized into administrative cities and counties. Kinmen was still designated as part of China's Fujian Province, of which the capital is Xiamen. It was a clever nuance. The upshot was that Chinese and Taiwanese officials could meet on Kinmen with minimum fuss because, technically, everyone recognized they were still in mainland China. Since the hotel opened in 2015, secret meeting after secret meeting had been held in this suite. The visiting Chinese were treated like royalty, with great food, expensive brandy, anything they wanted.

"Taiwan shows them face and respect," said Isaac. "I've never been sure that the Americans know how important face is to China. If you give face, pay respects and compliments, and keep the deal making under the table, like we do here, you can do business."

"And if you don't?"

"If you don't, it can end in blood."

"So, if there is a new war, whose side would you be on?"

"Taiwan knows it can't fight China," he said. "Even if the president orders the military to fire missiles from Kinmen, they won't be fired. The Kinmen people need China. It is our lifeblood."

"But what if America supports Taiwan against China? You feel Chinese. You feel Taiwanese. You feel American. What do you do?"

"Sure, I was born in Taiwan. I love the place to bits, so I hope the politicians won't be that crazy. So, if that happens, if war finds me, like Trotsky said, I tell you without doubt, I am an American citizen. My loyalty is to the United States and my president. I will do whatever is asked of me."

CHAPTER 17

THE HEART OF THE MATTER

A T THE CENTER OF THE SOUTH CHINA SEA DISPUTE ARE ISSUES THAT have caused much conflict over time—essentially trade, freedom of navigation, taxation and the interpretation of international law.

In the eighteenth century, American insurgents fighting British colonialism finally won independence in 1763 after a campaign lasting more than thirty years. The seeds of their discontent, however, had been sown more than a century earlier with the introduction of the Navigation Act, aimed at ensuring that all trade was carried out in the interests of Britain. Although amended and overtaken many times by new legislation, the principle remained throughout Britain's colonial conquests. From Mombasa to Mumbai to Shanghai, Britain designed systems to benefit itself, often at the expense of others. The Americans were the first to expel Britain from one of its foreign areas of control.

After victory, the newly independent nation concentrated on security within its own region of the western hemisphere. Latin America was becoming restless against its own European colonizers. Brazil was given self-government in 1815, then became a full republic in 1889; Argentina got its independence in 1816; Chile in 1818; Peru in 1821. But the United States believed these new nations would be susceptible to continuing hostile influence from European colonial powers.

So, in 1825, very much as China is acting now in Asia, America introduced the Monroe Doctrine banning European interference in the Caribbean and Latin America, an area that became known as "America's backyard." "It was in effect early America's way of saying 'hands off' to predatory outsiders," writes James Holmes of the US Naval War

College. "Latin America had largely cast off European rule early in the nineteenth century. US statesmen wanted to lock in these gains. They feared the European powers would attempt to reclaim lost empires in the New World, either through conquest or by creating client states."[135]

At the time, the United States had no navy or coast guard of any note, and President James Monroe bravely announced his new doctrine without having the wherewithal to enforce it. With the pragmatism that has come to underpin American foreign policy, the government hired the naval vessels of its old enemy, the British, to ward off intrusions by other Europeans testing America's resolve.

As the embryonic United States consolidated, fractures widened, and from 1861 to 1865 the growing pains of the new nation erupted into the Civil War. The issues were the economy, control, sovereignty, and of course slavery and race. Even after the Union won, it took another hundred years, until 1964, for the Civil Rights Act to make racial discrimination illegal. Race still remains a thorn in the American consciousness.

China has followed a comparable trajectory. Its rebellion against the American-backed nationalist government and the occupation by Western colonial powers lasted almost thirty years, until 1949, albeit interrupted by Japan's invasion in the 1930s. China immediately turned its mind to securing its territory, resulting in military action in Taiwan and Tibet and on the Korean Peninsula. There followed growing pains similar to America's, with the economic experiment of the Great Leap Forward of the 1950s that caused dire famine, and the quasi–civil war of the Cultural Revolution that pitted families against each other. It ended in 1976 when Mao Zedong died, but China still carries the scars.

America's path to becoming a superpower began in earnest in 1919 after the First World War and cemented itself with victory in the Second World War and the use of the nuclear bomb. China followed a less predictable track that was not defined by its wars. Reform followed the Cultural Revolution, but was interrupted in 1989 by democracy protests and the killing of activists, which temporarily made China an

---

135. James R. Holmes, "Monroe Doctrines in Asia," *The Diplomat*, June 2011.

international pariah. It picked up again in the early 1990s to bring China to where it is today.

There are similarities, too, in Russia's path. The 1917 revolution was the culmination of almost a hundred years of unrest, and its catalyst was the First World War. The overthrow of the czarist monarchy was followed by civil war and Russia taking control of neighboring territories to create a protective cordon around itself to form the Soviet Union, which became a superpower on the back of its Second World War victory. The Soviet Union ultimately failed, not so much because of its repressive system of government but because it did not integrate with the global economy, a lesson which China has learned. The other East Asian power, Japan, had its government torn down and rebuilt after the Second World War. Only India has undergone no revolutionary change. Its independence movement, despite appalling bloodshed, never evolved to full-scale war. It inherited and accepted the British parliamentary and judicial system through which it is governed today.

China's rise has been neither unpredictable nor a surprise. It has been evident for at least the past quarter century, following as it did on the economic success of East Asia as a whole. The United States only began to address the situation proactively in 2011 with its Pivot to Asia, an announcement that was mismanaged and seen as a military plan to contain China, immediately causing wires to become crossed between Beijing and Washington, DC.

Kurt M. Campbell, who as assistant secretary of state for East Asian and Pacific affairs worked with Secretary of State Hillary Clinton to design the Pivot, argues that the policy represented Asia's new high profile in the global balance. "It is the leading destination for US exports, outpacing Europe by more than 50 percent," he writes in *The Pivot: The Future of American Statecraft in Asia*. "The verdict on which economic principles will define the twenty-first century will be reached in Asia, home to three of the world's four largest economies and increasing levels of interdependence. On so many issues central to the world's future, Asia is at the center of the action."[136]

---

136. Kurt M. Campbell, *The Pivot: The Future of American Statecraft in Asia* (New York: Twelve, 2016).

The Asian giants of China, India, and Japan make up three of the four biggest global economies after the United States. The US National Intelligence Council estimates that, by 2030, Asia will be wealthier, have a bigger population and greater purchasing power, and spend more on defense than Europe and North America combined. The European, Japanese , and US share of global income is projected to fall from 56 percent today to well under half by 2030.[137]

Within the Pivot, however, the United States also raises the subject of democracy that for Beijing can be like a red flag to a bull. "[Asia's] militaries are drifting between conflict and peaceful coexistence. Its transitional states are deciding whether to embrace democracy or fall back on authoritarianism," Campbell writes. "A crucial and enduring component of the pivot will be to bend the arc of the Asian Century more toward the imperatives of Asian peace and prosperity and long-standing American interests. . . .Within Asia, the pivot reassured allies of the US presence and sent a clear signal to Beijing that America would remain engaged there for decades to come."[138]

The view from Beijing, however, was that the Pivot sent a wrong and confusing message. "It told Europe and the Middle East, 'You guys need to take care of things yourself now. We're leaving you for Asia,'" explained one senior Chinese official who didn't want me to use his name.

And then what happened? Russia took Crimea because it thought it could, and you had war in Ukraine. Japan nationalized the Diaoyu (Senkaku) Islands, and a week later there is the problem with Huángyán Dǎo (Scarborough Shoal) because the Philippines and Japan believed they could do what they wanted because America would come and help them. It has divided ASEAN countries, and damaged the US-China relationship. We ask them, "For what? What is this pivot?" They tell us that the United States only wants to reassure its allies in the region. We say, "For what? So, they can think they have Uncle Sam behind them so they can kick China around?"

---

137. "Global Trends, Paradox of Progress," National Intelligence Council, January 2017.
138. Ibid.,

In 2012, as China began intensifying its island building in reaction to the Pivot, two leading China scholars, Kenneth Lieberthal, director of the John L. Thornton China Center at the Brookings Institution, and Wang Jisi, dean of the School of International Studies at Beijing University, published a paper arguing that "strategic distrust" had become a central concern in US-China relations.

"Beijing realizes that China-US cooperation must be based on mutual strategic trust," they write. "Meanwhile, in Beijing's view, it is US policies, attitude and misperceptions that cause the lack of mutual trust between the two countries. Chinese strategic distrust of the United States is deeply rooted in history." Lieberthal and Jisi argue that from Beijing's viewpoint China's model of strong political leadership has managed social and economic affairs in a way that provides an alternative to Western democracy, adding, "Many Chinese political elites suspect that it is the United States that is on the wrong side of history."[139]

Harvard University professor Graham Allison reached far back into history with an article in *The Atlantic* entitled "The Thucydides Trap: Are the US and China Headed for War?" In 2017 he turned it into a book, Destined for War: Can America and China Escape Thucydides's Trap?, which received plaudits at the highest policy-making levels, including from former UN secretary-general Ban Ki-Moon, former US defense secretaries Ash Carter and William Cohen, and former CIA director David Petraeus.

Allison uses an example from the fifth century BC, when there were no nuclear weapons, smartphones, or satellites in space. It was the time of city-states when the expansion and growth of power in Athens alarmed Sparta, 130 miles to the southwest, to such an extent that it led to war. In all, Allison studied sixteen similar cases over a five-hundred-year period and found that twelve had ended in bloodshed. To avoid war, he concludes, there had to be "huge, painful adjustments in attitudes and actions" on both sides.[140] No such adjustment had accompanied the twentieth-century rises of Germany, Japan, and the So-

---

139. Kenneth Lieberthal, Wang Jisi "Addressing U.S.-China Strategic Mistrust," *Brookings*, March 2012.

140. Graham Allison, *Destined for War: Can America and China Escape Thucydides's Trap?* (Boston: Houghton Mifflin Harcourt, 2017).

viet Union. Each enveloped us in some kind of war. There was no indication that, with the entry of China, any adjustment was unfolding now
in the minds of either Beijing or Washington.

The concept of the Thucydides Trap has been discussed widely by
diplomats and academics. Chinese president Xi Jinping referred to it
when meeting a delegation of scholars, politicians, and businessmen in
the Great Hall of the People in 2013.[141] It is as if a four-letter word and
a mostly forgotten Athenian general have come to sum up the entwined
dangers looming between America and China.

Allison's use of a crisis that happened two and half thousand years
ago is also unsettling because it underlines that human nature itself has
failed to evolve along with our education, technology, and political
mechanisms. Thucydides argued that relations between states were constructed not on pragmatism but on fear and self-interest. If he was right,
we need to be worried.

IN 2016, THE security-minded RAND Corporation published *War with
China: Thinking Through the Unthinkable.* Among its many conclu-
sions was that the United States might be better off fighting a war now
than a decade hence when China's military would be much more advanced. "If hostilities erupted, both have ample forces, technology, industrial might, and personnel to fight across vast expanses of land, sea,
air, space, and cyberspace. Thus, Sino-US war, perhaps a large and
costly one, is not just thinkable; it needs more thought. Improvements
in Chinese military capabilities mean that a war would not necessarily
go the way US war planners plan it. Whereas a clear US victory once
seemed probable, it is increasingly likely that a conflict could involve
inconclusive fighting. The United States cannot expect to control a conflict it cannot dominate militarily."[142]

The report also calculated economic damage. "Although war
would harm both economies, damage to China's could be catastrophic
and lasting: on the order of a 25–35 percent reduction in Chinese gross

---

141. Gideon Rachman, *Easternisation: War and Peace in the Asian Century*,
Bodley Head, 2016.

142. David C. Gompert, Astrid Stuth Cevallos, Cristina L. Garafola, *War with
China Thinking Through the Unthinkable*, RAND Corporarion, Santa Monica, 2016.

domestic product in a yearlong war, compared with a reduction in US GDP on the order of 5–10 percent. Even a mild conflict, unless ended promptly, could weaken China's economy. A long and severe war could ravage China's economy, stall its hard-earned development, and cause widespread hardship and dislocation."[143]

In the same year, the Center for Naval Analysis published *Becoming a Great Maritime Power: A Chinese Dream*. The author, former Carrier Battle Group commander Mike McDevitt, concluded that by 2020 the Chinese Navy would be the biggest in the world. The China Coast Guard was already the world's largest maritime law enforcement fleet, with more than two hundred vessels, almost half of which weighed over a thousand tons. China's civilian cargo fleet had tripled in the past decade, and Beijing had identified thirty key trade routes, linking 1,200 ports in 150 countries, that it needed to keep secure. "Washington can do little that would be likely to deflect China from its goal," writes McDevitt. "The maritime power objective is inextricably linked to Chinese sovereignty concerns."[144]

There was also China's maritime militia, deployed as a lead military element in Beijing's South China Sea operations. The United States categorizes this as classic insurgency tactics, using civilians as soldiers, the difference being that this militia operates at sea and not on land in deserts or jungles. "It is irregular warfare at sea," Tom Culora of the Naval War College told me, comparing the militia to the unarmed troops used by Russia to take Crimea in 2014. "You don't have a very clear idea of who's a combatant and who's not a combatant and what role they're playing. It's hard to discern what people are doing, and that creates limitation on the norms of the Geneva Convention and the traditional law of war of what a navy can and cannot do."

China argues that the use of a civilian force in such as way is a legitimate tactic of war. "Victory comes from both the military and civilian quarter," General Xu Guangyu told me in Beijing. "We salute the Chinese fishermen who support the motherland."

---

143. Ibid.

144. Rear Admiral Michael McDevitt, USN (retired), *Becoming a Great Maritime Power: A Chinese Dream*. The Center for Naval Analysis, Arlington, June, 2016.

Xu also underlined the Communist Party military expansion policy announced in 2012: "We will develop six aircraft carriers and guided missile destroyers and attack submarines to lead our maritime force. We will have ten bases overseas, at least one on every continent. The United States and China do not want to have a war. But a small thing can cause trouble, and if you can't control it, it could become a big war, and if the Americans try to remove us from the Spratly Islands, if the Japanese occupy the Diaoyu (Senkaku) islands, there will be war."

War talk benefits militaries and allows defense contractors to apply for more funding. Yet new technologies and better weapons are never enough to take the war option completely off the table. That requires a change of mind-set on both sides, of the type that came about with the introduction of nuclear weapons and the concept of mutually assured destruction. The Pentagon refers to the current main threats from China, Iran, the Islamic State, North Korea, and Russia as the four-plus-one scenario for which the 2017 budget of $600 billion is inadequate. Yet the United States cannot afford to spend more, which in itself requires new thinking.

"Is the United States at such a stage that it seriously needs to deter and defeat Russia and China in a war?" asks defense analyst Harlan Ullman in *The Anatomy of Failure: Why America Loses Every War It Starts*. "In the twenty-first century, no one knows what it takes to deter. Consider China, Russia, Iraq, North Korea, and the Islamic State. What does it take to deter each, and from what?"[145]

There has been too little discussion about what to do after a war. If the United States wins, does it attempt complete defeat as with Germany and Japan, regime change as with Iraq and Libya, or containment as with the Soviet Union? None works and one billion Chinese would face a return to an era of humiliation which would be near impossible to manage.

"How does the US expect the billion surviving Chinese to respond?" asks Amitai Etzioni, Professor of International Relations at George Washington University. "Will they rebuild a nation focused on revenge, the same way the humiliated Germans did, leading to a regime like that of North Korea only 400 times larger?"[146]

---

145. Harlan Ullman, *The Anatomy of Failure: Why America Loses Every War It Starts*, Maryland, Naval Institute Press, 2017.

If China wins, does it tear down the current world order and, if so, does it have the institutions and wherewithal to build a new one from scratch? No, it does not. And if there's a stalemate, then what was the point?

The hostile talk from all sides about the South China Sea and China's renewed hostility with Japan is already impacting economic growth. "It has a negative effect," Nicholas Lardy of the Peterson Institute for International Economics told me. "How big it is, you can't say. It is raising eyebrows not just in the US government but also in private corporations that are thinking, do we want to invest more money in a country that is adopting expansionist and nationalistic positions with its nearby neighbors? China will ultimately pay a price if they continue down the current path."

It is interesting to note that Lardy's view is shared by economists in China itself. Like America in the early nineteenth century, China has reached a level of development where it needs to push out from its borders, but as yet it does not have the wherewithal to defend its policies militarily. Unlike America in 1825, however, it has no foreign gunboats to hire to do the job.

"The US still sits in the driver's seat," Liu Baocheng of the Center for International Business Ethics told me.

> We import more than eighty million metric tonnes of soybeans from the US, not to mention wheat and many agricultural products. One-fifth of the arable land of the US is there to grow food for China. The US is stronger. Its domestic economy and industrial and energy base would remain intact if there were war. China is not prepared. Chinese troops are not properly trained. The US has strong allies, while China maintains a nonallied diplomatic policy. If you count how many countries are China's friends, you don't really have a large list. The US has us encircled and could still impose strategic containment over China in terms of trade embargo and world financial market manipulation. Cyberspace is still heavily dependent on the US architecture, encryption codes, the Internet, the banking in-

---

146. Amitai Etzioni, "The Day After: China Edition Say the U.S. emerges as the victor in a war with China. What comes next", *The Diplomat*, May 11, 2017.

dustry, the financial world—all that is in the hands of the US. We are getting close to being equal to the US, even overtaking it in ten to fifteen years. Therefore, it is unthinkable that China would initiate such a war. Why would we?

Yet disagreement between China and the United States can very quickly dissolve into talk of missiles and conflict. In the first months of Donald Trump's presidency, the specter of war involving China was raised in North Korea, the South China Sea, and the Taiwan Strait. During the Korean standoff in the summer of 2017, China made clear that should the United States carry out a preemptive strike against North Korea it would ally itself with the regime.

As early as his confirmation hearings in January 2017, US secretary of state Rex Tillerson described China's building of South China Sea outposts as akin to Russia taking Crimea in 2014, adding, with a direct warning to Beijing, "Your access to those islands is not going to be allowed."[147] Although directed at his domestic American audience, Tillerson's threat was heard around the world. Beijing's government-controlled *Global Times* newspaper responded that the two sides had better prepare for a military clash.

WE ARE NOW in a very different era from that of the Soviet-US balance of power that emerged after the Cold War or the one that followed the collapse of communism and a misplaced sense that that one political system would envelop a global community operating under a single set of values and laws. The assumption then was that because a specific political formula worked in the West, it could be implanted in Africa, Asia, and Russia. As this experiment unfolded, China and Russia tended to stay quiet, and Western leaders pronounced shock and horror when one country or another descended into mayhem. There was little understanding of history, of the upheaval that had accompanied even America's own path forward.

The current system emerged from the Second World War and comprised the setting up of institutions like the Bretton Woods financial architecture, the UN, and the World Bank.[148] The First World War

---

147. Senate confirmation hearing Secretary of State Rex Tillerson, January 11, 2017.

had spawned the League of Nations, which quickly failed. It took only twenty years for trouble to flare up again. These attempts to balance power between nations date back to the 1648 Treaty of Westphalia, an agreement forged between various European governments to end wars that had been going on for more than thirty years. The cause then had been schisms between the Protestant Reformation in Europe and the Catholic Church. The Westphalian concept was to create a community of nations that controlled their own affairs under agreed international rule of law. "The Westphalian peace reflected a practical accommodation to reality, not a unique moral insight," writes Henry Kissinger in his book *World Order*. "It relied on a system of independent states refraining from interference in each other's domestic affairs and checking each other's ambitions through a general equilibrium of power." The Westphalian agreement became "the hallmark of a new system of international order," he argues.[149] A later attempt to forge a European peace came after the French Revolution and the Napoleonic Wars with the 1814–15 Congress of Vienna aimed at settling differences. A similar sense of a need for equilibrium had given rise to the electoral college system in the United States, whereby smaller states get an equalizing say in the choice of president, and in the European Union, whereby Estonia, with its population of 1.3 million, has a vote equal to that of Germany with its eighty-one million people. The aim is to prevent hegemony, in which powerful states hold unfair sway over smaller ones.

The United States argues that its presence in Asia prevents hegemony and that China should not be allowed undue influence over small countries. Given the savagery that has ripped through Europe since the seventeenth century, it is far from clear how successful the Westphalian system has been at keeping the peace. Nor has it been a successful export.

British politician Rory Stewart served as a provincial governor in southern Iraq after the 2003 invasion and in his book *Occupational Hazards: My Time Governing in Iraq* he describes how, too often, what

---

148. The Bretton Woods or UN Monetary and Financial Conference was held in Bretton Woods, New Hampshire in July 1944 to discuss mechanisms for a post-war international financial system.

149. Kissinger, Henry. *World Order*, New York, Penguin Press, 2014.

the West was attempting to deliver had little relevance on the ground. At one time, he was trying simultaneously to stop civil war breaking out between factions and to keep an oil refinery open to ensure his province had fuel. He wrote to his superiors asking if he could raise the salaries of oil workers. He got a response "telling us about democracy workshops and asking if we could provide Iraqi women to attend a women's conference. . . . They talked of Iraq's five-thousand-year-old civilization, insisted that Iraqis were educated middle-class people with secular, liberal sympathies, and attempted to build the utopia... re-branded corruption, crime and civil war as 'governance capacity building,' 'security-sector reform,' and 'conflict resolution.'"

Iraq and Libya are recent modern failures of exporting the West-phalian system into other cultures and China has skillfully eased itself into areas where the West's values and credibility have fallen short. "We are now moving into the Eastphalian system," Dr. Zhu Feng, a Chinese defense analyst, told me in Beijing. "Asian history is different from European history. Our thinking is different from yours. The Eastphalian system will adopt some kind of Asian way so that our history and traditions will be prioritized in world affairs."

This Eastphalian system would diminish American influence in Asia, and replace it with Chinese-led Asian values and the political mechanisms to implement them. It is notable that, as Malaysia and Singapore were advocating recognition of Asian values in the 1990s, there was little reference to India and South Asia. This is a Confucian East Asian initiative. As seen from Washington, the Westphalian view is a belief in democratic checks and balances, tempered by elections and the rule of law. The Eastphalian counterpart, as seen from Beijing, advocates a strong, appointed government where control flows from a politburo or a single leader, operating under a united governing party or the Mandate of Heaven as opposed to through the ballot box and the Will of the People.

In 1924 China's first president Sun Yat-sen, who led the overthrow of the imperial dynastic system, gave a speech in Japan laying out the difference in Asian and European thinking. He said European science

---

150. Stewart, Rory, *Occupational Hazards: My Time Governing in Iraq*, London, Picador, May 2007.

had used bombs and airplanes to oppress Asia and stop its progress. "European civilization is nothing but the rule of Might," he said,

> The rule of Might has always been looked down upon by the Orient. There is another kind of civilization superior to the rule of Might. The fundamental characteristics of this civilization are benevolence, justice and morality: This civilization makes people respect, not fear, it. Such a civilization is, in the language of the Ancients, the rule of Right or the Kingly Way. One may say, therefore, that Oriental civilization is one of the rule of Right. . . . Westerners consider themselves as the only ones possessed and worthy of true culture and civilization; other peoples with any culture or independent ideas are considered as Barbarians in revolt against Civilization. When comparing Occidental with Oriental civilization they only consider their own civilization logical and humanitarian. [151]

Much of Sun Yat-sen's sentiment of almost a hundred years ago is reflected among the Chinese leadership and academics today. "We don't need Bibles and guns," Liu Baocheng of the Center for International Business Ethics told me. "The US is exaggerating our differences. It's as if those guys feel they didn't finish the job after the Second World War. We do things a different way. We win friends by giving everyone a larger share of the benefits. This South China Sea dispute is a tiny issue. People will soon forget it."

But if he is right, China's hand would be strengthened, and to what extent the United States would resist or allow Eastphalian culture is one of the great unknowns, not least because of the unpredictable nature of its own democratic system.

Zhu headed a relatively new think tank, the China Center for Collaborative Studies of the South China Sea, which was set up in 2013. It is based at the University of Nanjing, which is also the home of China's prestigious People's Liberation Army Naval Command College, where many elements of its naval war plans are drawn up.

With one foot in academia and the other in military briefing

---

151. Sun Yat-sen, President Republic of China, speech on Pan-Asianism in Kobe, Japan November 28, 1924.

rooms, Zhu represents a new class of Chinese academic, at home in the coffee shops of Beijing and Washington, very much on the conference and panel circuit, and not afraid to take on the West's arguments, whether about democracy, economics, or power rivalry. A generation ago this style of advocacy did not exist in China, where you could spend a couple of affable hours speculating on what would cause a Sino-American nuclear war with someone very much tasked with ensuring that, if there were such a conflict, China would win.

Zhu and his colleagues contributed an added twist. Never before had there been such a high level of debate and interaction between two societies that appeared to be on such a collision course. Some 230,000 Chinese were studying in the United States in 2016.[152] In the same year, Chinese companies invested more than $50 billion there, an astonishing 360 percent surge on the previous year. It was as if the more hostile the rhetoric, the more Chinese money flowed into America. These were big-industry investments like movies, insurance, and hotels.[153] A critical number of investors were linked to China's most powerful families. A Bloomberg investigation in 2012 looked at descendants from the families of a group known as the "eight immortals," key figures like Deng Xiaoping who had been involved in the founding of the Chinese Communist Party in the 1920s. Of the 103 examined, twenty-three had been educated in the United States, eighteen had worked in American companies, and twelve owned property in America.

There were similarities here with the Russian billionaire oligarchs who capitalized on the collapse of Soviet communism in the 1990s. Ten years earlier these Chinese families, albeit keeping a lower profile, had begun taking advantage of this first wave of economic reform. "Someone was likely to get rich from this period of liberalization," explains Kerry Brown in his book *New Emperors: The Power and the Princelings in China*. "It might just as well have been the families of leaders who were in charge of the Party then, who were, after all, most trusted, and the ones who had sacrificed the most to get where they were. . . . Their longevity and the fact that they survived purges, dangers and challenges

---

152. Institute of International Education.

153. Ellen Sheng, "China Investment In The U.S. Hit An All-Time High In 2016, But Don't Expect The Same In 2017." *Forbes* magazine, December 18, 2016.

gifted them with immense political capital."[154]

But to what extent would any of this be enough to prevent conflict, whether over the clash of Westphalian and Eastphalian values or over remote islands of which few had ever heard? Western technology and investment had led to Japan's emergence as the first industrialized Asian power in the early twentieth century, and it became an enemy. American and British links with 1930s Germany had also been vast. Many influential Americans viewed the order that Adolf Hitler had brought to his broken country as a perfect barrier against Soviet communism. American industrialists saw it as such a good place to do business that Hitler presented automaker Henry Ford and IBM chairman Thomas Watson with the Grand Cross of the Supreme Order of the German Eagle.

China is far from being 1930s Germany or Japan, and there is no direct parallel, except perhaps the historical truth that, however unlikely it might seem at the time, things do fall apart. In her 1985 book *March of Folly: From Troy to Vietnam*, historian Barbara Tuchman wrote how governments did things directly against their own interests, making wrong choices despite the right alternatives being available. Within this debate, it is impossible to forget that the Iwo Jima Memorial near the Pentagon commemorates a battle in February–March 1945 that cost sixty-eight hundred American lives, caused by a new Asian power with ambitions to oust the United States from its region.

THE PAST DECADE has seen a shift in values in the West itself. Certainties about the free market and liberal democracy were diminished by the 2003 Iraq War and the 2007 financial crisis. The politics of populism saw the election of leaders as diverse as Donald Trump and the Philippines' Rodrigo Duterte, and a free trading culture known as globalization which had allowed Asia to become an economic powerhouse came under scrutiny.

Globalization has taken wealth from people in the richer countries and propelled it into the developing world, enabling countries like Brazil, China, and India to improve the lives of their citizens and be-

---

154. Brown, Kerry, *New Emperors: The Power and the Princelings in China*, New York, Tauris, 2014.

come regional powers. A single job for a Bangladeshi garment worker making shirts that would previously have been made in the United States opened up a chance for the family's education and health care, even though it might put an American worker onto food stamps. China and Asia championed globalization, while a critical mass within the Western democracies resented this spread of opportunity and blamed it for the fall in their own living standards.

A January 2017 report from Bocconi University in Italy found a direct link within Europe between levels of Asian trade that is associated with globalization and support for nationalism. It researched seventy-six legislative elections in fifteen European countries, from 1988, when the Cold War was winding down, to the financial crash in 2007. It found that those in areas exposed to a high level of imports from China were more inclined to vote for radical right-wing parties. "The unequal sharing of the welfare gains brought about by globalization has resulted in widespread concerns and a general opposition to free trade," wrote the report's authors, Italo Colantone and Piero Stanig. They described this as "economic nationalism," when political movements bundle "support for domestic free market policies with strong protectionist stances."[155]

A 2015 Oxfam study found that from 2009 to 2013 the number of Europeans living with "severe material deprivation" rose by 7.5 percent, to fifty million people. Oxfam blamed an increasing inequality in the distribution of wealth.[156]

These trends have been driven by the influx of refugees from the Middle East and sluggish economic performance. More than 8 percent of European adults were unemployed in 2017, and that figure rose to more than 20 percent among the young. The US figure is 5 percent, with 10 percent youth unemployment.[157] In 1960, according to the US Bureau of Labor Statistics, 24 percent of American workers had jobs in manufacturing, and today that figure is only 8 percent, five million

155. "The Trade Origins of Economic Nationalism: Import Competition and Voting Behavior in Western Europe," Italo Colantone and Piero Stanig, Baffi Carefin Centre Research Paper Series, January 2017.

156. "A EUROPE FOR THE MANY, NOT THE FEW Time to reverse the course of inequality and poverty in Europe", Oxfam Briefing Paper, September 9, 2015.

157. US Bureau of Labour Statistics.

jobs having been lost since 1994 when the North American Free Trade Agreement was signed with Canada and Mexico.[158]

Americans and Europeans are feeling themselves to be victims of globalization, leading to a cry to restrict borders and put the brakes on the free flow of goods and people. Elected largely on protectionist and anti-China rhetoric, Trump immediately shelved the embryonic Trans-Pacific Partnership and announced that he would redesign the North American Free Trade Agreement and build a wall between Mexico and the United States.

In a 2016 referendum Britain chose to leave the European Union, curb immigration, control its borders, and regain what many felt was its sovereignty. In both the British and US debates, campaign claims were proven, point by point, to be false. But that counted for nothing. The West was entering a political era where sentiment superseded fact. Earlier the impetus had been to sacrifice a measure of sovereignty for membership of larger groups operating under a shared set of rules that would deliver material gain. Among such groups were the Association of Southeast Asian Nations, NATO, the World Trade Organization, and the European Union itself, which had absorbed and democratized Europe's authoritarian nations after the Cold War.

During the Brexit campaign, professional after professional delivered advice warning that, should Britain sever its ties to such international institutions, living standards would suffer. But a key Brexit campaigner, cabinet minister Michael Gove, caught the public mood on both sides of the Atlantic when he said sharply, "People have had enough of experts."[159]

The repercussions of this thinking cannot be overestimated. "The idea that the expert was giving considered, experienced advice worth taking seriously was simply dismissed," writes US national security analyst Tom Nichols. "To reject the advice of experts is to assert autonomy, a way for Americans to demonstrate their independence. . . . They want to weigh in and have their opinions treated with deep respect and their preferences honored not on the strength of their arguments or on the evidence they present, but based on their feelings, emotions, and

---

158. US Bureau of Labour Statistics.
159. Michael Gove interview with Sky News June 3, 2016.

whatever stray information they may have picked up here or there along the way."[160]

The wealthy West had become a restless, unstable beast, with many of its citizens concluding that the system no longer delivered for them, that it was controlled by an unreachable and sophisticated elite who hoarded money and refused to spread wealth. Emotion supplanted material pragmatism. Bill Clinton's 1992 campaign slogan that it was all about "the economy, stupid" no longer applied. It was about raising dignity even if that meant lowering living standards, or, as the millionaire veteran film star Sir Michael Caine put it, "I would rather be a poor master than a rich servant."

The threat that this mood poses to the Westphalian democratic system is incalculable. Trust is collapsing, not only in experts and the elite but also in the elected representatives who rely on the advice of specialists and professionals to make policy and do their jobs. The Pew Research Center found that in 1958 73 percent of the population trusted the American government. In 2015, trust had dropped to just 19 percent.[161]

Into this uncertainty has stepped China's President Xi Jinping.

160. "How America Lost Faith in Expertise," Tom Nichols, *Foreign Affairs*, March/April 2017.

161. "Trust in Government: 1958-2015, Pew Research Center, November 23, 2015.

PART 5

GREAT POWER STATUS

"Nearly all men can stand adversity, but if you want to test a man's character, give him power."

—ABRAHAM LINCOLN, sixteenth president of the United States

CHAPTER 18

A PARALLEL WORLD ORDER

O N JANUARY 17, 2017, THREE DAYS BEFORE PRESIDENT DONALD Trump took office, Xi Jinping stepped onto the World Economic Forum podium at Davos, Switzerland, that beacon of Western capitalism, and held the banner high for values once championed by the democratic world. He advocated the ripping down of barriers and the boosting of international trade. He flew the flag for globalization, carrying the very same argument that two centuries earlier had brought British gunboats to Chinese ports demanding the right to buy and sell merchandise on Britain's terms and under its rules.

"Many people feel bewildered and wonder: What has gone wrong with the world?" Xi said, going on to deliver analysis that quoted Charles Dickens; name-checked the Arabian Nights; argued that world crises, such as Syrian refugees, had nothing to do with free trade; referred to inadequate global governance as a failure to meet people's expectations; and pointed out that globalization was "a natural outcome of scientific and technological progress, not something created by any individuals or any countries."[162]

His final words, a blend of Winston Churchill and Abraham Lincoln, were written to stir: "No difficulty, however daunting, will stop mankind from advancing. When encountering difficulties, we should not complain about ourselves, blame others, lose confidence or run away from responsibilities. We should join hands and rise to the challenge. History is created by the brave. Let us boost confidence, take action, and march arm-in-arm toward a bright future."[163]

---

162. Chinese President Xi Jinping speaking at World Economic Forum, Davos, January 17, 2017.
163. Ibid.

The Davos speech marked the end of China's attempt to forge what it had repeatedly described as a "new model of great power relations" between China and the United States, which led to the idea of the G2 relationship sitting at the pinnacle of the G8, G20, and other groupings of nations. During Xi's 2015 visit to the United States, the phrase was used time and again in trying to sell an idea of sharing influence between two superpowers, one that concentrated not on conflict and disagreement but on "mutual respect and mutually beneficial cooperation," in itself a very Asian concept. The model was never accepted by the United States. Too many in Congress, bruised and energized by constant horse trading and win-lose politics, were wary that Beijing was setting a trap to silence them on speaking out over Taiwan, democratic values, human rights and, indeed, the South China Sea.

China shelved the idea and, a month later, in February 2017, as the United States continued to turn inwards after Trump's inauguration, Xi established his nation as the champion of globalization. At a national security conference in Beijing, in typical Communist Party style, he announced his Two Guidances. The first was that China would "guide the international community to jointly build a more just and reasonable new world order." The second was that it would "guide the international community to jointly maintain international security."[164]

There it was—the launch of Eastphalian values onto the global stage. China would force reform of the postwar Westphalian system. Xi's reference to international security was a message to the United States not to mess with China's foreign policy, including its newly built bases in the South China Sea. China had claimed the moral torch of world leadership.

In May 2017 Xi reinforced his vision by hosting the Beijing summit on his infrastructure-building Belt and Road Initiative for twenty-nine heads of government and star attractions from the global autocracies. The other two Asian giants, India and Japan, kept their distance, wary about joining anything that resembled a Beijing-led strategic coalition. The Belt and Road Initiative talked up shared prosperity, open borders, free trade, and glittering skyscrapers, all derived

---

164. Zheping Huang, "Chinese president Xi Jinping has vowed to lead the "new world order" *Quartz,* February 22, 2017.

from legends of the ancient Silk Road that connected diverse civilizations. "Opening up brings progress while isolation results in backwardness," declared Xi. "Global growth requires new drivers, development needs to be more inclusive and balanced, and the gap between the rich and the poor needs to be narrowed."[165]

The summit exposed two opposing global views. One was that a swath of territory stretching between Beijing and Moscow may be coming under anti-American authoritarian control, thus conjuring up the specter of the Cold War. The other was that, at a time when there were not many big international visions around, this was one. The West was bereft of ideas and China was now appealing to the global imagination.

Acutely aware that others had trodden this path before, China was keen to show it was not a new colonial power. It was not trying to civilize weaker and poorer countries with any ideology, nor was the Belt and Road Initiative comparable to the postwar Marshall Plan, which poured billions into war-damaged Europe with the goal of bringing democracy and reviving the shattered Westphalian idea of balancing power between independent states.

"The Marshall Plan wanted to impose a system and values on others," Ruan Zhongzhe of the China Institute of International Studies told me. "It had conditionality. Do it or you won't receive aid. The Belt and Road Initiative is not the same kind of thing. We want to seek affinity in adjoining areas so we can cooperate with each other on a voluntary basis. You can choose yes or no. Its aim is to promote stability in the region. Many issues stem from poverty. Our greatest test is to help all those young people to be occupied by jobs. We want to create a secure corridor that will make a peaceful environment in a region of prosperity and stability. It cannot be created by China. We are just one country."

China's ambition is swept along on a tidal wave of self-belief that has left many of us asking how it could do so much so fast. Back in the 1990s, the chief engineer of Shanghai told me that by 2020 his city would have better infrastructure than New York. His enthusiasm was infectious, like that of a movie hero with the odds stacked against him,

165. Chinese President Xi Jinping keynote speech at Belt and Road forum in Beijing May 14, 2017 http://news.xinhuanet.com/english/2017-05/14/c_136282982.htm

yet it seemed only a fabricated Hollywood ending could make his dream a reality. Shanghai was then a mass of construction sites filled with thousands of cranes and bamboo scaffolding from which workers were creating a new skyline. They lived on-site in scrappy tents; they wore rags and rubber sandals and had no helmets, gloves, or safety harnesses. Men from whole villages traveled from a far-flung province and camped together to scrape together a living for their families as did the migrant farm workers in John Steinbeck's 1939 novel *The Grapes of Wrath*. At the time, I added skepticism to my reports on China's modernization. How could it ever happen? This was communist China. Only the developed democratic West knew how to build cities and run governments. I write this long before 2020, and anyone who rides both the New York and Shanghai subways can see that the chief engineer knew exactly what he was talking about.

But then China is no shining angel when it comes to how people are treated. Behind the much-hailed economic miracle lie numerous stories of staff being forced to work in regimented factories making high-tech products for Western multinational companies, in conditions so dismal that wire netting covers balconies and windows to prevent suicide; of lethal dangers in the construction, mining, and other industries; of an absence of health and safety provisions; of inhumane hours, physical abuse and bullying, and arbitrary payment, with wages deducted for food and shelter that leave workers with no or little income.[166] China's modernization has led to thousands of protests around the country. Land and labor disputes are common.

According to the BBC's former China editor, Carrie Gracie, China's modernization is controlled from the top with very little say given to those whose lives are turned upside down. Gracie has spent more than a decade tracking the transformation of a tiny farming community in western China into a modern city. In the White Horse Village series, she reported on the personal upheavals there, of family houses being demolished for high-rise blocks, of rice fields covered with highway concrete, of the building of schools and hospitals amid protests as land was expropriated and villagers forced to move.

---

166. Aditya Chakrabortty Forced Student Labour is Central to Chinese Economic Miracle, the Guardian, October 14, 2013.

White Horse Village lies in a narrow valley hemmed by daunting mountain peaks, and its way of life had not changed for centuries. Once a village of three thousand people, it has now become the fast-paced Wuxi New Town, population 200,000, with car showrooms, karaoke bars, and shining office blocks.

"This epic transformation is being replicated in thousands of villages all over China, the biggest urbanization in human history and a giant leap of faith in the name of progress," writes Gracie, explaining the motivation behind the Belt and Road Initiative. "The pressure is coming from the top. Chinese emperors once claimed to rule all under heaven. With the United States retreating from global leadership on free trade, President Xi has seized his chance. With no other country offering a big idea right now, this is the most ambitious bid to shape our century."[167]

It is worth noting that at the time that China announced its Belt and Road Initiative in 2013, it also closed the labor camps and prison farms where, at their peak, up to two million people were forced to work under an old communist policy known as "reeducation through labor." Human Rights Watch then estimated that the remaining camps held about 160,000 prisoners.[168] The closures coincided with a UN impetus for multinational companies to ensure their products were not contaminated by prison labor and showed how much China wanted to earn both access and respectability within the international trading system.

Parag Khanna, argues in *Connectography: Mapping the Future of Global Civilisation* that what is unfolding today with China's expansion cannot be compared to colonization because countries are no longer invaded. Instead they are bought.

"The path to wealth and peace is for trade to supersede the nation-state," he writes. "We need a more borderless world because we can't afford destructive territorial conflict, because correcting the mismatch of people and resources can unlock incredible human and economic potential. Human society is undergoing a fundamental trans-

---

167. Carrie Gracie, "Tales from the New Silk Road, *BBC News*, July 20, 2017 http://www.bbc.co.uk/news/resources/idt-sh/new_silk_road.

168. Malcolm Moore, "China Abolishes Its Labour Camps and Releases Prisoners", *The Telegraph*, January 2014.

formation by which functional infrastructure tells us more about how the world works than political borders."[169]

While Asia and China are talking about tearing down controls and borders, America and Europe are looking at tightening them, building checkpoints and walls. For many this raises issues such as patriotism and loyalty, questions that apply to Chinese studying in the United States, to staff at American factories in China such as those of Boeing and Motorola, and to the giant Taiwanese tech company Foxconn, which makes Apple products in China and sells them around the world. And what of the components inside the phone that come from France, Indonesia, Israel, the Philippines, and Singapore, an endless globalized list that grows all the time because China is now outsourcing its factories to cheaper labor markets in Bangladesh, Egypt, and Ethiopia. People, clothes, and gadgets have a shared, complex provenance. An iPhone is an American product, except it is not. It's a gadget from everywhere. Isaac Wang, my guide in Kinmen, is from China, Taiwan, and the United States, and that is comparatively straightforward. But what of a Chinese student who graduates from Columbia Business School in New York, joins a German bank, and is posted to Brazil, where she marries an information technology executive from Mexico who gets poached by Google and posted to Dubai, so she ends up working for the Chinese giant Ali Baba, with her children going to an international school? Where exactly does this family belong? Is their loyalty to their company, their countries—or, where?

"There is a new generation that finds its calling beyond national boundaries and pledges allegiance to the Independent Republic of the Supply Chain," Khanna sums up.[170]

As if to make the point, in April 2017, Beijing even took its Belt and Road Initiative as far as Britain when a train loaded with Scotch whisky, baby milk, and engineering equipment left London for eastern China. It arrived three weeks later, a month earlier than if it had made a similar journey by ship.

---

169. Parag Khanna, *Connectography: Mapping the Future of Global Civilisation* (New York: Random House, 2016).
170. Ibid.

THE CONNECTED WORLD routinely brings the polarized sides of the Sino-American relationship into a single room, nowhere more so than among the think tanks of Washington, DC. In late 2016, I attended a day-long conference entitled "China Power: Up for Debate" held by the Center for Strategic and International Studies. Among the experts sharing panels were the former US director of national intelligence, Admiral Dennis Blair; the former Carrier Battle Group commander, Admiral Mike McDevitt, from the Center for Naval Analyses; Tom Christensen, a former deputy assistant secretary of state; and a Chinese security expert, Zha Daojiong, from the University of Beijing.

Zha was also an adviser to the Communist Party and the Ministry of Foreign Affairs. He had worked at various times in Hong Kong, Japan, Singapore, and the United States. He was in early middle age, with gray-black hair and thin-rimmed spectacles, wearing a dark suit and a maroon patterned tie. He spoke with a tongue-in-cheek-smile and an easy turn of phrase that endeared him to his audience. He began by pointing out that he was Chinese, with English as a second language. "So, anything I say should not be held against me, or anyone else," he said, drawing a ripple of laughter. "One of the two points of difference between our two great countries is over what happens in the region. Sometimes we don't appreciate that peace has prevailed since 1975, and if you look at what's been going on in the Middle East and elsewhere, we should cherish that."

The conference room itself resembled a banquet hall without the food. We sat at large round tables with wall screens for PowerPoint presentations and roaming microphones for questions. Among us were a sprinkling of military uniforms, casually dressed young staff from congressional offices, consultants and lobbyists in formal suits and ties, the retired and the curious, and a handful of journalists like myself. The debates were being streamed live around the world.

Christensen countered Zha by arguing that the biggest source of instability from China had been its expanding navy and island building. "All of this raises concern that China is trying to create a functional lake in the South China Sea that would prevent foreign militaries from operating there freely," he said, advocating stepping up the pressure and testing China's resolve.

Former director of national intelligence Blair, who had also been commander of US forces in the Pacific, put forward a detailed prescriptive solution, spelling out what both the Chinese and US governments could do to keep the region peaceful. He even offered China a carrot by saying that the United States could "sharply reduce, if not eliminate its reconnaissance activities, surface and air, off the Chinese coast and notify China in advance of exercises that would take place in that area."

"Shipping would be off limits," he explained, adding,

> There would be no cutting of oil shipments to China or blocking shipments to Taiwan, and so on. We would formally or informally agree that this would be something both countries would adhere to even in conditions of conflict. China, for its part, would not further militarize any of the features it claims in the South China or East China seas. It would notify the US of military exercises, and both sides would continue to respond to crises. Anything outside that would mean something serious, and the other side would probably retaliate. If you were of a deal-making disposition, such a deal might be something interesting for both sides to consider.

In the audience was one of Zha's colleagues, Wu Shicun, who headed think tanks in China and the United States. One, the Institute for China-America Studies, had offices next to a fast food store on M Street in Washington, DC. The other was the much more lavishly appointed National Institute for South China Sea Studies in Hainan. Wu was a key official honing Beijing's South China Sea policy. His government gave him a fairly free rein to argue its case around the world. A few days earlier he had published a report accusing the United States of "unprecedented military deployments" in the Asia-Pacific. It had "carried out twelve hundred air and sea reconnaissance missions along China's coast in 2014, an increase of six times from 2009, making China America's number one surveillance target."

I interviewed him the next day at his small office at the Institute for China-America Studies, which declared that its mission was to "facilitate the exchange of ideas," particularly in areas "in need of greater mutual understanding." This was a Communist Party operation in the

American capital aimed at spreading soft power regarding its South China Sea policy.

Wu himself was a veteran of Sino-American tension. In April 2001 he was working with the Chinese Foreign Ministry on Hainan Island when a US Navy EP-3 Orion surveillance plane flying about seventy miles off the Chinese coast collided with a Chinese fighter pilot and had to make an emergency landing there. The pilot, who had been playing a game of chicken with the spy plane, died. The Chinese authorities detained the crew of twenty-one men and three women for eleven days. "The American press accused us of holding the crew hostage," he said. "But it wasn't like that at all. Nothing like this had happened before, and we were fighting among ourselves as to which government department should be in charge. Was it Hainan Province, the navy, the air force, the Public Security Bureau, the Foreign Ministry? Who?" He gave me a knowing smile. "This was China. These things take time. It is not always as the Americans think."

With his swept-back silver hair and furrowed brow, Wu looked like a cross between Albert Einstein and Dustin Hoffman. We talked in a long narrow room with two armchairs positioned beneath the American and Chinese flags, the full formal design of a Chinese meeting room except for its size, the Communist Party in miniature.

Wu began by explaining that his report on US military activities in the Asia-Pacific was the first of its kind. It had taken ten researchers six months to pull together the information from what he called "open sources," meaning there was nothing secret or classified in it. "The US insists on maintaining its supremacy in the Western Pacific," he said. "That is a worry for the whole international community as to whether China and the US will come to a war."

We talked for more than two hours, exploring again this concept of a new world order, with Wu insisting that if the United States wanted to retain the status quo, China and other nations needed to be better represented.

"China is now the world's second largest economy," he argued. "But the international system doesn't take into account our interests. The US economy is about eighteen trillion dollars and China's is ten trillion dollars, yet our stake in the International Monetary Fund is less than Britain's, less than France's, less than Japan's. The current international and regional architecture is still dominated by the US."

"So what, then, is the risk of war?" I asked.

"I don't think there is one," Wu replied genially. "These two countries have an obligation to work together to safeguard peace and stability for the international community."

"Then how would it work?"

"The US should keep to its commitment of taking no sides over the sovereignty issue in the South China Sea," Wu replied. "That is the first. Second, the US should convince the Chinese people that it has no intention of using the South China Sea dispute to contain China. And third, the US should refrain from conducting intelligence gathering activities very close to China's coast; that poses a threat to China's national security."

"So that's the US. What should China do?"

"China, as the owner of the South China Sea islands and as the country with the largest coast of the South China Sea, should respect the freedom of navigation enjoyed by the whole international community. Second, China should be prudent when it comes to island construction facilities which go beyond defensive needs. And third, China should not declare an Air Defense Identification Zone as it will undermine mutual trust between China and the United States. China now feels no security threat, so China doesn't need to announce it."

"But your report said the opposite," I noted. Wu's recent report had warned that China might set up an Air Defense Identification Zone around the Spratly Islands as it had done in 2013 in the Diaoyu/Senkaku Islands row with Japan.

"It said China could possibly set up an ADIZ if the US intensifies its patrols and keeps spying on us," said Wu. "But it doesn't need to, now."

I asked Wu what he thought of Admiral Blair's list of suggestions, including the United States curtailing its surveillance operations and an agreement to guarantee passage for shipping.

"I do not disagree completely," Wu responded thoughtfully.

With Blair and Wu, here were two figures who had the ear of their governments, with much common ground, who were both making detailed suggestions on how to stop a war in the South China Sea. It seemed so easy: freeze the prospect of conflict with a couple of informal arrangements, then set an agenda that would include China and other new powers in a reformed world order. Except, of course, things rarely work like that. There were politics and parliaments, and no one should kid themselves that arguments do not rage within the Chinese government just as they do within any American or European one. They are just not so public.

Blair's suggestions directly contradicted the view of one of his successors heading up the US Pacific Command. A couple of weeks earlier, Admiral Harry Harris had argued that he needed to keep track of China's new submarine-launched long-range ballistic missiles, which could target pretty much anywhere in the United States. "My obligation is to ensure that I know where those SSBNs are," said Harris. "Right now, I am aware of where they are and how many there are."[171]

Harris described China's claim to 90 percent of the South China Sea as outrageous and destabilizing for peace in the region. "They have manufactured land there at a staggering pace just in the last months," he told *Time* magazine. "No one should doubt our resolve to defend the territory of the United States, our people and our interests."[172]

THE UNITED STATES directly challenges China's South China Sea sovereignty claim by deploying warplanes or naval vessels close to its new outposts in the Spratly Islands in what is known as a "freedom of navigation" operation. If China's sovereignty was recognized under international law, the United States would not be allowed within twelve nautical miles of the islands without seeking permission. By sending its military into Chinese-claimed waters and airspace and refusing to leave when ordered, the United States is testing China's military resolve.

The administration of President Barack Obama was fraught with disagreement as to how these missions should be used. Harris wanted more, Obama less; and Trump ordered several in the first months of his presidency. China constantly warns that these operations could

---

171. Admiral Harry Harris at Defense One Leadership Briefing November 14, 2016.

172. Kirk Spitzer, "The New Head of the U.S. Pacific Command Talks to TIME About the Pivot to Asia and His Asian Roots", *Time* magazine, May 25, 2015 http://time.com/3895434/admiral-harry-harris-us-pacific-command-china-japan-asia/

spark something more serious, but for the time being they are carefully choreographed.

In 2015 CNN recorded a radio exchange on board a US Navy P-8A Poseidon surveillance plane patrolling the South China Sea. The Chinese radioed, "Foreign military aircraft, this is Chinese navy. You are approaching our military alert zone. Leave immediately in order to avoid misjudgment."

The Poseidon crew replied, "I am a United States military aircraft conducting lawful military activities outside national airspace with due regard to international law."[173]

Because of the risk of miscalculation, crews are careful not to say anything that could be misconstrued as being provocative. "The actual transits are heavily scripted," Mark E. Rosen, an international maritime lawyer at the US Center for Naval Analyses told me. "The crews are given talking points for when they are challenged or queried. Basically, they say, 'We are operating innocent passage in accordance with the 1983 United Nations Law of the Sea Convention.'"

China is challenging the very concept of international law as it is interpreted by Western democracies. As we saw from the reaction to the July 2016 Permanent Court of Arbitration ruling on the South China Sea claims, international law itself cannot do the business because there is no agreed-upon mechanism through which it is implemented. If anything, instead of giving room for the Southeast Asian governments to come to resolution themselves, the Hague ruling has drawn the United States much further into a dispute in which it claims neutrality. According to the tribunal, no nation has sovereignty over any of the Spratly Islands, yet Malaysia, the Philippines, and Vietnam, along with China, all have a presence there. The United States is making a point of testing China when there is no evidence that Beijing has any plans to interrupt international shipping. To even threaten such action would sever the very supply chains it is working to secure.

Western democracies have also been taken to international tribunals and rejected the judgments just as China had. Only the previous

---

173. Jim Sciutto, "Exclusive: China warns U.S. surveillance plane", CNN, September 15, 2015 http://edition.cnn.com/2015/05/20/politics/south-china-sea-navy-flight/index.html

year, in 2015, the same Permanent Court of Arbitration had ruled against Britain in a case that eerily resembled the one of the South China Sea. In 2010 Britain unilaterally set up a 400,000-square-mile Marine Protected Area around the Indian Ocean's Chagos Archipelago, whose sovereignty is disputed between Britain and the small island nation of Mauritius. The archipelago contains the controversial atoll of Diego Garcia, which once looked like the disputed reefs and rocks of the South China Sea. In the 1960s Britain leased it to the United States, which was looking for a foothold in the India Ocean, and America transformed it into the military base that it is today, like Mischief Reef, only much bigger. The United States forcibly evicted the Diego Garcia islanders to Mauritius and the Seychelles. In return, America helped Britain with its Polaris submarine program, giving it its first submarine-based nuclear missiles.[174]

Britain's declaration of a Marine Protected Area, ostensibly to safeguard fish stocks, was the last straw for Mauritius which, like the Philippines, took its dispute to the Permanent Court of Arbitration. After four years of hearings, the tribunal ruled that Britain had failed to give due regard to the rights of the Chagos islanders and had breached its obligations under the UN Convention on the Law of the Sea. Unlike China, Britain took part in the hearings and said it accepted the decision. But since then, apart from a single brief meeting when I last checked, nothing has happened. The ruling was ignored. Britain continued to intercept and order away fishing boats that entered the disputed area.

Thirty years earlier, Nicaragua took the United States to the International Court of Justice, also based in The Hague. The 1986 case revolved around the United States mining Nicaragua's harbors in its support of right-wing Contra rebels fighting to overthrow the government. The United States lost and immediately declared, just as China did in 2016, that the court had no jurisdiction.

Another judicial body in The Hague, the International Criminal Court, received a blow from the developing world in 2016 when three African governments, Burundi, Gambia, and South Africa, announced

---

174. "Stolen Island: the shameful story of Diego Garcia hits the stage," *The Guardian*, February 2012.

they would quit, claiming the court was biased in favor of white Europeans. "There are many Western countries, at least thirty, that have committed heinous war crimes against independent sovereign states since the creation of the International Criminal Court, and not a single Western war criminal has been indicted," said Gambian president Yahya Jammeh.[175] Under international pressure, South Africa later said it would retain its membership.

International law, therefore, has itself come under scrutiny. Judgments are ignored or adhered to only according to national interests, underlining a truth that the rule of law, legitimacy, military force, and other elements jostle together when balancing international power.

The ultimate arbiter of international law is the UN Security Council, but some resolutions, such as those passed against Israel, are routinely ignored, while those against Iran or North Korea tend to be enforced.[176] Hardeep Singh Puri, a former Indian ambassador to the UN who sat on the Security Council during his country's rotating membership from 2009 to 2013, argues that adherence to international law has reached a crisis point: "The structures for international peace and security are being tested as never before. It is in everyone's interest to reestablish the authority of the Security Council and reassert the primacy of law."[177]

But how could that happen, when the legitimacy of the Western-built system is under such strain? In June 2016, China and Russia joined forces to issue an unprecedented joint declaration "on the primacy of international law," pointing out that the concept of stability being guaranteed through nuclear weapons was now outdated. They emphasized that international law should be applied "on an equal footing" and that governments should "refrain from the threat or use of force." They condemned "unilateral military interventions." In a direct challenge to the US-led system, they ended resolving to uphold and promote international law, in "establishing a just and equitable international order."[178]

---

175. "Gambia announces withdrawal from International Criminal Court", *Reuters*, October 26, 2016.

176. "Israel has ignored resolution to stop settlements in Palestinian territories, UN says," *Independent*, March 2017.

177. Interview with author, June 6, 2017.

178. "Russia and China to Sign Joint Declaration on Principles of International Law," Kenneth Anderson, *Lawfare*, June 2016.

While the Permanent Court of Arbitration was deliberating on the South China Sea dispute, China announced that it had set up its own International Maritime Judicial Center that reported to the Supreme People's Court. In 2016 alone it had heard more than sixteen thousand cases over all maritime territory within its jurisdiction, meaning 90 percent of the South China Sea. And, like Britain in the Indian Ocean, since 1995 China has declared its own unilaterally protected areas with an annual fishing ban that runs from May to August.

"We have followed the letter of the law," defense analyst Ruan Zongze told me. "We adhered to article 298 of the Convention on the Law of the Sea, which allows a choice whether to accept arbitration or not. Thirty countries so far have refused arbitration, including Britain. So, it is not just China, and we said back in 2006 that we were not going to be subject to any kind of arbitration. We prefer to settle on a bilateral basis, case by case, which is how we have succeeded in solving twelve of our fourteen disputes on demarcated land borders." Those still unresolved are with Bhutan and India, and saw the Chinese and Indian armies standing off against each other in 2017.

Taiwan also lashed out against the Permanent Court of Arbitration ruling, which described its coast guard base in the Spratly Islands as neither a rock nor an island. President Tsai Ing-wen issued a blistering attack against the tribunal that its finding was unacceptable and had no legally binding force.[179]

Taiping, or Itu Aba Island, is Taiwan's only Spratly base, but it covers forty-six acres and is almost a mile long, with a twelve-hundred-foot runway. There are six hundred coast guard and support staff. It is also the best developed, with a solar power station, freshwater plant, Internet connection, and a post office. Taiwan has also released expenditure figures for the recent upgrading of the island, giving us an idea of how much China would be spending, too. Taiwan invested $23.3 million in a new runway, $66 million for the port and jetty, and a total of $1.1 billion for all modernization.[180] China's costs in building up seven islands from scratch would run into tens of billions of dollars.

---

179. "ROC position on the South China Sea Arbitration," Ministry of Foreign Affairs, July 2016.

180. To the author from Taipei representative office in London.

"We know how much maintaining a South China Sea base costs," said David Y. L. Lin, Taiwan's Foreign Minister from 2012-16. "It's very expensive."

The South China Sea dispute, therefore, goes to the core of Beijing's demand for an overhaul of the current global order. What legitimacy does America have to challenge China's foreign policy with warships because a tribunal of freelance lawyers has ruled one way or another in a court that is accountable to no international institution? Why should the head of the World Bank always be an American, and the head of the International Monetary Fund a European? And it is not only China asking these questions. Brazil, India, South Africa, and others are challenging the lopsidedness of global institutions and of the UN Security Council itself, which is the ultimate arbiter of international law.

CHAPTER 19

WHO IS IN CHARGE?

THERE IS OFTEN A MISCONCEPTION THAT BRITAIN, CHINA, FRANCE, Russia, and the United States have permanent UN Security Council seats because they were the original nuclear weapons states. That might have consolidated their positions, but in 1945, when the UN was created, only America had the bomb. The Soviet Union first carried out a test in 1949, Britain in 1952, France in 1960, and China in 1964. These countries were the five that had emerged as winners of the Second World War, and in any case, China at that time was controlled by the Kuomintang nationalist government which quickly became exiled to Taiwan. As horse trading for seats gathered speed, the United States had pushed for Brazil to become a permanent member, but Britain and the Soviet Union blocked it.

Yet more than seventy years later, this is how the world is still run despite men having walked on the moon; space probes on Mars; supersonic air travel; wars in Korea, Suez, Vietnam, Angola, Nicaragua, Bosnia, Chechnya, and the rest; coups in Iran, Chile, Fiji, and elsewhere; winds of change sweeping through the independent countries of the once-colonized world; the partition of India; the creation of Israel; the tearing down of the Berlin Wall; 9/11; the Second Iraq war; the Internet; and the fact that those born in 1945 would now be dead or in the evening of their lives. There is little wonder that the system is creaking at its outdated seams and the new kids on the block want a bigger slice of the pie.

As China's reforms began to work, particularly after it joined the World Trade Organization in 2001, Beijing recognized the benefits of being part of the American-led world order. But, with its newfound wealth, Beijing wanted more of a say.

Over the years there had been attempts to set up parallel institutions. None got off the ground enough to challenge the United States. China, with its Eastphalian vision, had not been as confident and rich as it was now, nor was America and its Westphalian one then seemingly so damaged. In 2001 the Shanghai Cooperation Organization was created to weld together Central Asia, China, and Russia. Its origins lay in the 1996 visit to Shanghai by Russian president Boris Yeltsin. China has also launched projects into Europe, like the 16+1 initiative, a project to persuade sixteen of the less well-off European countries to look east toward China for their growth. There is also the Regional Comprehensive Economic Partnership, a free trade project devised in 2011 when the US Pivot to Asia was announced. China sees it as a counterbalance to the US-led Trans-Pacific Partnership, which President Donald Trump promptly shelved after taking office.

One of the most contentious initiatives, however, has been the 2016 creation of the Asian Infrastructure Investment Bank (AIIB), which succeeded in creating a loud diplomatic split between the United States and its closest European ally, Britain. Here was a test of the legitimacy of the American vision and the extent to which the traditional "You're either with us or against us" maxim could be transferred from the so-called War on Terror to the rise of China. The bank was China's regional answer to the Asian Development Bank (ADB), a sister organization to the US-led World Bank. The AIIB would fund Asian infrastructure projects, including dams, roads, schools, and railways, and it would be run from Beijing. In an announcement that was met with apoplectic rage within Washington, DC, Britain announced without consultation that it would join as a founding member. Other European governments rushed in, and as of 2017 fifty-seven governments had joined. Japan and the United States were the only two significant countries refusing. The bank highlighted divisions, even among the closest Western allies, on how to handle China.

Britain, France, Germany, and South Korea signed up to the bank from the start. In March 2017 Canada became the latest G7 and NATO member set to join. The United States, by refusing to apply, also failed to keep its allies on its side. America argued that the AIIB failed to meet the exacting standards of international banking and investment, and accused it of undercutting quality control at the World Bank and the ADB. Why, it asked, was this alternative bank even necessary?

The US argument quickly fell apart when questioned by leading American economists. The ADB estimated the region would need $1.7 trillion a year until 2030 for infrastructure investment, and if that were to be met, more money had to be found. The AIIB, with authorized capitalization of $100 billion, could help. But—and this is politically important—the head of the ADB had always been Japanese, just as the World Bank was led by an American and the International Monetary Fund (IMF) by a European. This new bank would have a Chinese leader.

Even though China was the world's second biggest economy, it had very little representation in the financial architecture that now presided over the developing world, giving it no sense of ownership. Yet China had been responsible for more than half the reduction in global poverty over the past twenty-five years. The main obstacle to change was the US Congress. In 2010 a bill to give more voting rights in the IMF to emerging economies failed to get through, even though the shift would have been only for six 6 percent.

Former US Treasury secretary Lawrence Summers has noted that America's rejection of the AIIB might be remembered as the moment it had "lost its role as the underwriter of the global economic system."[181] His view is mostly shared by the former chairman of the Federal Reserve, Ben Bernanke, who deems it unfortunate that China felt it had to break off and go its own way. "It would be better to have a globally unified system and allow resources to go where they are needed," Bernanke notes. "I can understand why China and other countries might want to say, 'Well, we're going to set up our own system.'"[182] And Nobel Prize laureate in economics Joseph E. Stiglitz goes further, noting that the congressional vote reflected America's insecurity about its global influence. "It was not as if the US was offering an alternative source of funding," he explains. "It simply wanted hegemony. In an increasingly multipolar world, it wanted to remain the G-1."[183]

181, Lawrence Summers, "A global wake-up call for the U.S.?" *Washington Post*, April 5, 2015.

182. "US Congress pushed China into launching AIIB, says Bernanke," *Financial Times*, June 2, 2015.

183. Why America Doesn't Welcome China's New Infrastructure Bank," *The World Post*, April 2017

In economic and diplomatic terms, China's launch of the AIIB sits up there with its building of runways on the Spratly Islands. Both challenge the existing world order that Beijing did not trust to protect its interests, raising the question as to what red lines, if any, have been crossed as officials from Western democracies line up to get on its payroll.

Britain's representative at the bank is a young knight of the realm, Sir Danny Alexander, who until ejected by British voters in 2015 had been deputy finance minister in Her Majesty's government. He was a senior figure in Britain's third national party, the Liberal Democrats, a famous British politician and champion of Western democratic values who had moved his family to Beijing, with its austere buildings, red flags, walled compounds, and unaccountable decisions, the heart of authoritarianism where the vision for a new Eastphalian world order was being put into practice.

Sir Danny has a youthful face, thick red hair, and a ready smile skillfully deployed to deflect difficult questions. He chuckled when I asked him about Eastphalia, and countered with the G-Zero concept, coined by political scientist Ian Bremmer in his 2012 book, whose title is self-explanatory: *Every Nation for Itself: What Happens When No One Leads the World*.[184] We agreed that G-Zero might be more apt for where we are now—that is, if Europe and the United States continue to be more inward-looking.

The AIIB was still embryonically young, as was evident in the expanse of space in its Beijing headquarters, equipped with desks, computer screens, and conference tables but barely any staff. It reminded me of empty multilane highways in far-flung Chinese provinces built with a mix of hope, anticipation, confidence, planning, and corruption. Some, flanked by half-built luxury mansions and empty factories, resembled a dystopia of failure. Others did well, showing foresight and ambition. Arterial roads barely used a decade earlier were now busy, but with traffic flowing smoothly because of forward planning that anticipated all Chinese wanting to own a car.

The bank had taken vast office space for the future, and Sir Danny was vice president and corporate secretary, deciding how this new in-

---

184. Ian Bremmer, *Every Nation for Itself: What Happens When No One Leads the World* (New York: Portfolio, 2012).

stitution should unfold. In his last job, as a junior left-leaning coalition partner in an austerity-driven government tasked to cut public funding, he had endured daily political backbiting and voters' wrath. Now his mission was to lend money from the Mediterranean to the Pacific, building bridges, roads and waterways that would lift people out of poverty, make cities habitable and connect the world. Enthusiastically, he reeled off contracts already signed: power to twenty-five million Bangladeshis, upgrading Indonesia's slums, hydroelectric projects in Pakistan, a gas power station in Myanmar, and a railway and port in Oman. The bank's projects were wrapped into the Belt and Road Initiative, now the engine of Beijing's influence-spreading policy aimed at diluting the dominance of India, Japan and the United States.

So why was it, I asked, that Britain, holding itself up as the mother of democracy and a close American ally, was now at the heart of China's ambition to undermine those values? And where did Sir Danny stand, working in this nondemocratic system when he was cheerleader for his own party, which carried the very name of liberal democracy?

"I'm not sure if your continuum is a straight line," he said. "Britain decided to join the bank because we saw a serious effort to create an international institution investing in infrastructure that we believed in. The initiative is really important because China is showing it can work closely with fifty-six other countries to build an institution that everyone recognizes runs according to high global standards."

Sir Danny explained that those high standards were so exact that the AIIB and the World Bank were able to rely on each other's due diligence reports to ensure that work would get done without bribes, favors, or cutting corners even though the World Bank's track record was littered with projects that failed, wasted money, and bloated budgets. China was now financing infrastructure that the World Bank had failed to do during the two decades after the Cold War, when there was an empty canvas on which it was able to work, free of competition. For the past decade, long before the AIIB was created, China has been financing more projects in poorer countries than the World Bank.[185]

Because of that, Sir Danny's AIIB symbolized the divisions among

---

185. Geoff Dyer, Jamil Anderlini, Henry Sender, "China's lending hits new heights" *Financial Times*, January 17, 2011.

developed countries on how to handle China. Given that he had been one of the most recognizable figures in British politics, I asked him again if his doing this job here in Beijing undermined democratic ideals.

He gave it not a second's thought. "No, of course it doesn't," he said. "The United Kingdom works closely with countries around the world to support these agendas—"

"But have you compromised your own values?"

"No. The UK is a member of the UN and all sorts of international institutions with aid programs with different political systems. You gain much more by finding ways to work together, share ideas, and collaborate."

"How, then, do you see the current tension with the US over so many issues panning out?"

"You're asking me to stare into a crystal ball, which I don't have."

"But you're putting money into very long-term projects, so you have to look into that crystal ball."

Sir Danny looked out of his large high-rise window over the city, then said: "Are the cities of the future—where another billion are going to move—livable, clean places, easy to get around for people, goods, and services, easy to move between Europe, Asia, the Americas, and other parts of the world?"

He continued laying out his vision. Infrastructure was about building bridges, not putting up walls. He had once been the face of a center-left coalition partnership with the right until the 2015 election, when the Conservative Party won an absolute majority and the Liberal Democrats were decimated to a handful. Then came Britain's vote to leave the European Union, Trump's victory in the United States, and the anti-immigration xenophobia and anti-globalization fervor that came with them. Sir Danny was part of the vacuum into which China had stepped. He had come to Beijing to champion higher living standards, freer trade, and globalization.

Outside the bank's windows, smog covered the city so that all we could see were the tops of buildings poking like plants out of a yellow-gray blanket. "It comes and goes," said Sir Danny, plucking my coat from the stand as I left. "If you'd come yesterday, there was beautiful clear blue sky."

Back downstairs, my chest tightened in the ice-cold polluted air.

Fast-walking office workers wearing a spectrum of masks passed back and forth. In the place I was staying, intricate instructions about air purifiers were pinned to the wall. I started checking my phone, then remembered that the panoply of communication tools— Google, Skype, WhatsApp, and others—were all blocked. Those visiting China on government or business-sensitive trips often go with fresh phones or strip theirs out to factory settings so hackers can't get in and steal personal details. In Guangzhou the staff at my hotel had downloaded software onto my laptop, a virtual private network (VPN), to bypass firewalls simply to get e-mail. By July 2017 Apple and several other multinationals had removed VPN software from their products to comply with tighter Chinese government regulations.

Beijing is not like Shanghai or Xiamen. It is part old communist bricks and concrete and part bright lights and neon billboards. Glitter and ostentation do not predominate, as in so many Asian megacities, or even in Times Square or Piccadilly Circus. Designer names and international hotel chains are subordinated to a kind of pastel gray cream and maroon that washes through the streetscape of buildings. It is an austere city, with slabs of office blocks lining wide boulevards designed to accommodate tanks. There are modern signs of I. M. Pei and other pioneering architects trying to break through. There is also an almost Germanic whiff of Albert Speer's politicized architecture, certainly in Tiananmen Square, with its intimidating monuments built even as Mao Zedong was fighting with India, South Korea, and Taiwan and starving his own people.

In Beijing the roads are wide, but the traffic crawls. You can't go anywhere in much less than an hour. We passed through Tiananmen Square, that evocative badge of Chinese communist power. If China has been right about development, is it also right about how many opponents need to be jailed, how many restrictions imposed on citizens, how much opinion is stifled to lift millions out of poverty? Is that how it has to work? Were Iraq and Libya just fantasies hatched by Western politicians who did not have a clue, a populist move within a short electoral cycle, to make those in office look good? Or has it always been thus as societies develop, only we have forgotten? America has its Civil War, its race riots, gunfights, and infrastructure building. Between 1904 and 1914, the United States built the Panama Canal, cutting a forty-eight-mile shipping lane that linked the Atlantic and Pacific Oceans, taking over from the French, whose plans were riddled with inefficiency and corruption. Was this the equivalent of China's Belt and Road Initiative, moving in to build new trade routes where others had failed?

Driving through Tiananmen Square we passed queues outside the National History Museum, newly renovated at a cost of $400 million. Exhibits inside tell China's story, leaving certain bits out, like any good storyteller, cutting out the dull and any segments that veer from the overarching narrative of struggle, moral good, and triumph. Confined to the airbrush of history are the murderous Cultural Revolution, the famine of the Great Leap Forward that killed tens of millions, and the Tiananmen Square killings of prodemocracy activists that took place on June 4, 1989, right outside the museum.

Is this a nation unable to confront its own history, an accusation that China so readily levels against Japan, and that the United States levels against China? Or is this what all nations do—lie and forget in order to succeed? In my own school classes, teachers not only failed to tell me about the Opium Wars but also omitted mentions of a raft of other methods Britain had used in its control of other countries. I was taught about the 1415 Battle of Agincourt and the 1860s American Civil War, but not Britain's 1814 burning of the White House in the War of 1812. There was no mention either of the 1919 massacre of civilians in Amritsar, when Colonel Reginald Dyer ordered the continuous shooting for ten minutes of civilians, resulting in the murder of 379 people; and nothing of atrocities against Mau Mau insurgents in Kenya in the 1950s and 1960s. In 2013 Britain agreed to pay $30 million in compensation to a trust set up for the victims' families in Kenya for carrying out "unspeakable and horrific gross violation of human rights," including "massacres, torture and sexual violence."[186] And when Mao Zedong is condemned for the famine of the Great Leap Forward, there is usually no reference to the comparable famine in Bengal in 1943 when, under British rule, three million died, allegedly because Winston Churchill refused to ship in food supplies.[187]

---

186. "Mau Mau torture victims to receive compensation–Hague," *BBC*, June 6, 2013.

187. Soutik Biswas "How Churchill Starved India," BBC, October 28, 2010.

At the southern end of Tiananmen Square, opposite the huge portrait of Mao, is his mausoleum. Near it stands the granite Monument to the Martyrs of the People, thirty meters tall, with 170 life-size figures and a plinth inscribed, in Mao's own handwriting, "Eternal Glory to the People's Heroes." The pillars and steps of the Great Hall of the People stretch more than three hundred meters along the western side of the square. Inside, where Philippines president Ronaldo Duterte declared that he had dumped America in favor of China, is a banquet hall for five thousand guests and rooms dedicated to Hong Kong, Macau, and Taiwan, the territories China lost during its Century of Humiliation. Two territories have been returned; Taiwan is yet to come.

To the north stands the Gate of Heavenly Peace, where Mao proclaimed an end to humiliation and began restoring a sense of destiny to China, refreshed by its new emperor and his Mandate of Heaven. Five bridges run from there to the gates of the Forbidden City, now open to all, a museum of nine thousand rooms in a spread of wooden buildings with yellow-glazed tiled roofs and white marble terraces, once staffed by seventy thousand imperial eunuchs, behind walls that are nearly ten meters high.

While the Forbidden City was the reference point for old China, a few hundred meters to the west now rise the high red walls of the current center of Chinese power, the compound of Zhongnanhai, meaning "central and southern seas," sometimes referred to as the Sea Palace.

The outside walls are decorated with party slogans: "Long Live the Unbeatable Thoughts of Chairman Mao" and "Long Live the Great Chinese Communist Party." Taxis are not permitted to pull up outside, and green-uniformed armed soldiers of the Central Guards Regiment, the equivalent of the US Secret Service, are charged with protecting China's leaders. They do a good job. None has ever been assassinated.

Inside are broad uncluttered roads, reception rooms, luxurious accommodations, and drooping willows beside ornamental lakes. It is here that decisions have been made about where and when to order troops across the disputed line into India, how to irritate Japan over the Diaoyu/Senkaku Islands, how to leverage the United States over North Korea, how to squeeze, coax or muscle Taiwan back, and how to use the new military bases in the South China Sea. It is from inside these walls that the vision to realize a Chinese world order is being planned.

CHAPTER 20

A FAULT-LINE GAMBLE

THE DISPUTED SOUTH CHINA SEA ISLANDS PRESENT US WITH A ONCE-in-a-generation opportunity. Beijing has no more reason to use its islands to threaten international shipping than America has reason to take them out with air strikes. Beijing needs the trade routes to stay open. The United States needs China for a myriad of issues that stretch far beyond seven garrisoned outposts in international waters.

The standoff, and its accompanying rhetoric, is a mark of how carefully both governments need to choreograph their disagreements to avoid sudden conflict, because any open hostility risks global turmoil. The advantage offered by the islands is that they are garrisoned, uninhabited, or very sparsely populated. In news terms, this is not a story in which human suffering propels foreign policy, as has happened often in the Middle East, allowing for decisions to be made on a clearer and more pragmatic canvas.

China has propelled itself, rocket-like, from being a shambolic near-failing state to becoming the factory of the world. It is now a crucible for ideas, a juggernaut of which almost everyone wants to be part. Beijing's five-year plan to 2020 includes an ambition to lead in computer chips, robotics, satellites, and aviation equipment. China's technology in clean-air products, electric cars, and solar energy is already competing head-on with developed countries, and it is significant that the United States is currently reversing laws from the era of President Barack Obama in order to bring back more polluting measures, such as coal-fired power. Automation, artificial intelligence, and robots are at the heart of sweeping reforms to its factories and manufacturing industries, and the United States concedes that China is already ahead in areas such as high-speed rail, supercomputing, and advanced energy technologies.

Yet none of that would have been possible without the US-led world order that provided a security umbrella and the rule of law through which China could regain its historical strength and become rich.

By challenging this world order before it is ready, Beijing is taking a gamble and, for their part, Western democracies are being too slow to adapt to the new reality that China presents. The South China Sea island building is symbolic in that it allows the world's most populous country to move away from its Century of Humiliation and embrace an era of opportunity. They are symbols of dignity. Mischief Reef, with its harbor and twenty-six-hundred-meter runway, underlines the restoration of China's vigor and renders irrelevant the argument over maps, history, possession, and court rulings on tidal flows. As America and Europe before it, China has done what it has because it can.

The islands serve as a reminder of what could go wrong, how it might spread and the catastrophe a bad decision could bring. They are also a political reality for China's neighbors who are having to think carefully about where their long-term future and allegiance really lie and balance accordingly.

The past few years have proven that money and development are not enough, either in the West or in Asia. The overarching concept of dignity needs to be addressed, posing the challenge of how to slot Eastphalia into Westphalia without conflict.

During the writing of *Asian Waters*, each regional fault line has been tested. Chinese and Indian troops have been deployed to the disputed border in the Himalayas. Chinese war planes have buzzed Taiwanese military exercises in the Taiwan Strait. Chinese and Japanese ships and planes have skirted closely around each other in the East China Sea. North Korea has tested nuclear bombs and missiles while Japan, South Korea, and the United States drew up plans to invade. China and the United States have challenged each other in the South China Sea. China has threatened Vietnam with military action over contested drilling near the Paracel Islands. And so on, and so on, amid repeated warnings about risks of miscalculation.

Historically, major reforms to the global system have been implemented only after war. Both the 1815 Congress of Vienna after the defeat of Napoleonic France and the 1919 Treaty of Versailles that ended the First World War failed to keep a lasting peace. The 1947 Treaties of Paris and the 1951 Treaty of San Francisco were drawn up after the Second World War and have been more enduring, leading to the creation of the UN, NATO, the European Union, and other financial and political institutions. This is the system from which China has benefited and against which it is now rebelling.

A clamor for reform goes far beyond China and coincides with increased connectivity through the Internet, air travel, and infrastructure that is diminishing the relevance of frontiers, diluting national identity and creating a more transparent, borderless system that controls so much now in trade and politics. But it comes during a political cycle when America and Europe are having to address unrest among their own citizens over damaged economies, disparities of wealth, and a political class perceived as being privileged, out of touch, and ineffective.

There is a growing, albeit exaggerated, perception that the West lies weakened against a rising China, filled with ideas about building a rival system to liberal democracy, one of a wealth-creating, infrastructure-building, high-achieving, hard-driving one-party state.

In the long term the Communist Party will need to update its pact with its citizens and make itself more accountable and transparent, but it is no longer enough for Western democracies to say that China is at fault because it is not a democracy. Nor can the West keep arguing that liberal democracy is the only government system that all successful nations should follow. For billions around the world, Winston Churchill's maxim that democracy is the worst form of government except for all others has been proven wrong.

These contradictions of how the world currently operates underline the need for change. The economic system jumps across frontiers, while the political one still emanates from the writ of nation-states ultimately controlled by five countries that won a war more than seventy years ago. It is too outdated to last. In 2018, as the United States was still fighting the Korean War, Beijing was laying down its big future vision of a modern global society.

Through that prism, the South China Sea islands lie not so much in one or another's sovereign territory but in international trade routes of which China will become the ultimate guarantor. It is an issue less about borders and more of responsibility, and it has nothing whatsoever to do with the long-ago unfurling of flags by colonial sea captains.

While this challenge can be compared to the emergence of Germany in the early twentieth century, or the rise of Athens that threatened Sparta in the fifth century BC, China's method of step-by-step salami slicing can also be used to avoid war. China claims it wants respect, security for its supply chains, and a bigger seat at the top table that controls the world order. But if the United States will not let it fully inside the tent, China will go it alone and build its own. It has now abandoned its "new model" of great power relations' to concentrate on the Belt and Road Initiative, the AIIB and a raft of other projects which signal its determination.

That, in itself, creates a more confrontational slant, reaffirming that the 1940s-designed world order is crying out for change and that to delay longer could make the world a more dangerous place. Any initiative to restructure the UN and its related institutions should begin now before major conflict breaks out rather than afterward, when cities have been flattened and the lives of millions lost or ruined.

Trade negotiations are an example of how it could work. Sessions of the General Agreement on Tariffs and Trade began in 1947. They became the World Trade Organization, which has instilled order in global trade with a constant regeneration of ideas and change through continuing negotiation. A similar forum could be created to examine the international architecture and its myriad of financial, political, and humanitarian institutions.

Some would try to block reform. Others would describe it as naïve nonsense. Why, when America is the top dog, should it concede ground to a potential enemy? Some would cry appeasement, unfurling the banners of democracy and pointing to China's bans on religion and discussion, to its prison camps, executions, and rubber stamp parliaments. In the long term they may be right. But China is not Germany in the early twentieth century or Japan in the 1930s, nor the Soviet Union in the 1940s or Iraq or Libya in the early twenty-first century. Nor is it an expanding ancient Athens, any more than the United States is a retreating ancient Sparta. China is claiming great power status, and the West should address it exactly for what it is.

Negotiations to restructure the world order would be best based on pragmatism rather than fear and self-interest, and they would take decades. Everyone, whether an American or Chinese president, a Brazilian sugarcane cutter, Indian brick kiln worker, or a Vietnamese fisherman, should feel in some way involved. Such a forum would be fraught with obstacles, breakdowns, and challenges. But even if progress runs at a snail's pace and is so incremental to be barely noticed, it would show that change was underway.

Without such a project the drums of war will get louder because the human race, when faced with insecurity, has a tendency to fight. Black swans will circle, and one will strike, as it did in 1914, 1941, and 2001. The West talks about accommodating China's rise, and Asia talks about the West's descent. There is no need to see it through such a prism. Managed skillfully, the transition could be seamless. Managed badly, and we would have to think the unthinkable.

If China does sees itself as the new force in the world, it is up to China to get it right. The first step would be to initiate a peaceful and pragmatic end to the disputes in Asian waters.

SELECTED BIBLIOGRAPHY

Allison, Graham, *Destined for War: Can America and China Escape Thucydides's Trap?*, Boston: Houghton Mifflin Harcourt, 2017.

Bhatia, Shyam. *Goodbye Shahzadi: A Political Biography of Benazir Bhutto*. Bhutto, New Dehli: Roli, 2008.

Bremmer, Ian. *Every Nation for Itself: What Happens When No One Leads the World*. New York: Portfolio, 2012.

Brown, Kerry. *CEO, China: The Rise of Xi Jinping*. New York: Tauris, 2016.

———. *China's World: The Global Aspiration of the Next Superpower*. New York: Tauris, 2017.

———. *New Emperors: The Power and the Princelings in China*, New York, Tauris, 2014

Buckley, Michael. *Meltdown in Tibet: China's Reckless Destruction of Ecosystems from the Highlands of Tibet to the Deltas of Asia*. Basingstoke, England: Palgrave Macmillan, 2014.

Campbell, Kurt M. *The Pivot: The Future of American Statecraft in Asia*. New York: Twelve, 2016.

Caplan, Robert D. *Asia's Cauldron: The South China Sea and the End of a Stable Pacific*. New York: Random House, 2014.

Ching, Frank. *Ancestors: The Story of China Told through the Lives of an Extraordinary Family*. London: Ebury, 2011.

Clark, Duncan. *The House That Jack Ma Built*. London: Ecco, 2016.

Clinton, Hillary. "America's Pacific Century." *Foreign Policy*, October 11, 2011.

Cole, Bernard D. *China's Quest for Great Power: Ships, Oil, and Foreign Policy*. Annapolis, MD: Naval Institute Press, 2016.

Dervis, Kermal. *Reflections on Progress: Essays on the Global Political Economy.* Washington, DC: Brookings Institution Press, 2016.

Easton, Ian. *The Chinese Invasion Threat: Taiwan's Defense and American Strategy in Asia.* Arlington, VA: Project 2049 Institute, 2017.

Emmott, Bill. *Fate of the West: The Decline and Revival of the World's Most Valuable Political Idea.* London: Economist Books, 2017.

———. *Rivals: How the Power Struggle between China, India, and Japan Will Shape Our Next Decade.* Boston: Mariner, 2009.

Etzioni, Amitai. *Avoiding War with China: Two Nations, One World.* Charlottesville: University of Virginia Press, 2017.

Fenby, Jonathan. *Will China Dominate the 21st Century? (Global Futures),* Oxford: Polity Press; 2nd Revised edition, 2017.

———. *Tiger Head, Snake Tails: China today, how it got there and why it has to change.* London: Simon & Schuster UK, 2013.

Feng, Zhu, John G. Ikenberry, and Wang Jisi, Wang, eds. *America, China, and the Struggle for World Order: Ideas, Traditions, Historical Legacies, and Global Visions.* London: Palgrave Macmillan, 2015.

Ferejohn, John, and Frances M. Rosenbluth. *Forged through Fire: War, Peace, and the Democratic Bargain.* New York: Liveright, 2016.

Fidler, David P., Sumit Ganguly, and Sung W. Kim. *Eastphalia Rising? Asian Influence and the Fate of Human Security.* Bloomington, IN: World Policy Journal, 2009.

Flynn, Michael T., and Michael Ledeen. *The Field of Fight.* New York: St Martin's, 2016.

French, Howard W. *Everything under the Heavens: How the Past Helps Shape China's Push for Global Power.* New York: Knopf, 2017.

Fukuyama, Francis. *The End of History and the Last Man.* New York: Free Press, 1992.

Gertz, Bill. *iWar: War and Peace in the Information Age.* New York: Threshold, 2017.

Gewirtz, Julian. *Unlikely Partners: Chinese Reformers, Western Economists, and the Making of Global China.* Cambridge, MA: Harvard University Press, 2017.

Green, Michael J. *By More than Providence: Grand Strategy and Amer-*

ican Power in the Asia Pacific since 1783. New York: Columbia University Press, 2017.

Hadfield, Gillian K. *Rules for a Flat World: Why Humans Invented Law and How to Reinvent It for a Complex Global Economy.* Oxford: Oxford University Press, 2016.

Harvey, Brian. *China in Space: The Great Leap Forward.* New York: Springer, 2013.

Hayton, Bill. *The South China Sea: The Struggle for Power in Asia.* New Haven, CT: Yale University Press, 2014.

Heydarian, Richard J. *Asia's New Battlefield: The USA, China and the Struggle for the Western Pacific.* London: Zed, 2015.

Jinping, Xi. *The Governance of China.* Beijing: Foreign Language Press, 2014.

Kausikan, Bilahari. *Dealing with an Ambiguous World.* Toh Tuck, Singapore: World Scientific, 2016.

Khanna, Parag. *Connectography: Mapping the Global Revolution.* New York: Random House, 2016.

Kissinger, Henry. *World Order,* New York, Penguin Press, 2014

Lanteigne, Marc, and Su Ping. *China's Arctic Diplomacy: China and the Struggle for Power in the Polar North.* New York: Taurus, 2017.

Lardy, Nicholas. *Markets over Mao: The Rise of Private Business in China.* Washington, DC: Peterson Institute for International Economics, 2014.

Lovell, Julia. *The Opium War: Drugs, Dreams and the Making of China.* New York: Picador, 2011.

Luce, Edward. *The Retreat of Western Liberalism.* London: Little, Brown, 2017.

Manicom, James. *Bridging Troubled Waters: China, Japan, and Maritime Order in the East China Sea.* Washington, DC: Georgetown University Press, 2014.

McCoy, Alfred W. *In the Shadows of the American Century: The Rise and Decline of US Global Power.* Chicago: Haymarket, 2017.

McGregor, James. *No Ancient Wisdom, No Followers: The Challenges of Chinese Authoritarian Capitalism.* New Haven, CT: Prospecta, 2012.

McGregor, Richard. *Asia's Reckoning: China, Japan, the US, and the Struggle for Global Power*. New York: Viking, 2017.

Mearsheimer, John J. *The Tragedy of Great Power Politics*. New York: Norton, 2003.

Menon, Shivshankar. *Choices: Inside the Making of India's Foreign Policy*. Washington, DC: Brooking Institution Press, 2016.

Mishra, Pankaj. *Age of Anger*. London: Lane, 2017.

Mukerjee, Madhusree. *Churchill's Secret War: The British Empire and the Ravaging of India during World War II*. New York: Basic Books, 2010.

Oros, Andrew L, *Japan's Security Renaissance: New Policies and Politics for the Twenty-first Century,* Columbia, 2017.

Pomfret, John. *The Beautiful Country and the Middle Kingdom: America and China, 1776 to the Present*. New York: Holt, 2016.

Rachman, Gideon. *Easternisation*. London: Bodley Head, 2016.

Rands, H. W. B. *The General vs. The President: MacArthur and Truman at the Brink of Nuclear War*. New York: Doubleday, 2016.

Reardon-Anderson, James. *Reluctant Pioneers: China's Expansion Northward, 1644–1937*. Palo Alto, CA: Stanford University Press, 2005.

Roberts, Adam. *Superfast Primetime Ultimate Nation: The Relentless Invention of Modern India*. London: Profile, 2017.

Short, Philip. *Mao: The Man Who Made China*. New York: I. B. Taurus, 2016.

Smith, Jeff M. *Cold Peace: China-India Rivalry in the Twenty-First Century*. Lanham, MD: Lexington, 2013.

Stewart, Rory, *Occupational Hazards: My Time Governing in Iraq,* London, Picador, May 2007

Stuenkel, Oliver. *Post-Western World: How Emerging Powers are Remaking Global Order*. Cambridge: Polity, 2016.

Subramanian, Arvind. *Eclipse: Living in the Shadow of China's Economic Dominance*. Washington, DC: Institute of International Economics, 2011.

Trenin, Dmitri. *Should We Fear Russia?* Cambridge: Polity, 2016.

Trump, Donald, with Tony Schwartz. *The Art of the Deal*. New York: Ballantine, 2016.

Ullman, Harlan, *Anatomy of Failure: Why America Loses Every War It Starts*, Maryland, Naval Institute Press, 2017

Von Hippel, Karin. *Democracy by Force: US Military Intervention in the Post-Cold War World*. Cambridge: Cambridge University Press, 1999.

Welsh, Jennifer. *The Return of History*. Toronto: House of Anansi, 2016.

Winchester, Simon. *Pacific*. New York: Harper, 2016.

Zetter, Kim. *Countdown to Zero Day: Stuxnet and the Launch of the World's First Digital Weapon*. New York: Crown, 2014.</BIB>

ACKNOWLEDGMENTS

A HUGE CAST OF KNOWLEDGEABLE AND EXPERIENCED PEOPLE GAVE their time and insight during the writing of Asian Waters for which I am deeply indebted. Through the years hundreds have contributed to my own thoughts in trying to make sense of Asia and its impact on all our lives. All errors and miscalculations are, of course, my own.

From the Center for Strategic and International Studies, thank you to Bonnie Glaser, who runs the China Power Project; Greg Poling of the Asia Maritime Transparency Initiative; Murray Hiebert, deputy director of the Southeast Asia Program, and Scott Kennedy, director of the Project on Chinese Business and Political Economy. Thanks also to Nicholas R. Lardy at the Peterson Institute for International Economics; Shihoko Goto, Northeast Asia Associate at the Woodrow Wilson Center's Asia Program; Nong Hong of the Institute for China-America Studies; and Michael McDevitt, Mark E. Rosen, Peter Swartz, and James Clad at the Center for Naval Analyses. Harlan Ullman of the Killowen Group introduced me to the US Naval War College, where Jeff Harley, its fifty-sixth president, gave me access to naval and Asian experts. Thanks to Peter Dutton, who leads the China Maritime Studies Institute and to Tom Culora, Andrew Erickson, Tommy Groves, Kelley Hinderer, James Kelly, Don Marrin, Terence Roehrig, Kathleen Walsh, and Toshi Yoshihara; to Elizabeth Delucia and Rob Duane for their historical perspective at the Naval War College Museum; and to Barbara Mertz and Daniel Marciniak for flawlessly arranging my visit to the college. I have drawn on research from many other institutions, notably the Atlantic Council, the Brookings Institution, the Foreign Affairs

Council, the Heritage Foundation, and the Universal Peace Federation, specifically for help on the Korean Peninsula. In Britain I drew heavily from Chatham House (the Royal Institute of International Affairs), and am grateful to the late Lord Williams of Baglan and to Bill Hayton and at the Royal United Service Institute, to Michael Clarke, Karin von Hippel, Shashank Joshi, and Veerle Nouwens; and at the International Institute for Strategic Studies, to Nick Childs and Nigel Inkster; to Kerry Brown from Kings College, London; to the BBC, where I have been helped by many colleagues on Asian Waters stories over the years, including John Boon, Alistair Burnett, Darren Conway, Anne Dixey, Malcolm Downing, Carrie Gracie, Don Gummerson, Amanda Gunn, Tony Grant, Tony Hall, Peter Hanington, Mary Hockaday, Dominic Hurst, Stephen Mulvey, Jonathan Patterson, Mark Perrow, Kate Peters, Joc Phua, Tim Platt, Vin Ray, Tim Rex, Andrew Roy, Paul Royall, Baskar Solanki, Fred Scott, Simon Smith, James Stephenson, Francesca Unsworth, Anna Williams, Rupert Wingfield-Hayes, Chris Wylde, and many more.

In China I am indebted to Christine Yu and Edera Liang Yan for logistical help; also to Wu Shicun of the National Institute for South China Sea Studies; Pu Ruoqian and Milton Nong Ye at Jinan University; students Wilson Lu Chuhau and Duran Wu Yusen; Liu Baocheng at the Center for International Business and Economics; Ruan Zongze of the China Institute of International Studies; Andy Qingan Zhou at the School of Journalism and Communication; Xu Guangyu of the Chinese Military Disarmament Control Council; Shi Yinhong of Renmin University; Danny Alexander at the Asian Infrastructure Investment Bank; Carnegie Institute director Paul Haenle, and others who would prefer to remain anonymous.

For Taiwan, thanks to David Yung Lo Lin and Jo Y. C. Hsu in London, for insight and logistical help; to Daniel Chen and Isaac Wang on Kinmen Island; to Hsu Shao-liang, Lee Su-ching and their teams on Dongsha Island; and, in Taipei, Roy Chun Lee at the Chung-Hua Institution for Economic Research, defense analysts Chong-pin Lin and Edward Chen, and Paul Kuoboug Chang, Michael Chen, Jeff Lee, Hu Wei-ting, and their teams from the Ministry of Foreign Affairs.

Ambassador Vu Quang, Linh Hoang Do, and Nguyen Ngoc Huan at the Vietnamese embassy in London helped smooth my way to Danang, Hanoi, and Ly Son. Thanks in Vietnam to my guide and interpreter, Luoang Hoang Giap; to Nguyen Can Dong and Tran Cong Truc, who explained borders and Vietnam's view of China; to others would prefer to remain anonymous; to Vu Vanh King, commander of the Quang Ngai Coast Guard; to Tran Ngoc Nguyen and his team on Ly Son Island, and to Vo Van Giau and his fellow fishermen there.

In the Philippines, Marites Vitug referred me to Purple Romero who doggedly arranged an itinerary. Thanks there to John Forbes and Ebb Hinchliffe at the American Chamber of Commerce; General Guillermo A. Molina Jr. and his team at Camp Aguinaldo; Defense Secretary Delfin Lorenzana; Foreign Secretary Perfecto Yasay, and diplomats at the American embassy; Senator Gregorio Honasan; Speaker Jose de Vanecia Jr.; Jay Batongbacal at the Institute for Maritime Affairs and the Law of the Sea, University of the Philippines; Kristine Leilani Salle and her team at the Philippine Embassy in London; and others who would prefer their names not be mentioned.

On South Asia, thanks to William A. Avery, Brahma Chellaney, Namita Gokhale, Ashok Mehta, Hardeep Singh Puri, Navtej Sarna, Mihir Sharma, Navdeep Suri, and Vikas Swarup for steering me through the complexities there. On the ground in India, I am indebted to Sudhir Katiyar, Jignesh Mevani, Aeshalla Krishna and their teams from the Prayas Center for Labor Research; to Andy Griffiths, Matthew Joji, and Rosean Rajan from the International Justice Mission, who introduced me to Dialu Nial and the late Nilambar Mahji, just two of the tens of millions in South Asia born into dreadful lives of near slavery. Chandan Kumar from Action Aid helped in the Indian Tea Plantations, and thanks there to Vedprakash Gautam and Caroline den Dulk from the UN's child protection agency, UNICEF; Sarah Roberts and Rohinton Babaycon of the Ethical Tea Partnership; campaigners Partha Pratim Sarkar, Anil Bomjon Chay, and Raju Thapa, from the Banda Pani Tea Garden; and plantation growers Samar Jyoti Ghaliha from the Dikom Tea Estate and Vijay Dalmia from the Merry View Estate. I worked closely with Andrew Brady from Britain's Union Solidarity International, who set up the Blood Bricks campaign, and have learned much from Peter McAllister of the Ethical Trading Initiative, Peter Frankel from Amnesty International, and many others.

Colleagues and former colleagues gave time and insight, including including Nayan Chanda, Bob and Frankie Drogin, Susan Froetschel, Richard and Candy Gourlay, Hugo Gurdon, Steve Erlanger, Karin Landgren, Nancy Langston, Jonathan Mirsky, Cait Murphy, Rita and Geoff Payne, Gwen Robinson, Claudia Rosette, and Raymond Whitaker. Thanks also to the BBC, *Nikkei Asian Review, Yale Global* and others who used my journalism while reasearching Asian Waters.

Any book requires hard, professional teamwork, and I am grateful to David Aretha and Mary Sandys for tidying up the manuscript and prompting me to clarify arguments, descriptions, and explanations. Thanks to John Elliott for guiding me on India, Lesley Downer for her context and deep knowledge of Japan, and Adam Williams and Hong Ying for their help and insight into the intricacies of China's history and vision.

Thank you to David Grossman, my agent for more than twenty years, who introduced me to the legendary Peter Mayer, owner of Duckworth Overlook. *Asian Waters* was Peter's idea and throughout the process he prodded, suggested and challenged to make it a much better book. My appreciation too, to Tracy Carns, Matt Casbourne, Adam O'Brien and their colleagues at Duckworth Overlook.

ABOUT THE AUTHOR

HUMPHREY HAWKSLEY IS A FOREIGN CORRESPONDENT, AUTHOR, FILM-maker with vast experience in Asia, having taken BBC postings to Colombo, Delhi, Hong Kong, Manila, and Beijing, where he also reported for US BBC affiliates, ABC, and National Public Radio. His "future-history" scenarios about conflict in Asia have been international best-sellers and his journalism has been published in most mainstream British and American publications. His documentary films include *Aid under Scrutiny*, on the failures of international development; the award-winning *Bitter Sweet*, on human rights abuses in the confectionary supply chain; and *Danger: Democracy at Work*, on the risks of bringing Western-style democracy too quickly to some societies. He has given lectures at many universities including Cambridge University, Columbia University, Jinan University, the London Business School, and University College London. He is a regular speaker and panelist.

INDEX